Stochastic Sorcerers: Variational Autoencoders

Jamie Flux

https://www.linkedin.com/company/golden-dawn-engineering/

Collaborate with Us!

Have an innovative business idea or a project you'd like to
collaborate on?
We're always eager to explore new opportunities for growth and
partnership.
Please feel free to reach out to us at:

https://www.linkedin.com/company/golden-dawn-
engineering/

We look forward to hearing from you!

Contents

3

Chapter 1

Basic Variational Autoencoder for MNIST

In this chapter, we introduce the fundamental concepts of Variational Autoencoders by constructing a simple VAE in Python. We load the MNIST dataset, define an encoder network that maps images to a latent distribution, and a decoder that reconstructs images from latent samples. We show how to implement the reparameterization trick, optimize the ELBO (Evidence Lower Bound) loss, and evaluate reconstruction quality. By the end, you'll have a clear understanding of the core VAE architecture and training pipeline.

- We define an encoder to map input images to latent parameters (mean and log-variance).

- The decoder reconstructs the original images from the latent samples.

- During training, we use the reparameterization trick to backpropagate through the sampling step.

- Our objective is to minimize the ELBO, composed of the reconstruction loss plus the KL divergence between the approximate posterior and the prior.

Python Code Snippet

```python
import torch
import torch.nn as nn
import torch.optim as optim
from torch.utils.data import DataLoader
from torchvision import datasets, transforms
import matplotlib.pyplot as plt
import numpy as np
import os

# ---------------------------------------------------
# 1) VAE Model Definition
# ---------------------------------------------------

class VAE(nn.Module):
    """
    A basic Variational Autoencoder for MNIST.
    The encoder maps an image to (mu, log_var).
    The decoder reconstructs the original image from the latent
    ↪  code.
    """
    def __init__(self, latent_dim=20):
        super(VAE, self).__init__()
        self.latent_dim = latent_dim

        # Encoder: simple feed-forward MLP (784 -> 400 -> latent_dim
        ↪  * 2)
        self.encoder = nn.Sequential(
            nn.Linear(784, 400),
            nn.ReLU(inplace=True)
        )
        self.enc_mu = nn.Linear(400, latent_dim)
        self.enc_logvar = nn.Linear(400, latent_dim)

        # Decoder: MLP (latent_dim -> 400 -> 784)
        self.decoder = nn.Sequential(
            nn.Linear(latent_dim, 400),
            nn.ReLU(inplace=True),
            nn.Linear(400, 784),
            nn.Sigmoid()  # We assume input is in [0,1], so Sigmoid
            ↪  is appropriate
        )

    def reparameterize(self, mu, log_var):
        """
        Reparameterization trick:
        z = mu + sigma * epsilon, where epsilon ~ N(0,1).
        """
        std = torch.exp(0.5 * log_var)
        eps = torch.randn_like(std)
        return mu + eps * std
```

```python
def forward(self, x):
    """
    Encodes x into a latent distribution, then reparameterizes
    ↪  and decodes.
    Returns reconstructed image and the latent distribution
    ↪  parameters.
    """
    # Flatten input
    x = x.view(-1, 784)

    # Encode
    h = self.encoder(x)
    mu = self.enc_mu(h)
    log_var = self.enc_logvar(h)

    # Reparameterize
    z = self.reparameterize(mu, log_var)

    # Decode
    x_recon = self.decoder(z)

    # Reshape output back to image dimensions (B, 1, 28, 28)
    x_recon = x_recon.view(-1, 1, 28, 28)
    return x_recon, mu, log_var


# -----------------------------------------------------
# 2) Loss Function: ELBO
# -----------------------------------------------------

def vae_loss_fn(x_recon, x, mu, log_var):
    """
    ELBO = Reconstruction Loss + KL Divergence
    - Reconstruction Loss: we use binary cross-entropy
    - KL Divergence: measures the distance between approximate
    ↪  posterior q(z|x) and prior p(z)
    """
    # Binary cross-entropy as reconstruction loss
    bce = nn.functional.binary_cross_entropy(
        x_recon, x, reduction='sum'
    )

    # KL divergence
    # KL = 0.5 * sum(1 + log_var - mu^2 - exp(log_var))
    kl = -0.5 * torch.sum(1 + log_var - mu.pow(2) -
    ↪  torch.exp(log_var))

    # Return average per batch item, although sum is commonly used
    ↪  as well
    return (bce + kl) / x.size(0)


# -----------------------------------------------------
# 3) Training and Testing Procedures
```

```
# -----------------------------------------------------

def train_epoch(model, dataloader, optimizer, device):
    model.train()
    total_loss = 0
    for images, _ in dataloader:
        images = images.to(device)

        optimizer.zero_grad()
        x_recon, mu, log_var = model(images)
        loss = vae_loss_fn(x_recon, images, mu, log_var)
        loss.backward()
        optimizer.step()

        total_loss += loss.item()
    return total_loss / len(dataloader)

def test_epoch(model, dataloader, device):
    model.eval()
    total_loss = 0
    with torch.no_grad():
        for images, _ in dataloader:
            images = images.to(device)
            x_recon, mu, log_var = model(images)
            loss = vae_loss_fn(x_recon, images, mu, log_var)
            total_loss += loss.item()
    return total_loss / len(dataloader)

# -----------------------------------------------------
# 4) Utility: Visualization of Reconstructions
# -----------------------------------------------------

def visualize_reconstructions(model, dataloader, device, epoch):
    """
    Plots original images next to their reconstructions.
    """
    model.eval()
    images, _ = next(iter(dataloader))
    images = images.to(device)
    with torch.no_grad():
        x_recon, _, _ = model(images)

    # Move tensors to CPU for plotting
    images = images.cpu().numpy()
    x_recon = x_recon.cpu().numpy()

    # Plot a few samples
    n = 6
    fig, axes = plt.subplots(2, n, figsize=(12, 4))
    for i in range(n):
        # Original
        axes[0, i].imshow(images[i][0], cmap='gray')
        axes[0, i].axis('off')
```

```python
            # Reconstructed
            axes[1, i].imshow(x_recon[i][0], cmap='gray')
            axes[1, i].axis('off')

    os.makedirs('vae_results', exist_ok=True)
    plt.savefig(f'vae_results/reconstruction_epoch_{epoch}.png')
    plt.close()


# ----------------------------------------------------
# 5) Main - Putting it all Together
# ----------------------------------------------------

def main():
    # Hyperparameters
    batch_size = 64
    latent_dim = 20
    epochs = 5
    learning_rate = 1e-3

    device = torch.device("cuda" if torch.cuda.is_available() else
    ↪ "cpu")

    # Dataset and Loader
    transform = transforms.Compose([
        transforms.ToTensor()
    ])

    train_dataset = datasets.MNIST(
        root='data', train=True, download=True, transform=transform
    )
    test_dataset = datasets.MNIST(
        root='data', train=False, download=True, transform=transform
    )

    train_loader = DataLoader(train_dataset, batch_size=batch_size,
    ↪ shuffle=True)
    test_loader = DataLoader(test_dataset, batch_size=batch_size,
    ↪ shuffle=False)

    # Model, optimizer
    model = VAE(latent_dim=latent_dim).to(device)
    optimizer = optim.Adam(model.parameters(), lr=learning_rate)

    # Training loop
    for epoch in range(1, epochs+1):
        train_loss = train_epoch(model, train_loader, optimizer,
        ↪ device)
        test_loss = test_epoch(model, test_loader, device)

        print(f"Epoch [{epoch}/{epochs}], Train Loss:
        ↪ {train_loss:.4f}, Test Loss: {test_loss:.4f}")
```

```
# Visualization of reconstructions
visualize_reconstructions(model, test_loader, device, epoch)

print("Training complete. Reconstruction samples have been saved
↪  to 'vae_results' folder.")

if __name__ == "__main__":
    main()
```

Key Implementation Details:

- **Encoder and Decoder Networks:** The `VAE` class comprises a simple MLP encoder that produces `mu` and `log_var`, and a decoder that expands the latent code back to the input dimension.

- **Reparameterization Trick:** The `reparameterize` function draws samples from the latent distribution using `z = mu + std * eps`, enabling backpropagation through the sampling process.

- **ELBO Loss:** Implemented by `vae_loss_fn`, combining binary cross-entropy reconstruction loss and the KL divergence between the approximate posterior and the unit Gaussian prior.

- **Training and Evaluation:** `train_epoch` and `test_epoch` loop over data, calculate losses, and update the model parameters.

- **Visualizing Reconstructions:** `visualize_reconstructions` saves side-by-side comparisons of original images and their reconstructions, offering a quick qualitative evaluation of VAE performance.

Chapter 2

Convolutional VAE for Image Denoising

Building on the concepts from the basic VAE, we apply convolutional layers to handle image data more effectively. We collect or create noisy images, construct a CNN-based encoder and decoder, and train the model to denoise images. This chapter explains how to adapt the architecture to larger images, manage memory usage, and tune hyperparameters such as convolution kernel size, learning rate, and noise levels. You will learn how to leverage PyTorch or TensorFlow for building deeper CVAE modules that yield cleaner reconstructions.

Python Code Snippet

```python
import torch
import torch.nn as nn
import torch.optim as optim
import torchvision
import torchvision.transforms as transforms
from torch.utils.data import DataLoader
import matplotlib.pyplot as plt
import os

# -------------------------------------------------------------
# 1) Convolutional VAE Model Definition
# -------------------------------------------------------------
class ConvEncoder(nn.Module):
    """
    A convolutional encoder that outputs both mean and log variance
```

```python
    for the VAE's latent distribution.
    """
    def __init__(self, latent_dim=16):
        super(ConvEncoder, self).__init__()
        # in_channels=1 for grayscale (MNIST), adjust if using RGB
        self.conv_layers = nn.Sequential(
            nn.Conv2d(in_channels=1, out_channels=32, kernel_size=4,
            ↪  stride=2, padding=1),
            nn.BatchNorm2d(32),
            nn.LeakyReLU(0.2, inplace=True),

            nn.Conv2d(in_channels=32, out_channels=64,
            ↪  kernel_size=4, stride=2, padding=1),
            nn.BatchNorm2d(64),
            nn.LeakyReLU(0.2, inplace=True),

            nn.Conv2d(in_channels=64, out_channels=128,
            ↪  kernel_size=3, stride=1, padding=1),
            nn.BatchNorm2d(128),
            nn.LeakyReLU(0.2, inplace=True)
        )

        # After two 2-stride convs: 28x28 -> 7x7 if using MNIST
        self.flatten = nn.Flatten()

        # We assume the final spatial size is 7x7 with 128 channels
        self.fc_mu = nn.Linear(128*7*7, latent_dim)
        self.fc_logvar = nn.Linear(128*7*7, latent_dim)

    def forward(self, x):
        x = self.conv_layers(x)
        x = self.flatten(x)
        mu = self.fc_mu(x)
        logvar = self.fc_logvar(x)
        return mu, logvar

class ConvDecoder(nn.Module):
    """
    A convolutional decoder that reconstructs images from latent
    ↪  vectors.
    """
    def __init__(self, latent_dim=16):
        super(ConvDecoder, self).__init__()

        # We will project the latent vector back to a conv feature
        ↪  map.
        self.fc = nn.Linear(latent_dim, 128*7*7)

        # Deconvolution layers to upsample back to 28x28.
        self.deconv_layers = nn.Sequential(
            nn.ConvTranspose2d(128, 64, kernel_size=4, stride=2,
            ↪  padding=1),
            nn.BatchNorm2d(64),
```

13

```python
            nn.LeakyReLU(0.2, inplace=True),

            nn.ConvTranspose2d(64, 32, kernel_size=4, stride=2,
            ↪  padding=1),
            nn.BatchNorm2d(32),
            nn.LeakyReLU(0.2, inplace=True),

            # Final layer outputs a single channel (grayscale),
            # use Sigmoid or Tanh if you prefer a specific range.
            nn.Conv2d(32, 1, kernel_size=3, padding=1),
            nn.Sigmoid()
        )

    def forward(self, z):
        x = self.fc(z)
        x = x.view(-1, 128, 7, 7)
        x = self.deconv_layers(x)
        return x

class ConvVAE(nn.Module):
    """
    Combines the convolutional encoder and decoder into a single VAE
    ↪  module.
    """
    def __init__(self, latent_dim=16):
        super(ConvVAE, self).__init__()
        self.encoder = ConvEncoder(latent_dim=latent_dim)
        self.decoder = ConvDecoder(latent_dim=latent_dim)

    def reparameterize(self, mu, logvar):
        """
        Reparameterization trick:
        z = mu + std * eps, where eps ~ N(0,1).
        """
        std = torch.exp(0.5 * logvar)
        eps = torch.randn_like(std)
        return mu + eps * std

    def forward(self, x):
        mu, logvar = self.encoder(x)
        z = self.reparameterize(mu, logvar)
        recon = self.decoder(z)
        return recon, mu, logvar

# ----------------------------------------------------------------
# 2) Custom VAE Loss (Reconstruction + KL Divergence)
# ----------------------------------------------------------------
def vae_loss(recon, x, mu, logvar):
    """
    Standard VAE loss:
      1) Reconstruction loss (MSE or BCE)
      2) KLD = -0.5 * (1 + logvar - mu^2 - exp(logvar))
    """
```

14

```python
        recon_loss = nn.functional.mse_loss(recon, x, reduction='sum')

        # KL divergence
        kld = -0.5 * torch.sum(1 + logvar - mu.pow(2) - logvar.exp())

        return (recon_loss + kld) / x.size(0)

# ------------------------------------------------------------------
# 3) Training and Testing Routines
# ------------------------------------------------------------------
def train_epoch(model, dataloader, optimizer, device,
        noise_factor=0.5):
    model.train()
    epoch_loss = 0.0
    for images, _ in dataloader:
        images = images.to(device)

        # Add Gaussian noise to the images for denoising
        noisy_images = images + noise_factor *
            torch.randn_like(images)
        # Clamp the values to be in [0,1]
        noisy_images = torch.clamp(noisy_images, 0., 1.)

        optimizer.zero_grad()
        recon, mu, logvar = model(noisy_images)
        loss = vae_loss(recon, images, mu, logvar)
        loss.backward()
        optimizer.step()

        epoch_loss += loss.item()
    return epoch_loss / len(dataloader)

def test_epoch(model, dataloader, device, noise_factor=0.5):
    model.eval()
    epoch_loss = 0.0
    with torch.no_grad():
        for images, _ in dataloader:
            images = images.to(device)

            # Add the same level of Gaussian noise
            noisy_images = images + noise_factor *
                torch.randn_like(images)
            noisy_images = torch.clamp(noisy_images, 0., 1.)

            recon, mu, logvar = model(noisy_images)
            loss = vae_loss(recon, images, mu, logvar)
            epoch_loss += loss.item()
    return epoch_loss / len(dataloader)

# ------------------------------------------------------------------
# 4) Utility for Visualizing Denoising
# ------------------------------------------------------------------
```

```python
def visualize_denoising(model, dataloader, device, noise_factor=0.5,
 ↪  num_images=6):
    model.eval()
    os.makedirs("denoising_results", exist_ok=True)
    with torch.no_grad():
        images, _ = next(iter(dataloader))
        images = images.to(device)

        noisy_images = images + noise_factor *
        ↪  torch.randn_like(images)
        noisy_images = torch.clamp(noisy_images, 0., 1.)

        recon, _, _ = model(noisy_images)

        # Convert to CPU for plotting
        images = images.cpu()
        noisy_images = noisy_images.cpu()
        recon = recon.cpu()

        fig, axes = plt.subplots(nrows=3, ncols=num_images,
        ↪  figsize=(num_images*2, 6))
        for i in range(num_images):
            # Original
            axes[0][i].imshow(images[i].squeeze(), cmap='gray')
            axes[0][i].set_title("Original")
            axes[0][i].axis('off')

            # Noisy
            axes[1][i].imshow(noisy_images[i].squeeze(),
            ↪  cmap='gray')
            axes[1][i].set_title("Noisy")
            axes[1][i].axis('off')

            # Reconstructed
            axes[2][i].imshow(recon[i].squeeze(), cmap='gray')
            axes[2][i].set_title("Reconstructed")
            axes[2][i].axis('off')

        plt.tight_layout()
        plt.savefig("denoising_results/sample_denoising.png")
        plt.close()

# ----------------------------------------------------------------
# 5) Main Script
# ----------------------------------------------------------------
def main():
    device = torch.device("cuda" if torch.cuda.is_available() else
    ↪  "cpu")
    print(f"Using device: {device}")

    # Hyperparameters
    latent_dim = 16
    batch_size = 64
```

```
epochs = 5
learning_rate = 1e-3
noise_factor = 0.5  # Controls how severely images are corrupted

# Dataset and DataLoaders (using MNIST as an example)
transform = transforms.Compose([
    transforms.ToTensor(),
])
train_data = torchvision.datasets.MNIST(
    root='data', train=True, download=True, transform=transform)
test_data = torchvision.datasets.MNIST(
    root='data', train=False, download=True,
    ↪  transform=transform)

train_loader = DataLoader(train_data, batch_size=batch_size,
↪  shuffle=True)
test_loader = DataLoader(test_data, batch_size=batch_size,
↪  shuffle=False)

# Initialize the VAE model, optimizer
model = ConvVAE(latent_dim=latent_dim).to(device)
optimizer = optim.Adam(model.parameters(), lr=learning_rate)

# Training loop
for epoch in range(epochs):
    train_loss = train_epoch(model, train_loader, optimizer,
    ↪  device, noise_factor=noise_factor)
    val_loss = test_epoch(model, test_loader, device,
    ↪  noise_factor=noise_factor)
    print(f"Epoch [{epoch+1}/{epochs}] | Train Loss:
    ↪  {train_loss:.4f} | Val Loss: {val_loss:.4f}")

    # Visualization of denoising after each epoch
    visualize_denoising(model, test_loader, device,
    ↪  noise_factor=noise_factor, num_images=6)

print("Training completed!")

if __name__ == "__main__":
    main()
```

Key Implementation Details:

- **VAE Architecture:** The ConvVAE consists of a convolutional encoder (ConvEncoder) and a convolutional decoder (ConvDecoder). The encoder outputs the mean and log-variance for the latent distribution.

- **Reparameterization Trick:** Within the reparameterize

function, samples are generated as $\mu + \sigma \times \epsilon$, ensuring gradients flow properly through the mean and variance.

- **Denoising Setup:** We add noise in the `train_epoch` and `test_epoch` routines by combining images with Gaussian noise, showing how the CNN-based VAE can learn to reconstruct clean images from noisy inputs.

- **Loss Function:** The `vae_loss` combines a reconstruction term (ℓ_2 or MSE) with the KL divergence to maximize the Evidence Lower Bound (ELBO).

- **Training Loop:** Each epoch calls `train_epoch` to backpropagate the VAE loss and `test_epoch` to evaluate on unseen data. The model parameters are updated with Adam at a user-specified learning rate.

- **Visualization:** The `visualize_denoising` function saves a grid showing the original image, noisy input, and reconstructed output for multiple examples, thereby verifying the denoising efficacy.

Chapter 3

VAE for Dimensionality Reduction

This chapter focuses on using VAEs as a powerful method for non-linear dimensionality reduction. We show how to adapt the encoder to produce a compact latent embedding and use that embedding for visualization or further downstream tasks. You will implement a feed-forward encoder and decoder, prepare a dataset of high-dimensional vectors, and observe how a VAE uncovers meaningful structure in data. The chapter highlights how to scale the network for larger feature counts and introduces tips for selecting the latent space dimensionality.

Python Code Snippet

```python
import torch
import torch.nn as nn
import torch.optim as optim
from torch.utils.data import DataLoader
import torchvision
import torchvision.transforms as transforms
import matplotlib.pyplot as plt
import numpy as np

# ------------------------------------------------------------
# 1) Define the VAE architecture
```

```
# --------------------------------------------------------------
class VAE(nn.Module):
    """
    A Variational Autoencoder for dimensionality reduction.
    Encoder: Feed-forward network producing mu and logvar.
    Decoder: Feed-forward network reconstructing data from latent
    ↪  space.
    """

    def __init__(self, input_dim=784, hidden_dim=256, latent_dim=2):
        super(VAE, self).__init__()

        # Encoder: maps input to mu, logvar
        self.encoder = nn.Sequential(
            nn.Linear(input_dim, hidden_dim),
            nn.ReLU(inplace=True),
            nn.Linear(hidden_dim, hidden_dim),
            nn.ReLU(inplace=True),
        )

        self.fc_mu = nn.Linear(hidden_dim, latent_dim)
        self.fc_logvar = nn.Linear(hidden_dim, latent_dim)

        # Decoder: maps latent vector to reconstruction
        self.decoder = nn.Sequential(
            nn.Linear(latent_dim, hidden_dim),
            nn.ReLU(inplace=True),
            nn.Linear(hidden_dim, hidden_dim),
            nn.ReLU(inplace=True),
            nn.Linear(hidden_dim, input_dim),
            nn.Sigmoid()  # scaled to [0,1] for MNIST
        )

    def encode(self, x):
        h = self.encoder(x)
        mu = self.fc_mu(h)
        logvar = self.fc_logvar(h)
        return mu, logvar

    def reparameterize(self, mu, logvar):
        """
        Reparameterization trick to sample from N(mu, var) from
        N(0,1) samples. We compute std from logvar as exp(0.5 *
        ↪  logvar).
        """
        std = torch.exp(0.5 * logvar)
        eps = torch.randn_like(std)
        return mu + eps * std

    def decode(self, z):
        return self.decoder(z)

    def forward(self, x):
        """
```

```python
    Full VAE forward pass: encode, reparameterize, then decode.
    """
    mu, logvar = self.encode(x)
    z = self.reparameterize(mu, logvar)
    x_recon = self.decode(z)
    return x_recon, mu, logvar


# --------------------------------------------------------------
# 2) Define the VAE loss function
# --------------------------------------------------------------
def vae_loss_function(x_recon, x, mu, logvar):
    """
    Standard VAE loss = Reconstruction loss + KL Divergence.
    We'll use binary cross-entropy for reconstruction,
    suitable for normalized [0,1] MNIST pixel values.
    """
    bce = nn.functional.binary_cross_entropy(x_recon, x,
    ↪  reduction='sum')

    # KL divergence term
    # KL = 0.5 * sum(1 + logvar - mu^2 - exp(logvar))
    # across all dimensions
    kld = -0.5 * torch.sum(1 + logvar - mu.pow(2) - logvar.exp())

    return (bce + kld) / x.size(0)


# --------------------------------------------------------------
# 3) Training and evaluation loops
# --------------------------------------------------------------
def train(model, dataloader, optimizer, device):
    model.train()
    total_loss = 0
    for batch_idx, (data, _) in enumerate(dataloader):
        data = data.view(data.size(0), -1).to(device)  # flatten
        optimizer.zero_grad()

        x_recon, mu, logvar = model(data)
        loss = vae_loss_function(x_recon, data, mu, logvar)
        loss.backward()

        optimizer.step()
        total_loss += loss.item()
    return total_loss / len(dataloader)

def evaluate(model, dataloader, device):
    model.eval()
    total_loss = 0
    with torch.no_grad():
        for batch_idx, (data, _) in enumerate(dataloader):
            data = data.view(data.size(0), -1).to(device)
            x_recon, mu, logvar = model(data)
            loss = vae_loss_function(x_recon, data, mu, logvar)
            total_loss += loss.item()
```

```python
        return total_loss / len(dataloader)

# ----------------------------------------------------------------
# 4) Utility to see 2D latent space (for dimensionality reduction)
# ----------------------------------------------------------------
def visualize_latent_space(model, dataloader, device):
    """
    Use the encoder to map data points to 2D latent space
    and visualize a scatter plot.
    """
    model.eval()
    latents = []
    labels = []

    with torch.no_grad():
        for data, target in dataloader:
            data = data.view(data.size(0), -1).to(device)
            mu, logvar = model.encode(data)
            z = model.reparameterize(mu, logvar)
            latents.append(z.cpu().numpy())
            labels.append(target.numpy())

    latents = np.concatenate(latents, axis=0)
    labels = np.concatenate(labels, axis=0)

    plt.figure(figsize=(6,6))
    scatter = plt.scatter(latents[:, 0], latents[:, 1], c=labels,
    ↪   alpha=0.7, cmap='tab10')
    plt.colorbar(scatter, ticks=range(10))
    plt.title("2D Latent Space Visualization")
    plt.xlabel("z1")
    plt.ylabel("z2")
    plt.show()


# ----------------------------------------------------------------
# 5) Main script: load data, train the VAE, visualize latents
# ----------------------------------------------------------------
def main():
    device = torch.device("cuda" if torch.cuda.is_available() else
    ↪   "cpu")

    # Hyperparameters
    batch_size = 128
    epochs = 5
    input_dim = 784          # 28x28
    hidden_dim = 256
    latent_dim = 2           # We visualize data in 2D

    # Load MNIST dataset
    transform = transforms.Compose([
        transforms.ToTensor()
    ])
```

```
train_dataset = torchvision.datasets.MNIST(
    root="./data", train=True, download=True,
    ↪  transform=transform
)
test_dataset = torchvision.datasets.MNIST(
    root="./data", train=False, download=True,
    ↪  transform=transform
)

train_loader = DataLoader(train_dataset, batch_size=batch_size,
↪  shuffle=True)
test_loader = DataLoader(test_dataset, batch_size=batch_size,
↪  shuffle=False)

# Initialize VAE model
model = VAE(input_dim=input_dim, hidden_dim=hidden_dim,
↪  latent_dim=latent_dim).to(device)

# Optimizer
optimizer = optim.Adam(model.parameters(), lr=1e-3)

# Training loop
for epoch in range(1, epochs + 1):
    train_loss = train(model, train_loader, optimizer, device)
    val_loss = evaluate(model, test_loader, device)
    print(f"Epoch [{epoch}/{epochs}], Train Loss:
    ↪  {train_loss:.4f}, Val Loss: {val_loss:.4f}")

# Visualize the 2D latent space
visualize_latent_space(model, test_loader, device)

if __name__ == "__main__":
    main()
```

Key Implementation Details:

- **Encoder and Decoder:** Our `VAE` class provides a feed-forward `encoder` that outputs `mu` and `logvar`, and a `decoder` which reconstructs input from the latent variable.

- **Reparameterization Trick:** The method `reparameterize` samples z from the learned distribution by combining `mu` and `std = exp(0.5 * logvar)`, ensuring the model is differentiable end-to-end.

- **Loss Function:** The `vae_loss_function` combines the binary cross-entropy reconstruction term and the KL divergence to encourage a continuous latent space.

- **Data Pipeline:** We load the MNIST dataset as an example of high-dimensional input (784 features), flatten each 28×28 image into a 1D vector, and train the network to reconstruct these vectors.

- **Dimensionality Reduction:** We set `latent_dim=2` so we can visualize the learned embedding in two dimensions, observing meaningful clusters or structures in this latent space.

- **Visualization:** The function `visualize_latent_space` shows how to map data into the 2D latent representation and provides a scatter plot colored by class labels.

Chapter 4

Conditional VAE for Image Synthesis

Here, we introduce condition labels into the VAE framework to guide the reconstruction and generation process. You will load an image dataset with class labels, modify the encoder and decoder to accept label embeddings, and generate class-specific samples. This chapter demonstrates how to incorporate labels into the loss function, handle different label formats, and balance the KL divergence with reconstruction objectives. By the end, you'll have a working implementation capable of synthesizing images based on a specified category.

- We begin by loading a labeled image dataset (e.g., MNIST) and structuring the images along with their numeric class labels.

- We design both the encoder and the decoder to include label embeddings alongside image features. The encoder merges this label information before projecting into a latent distribution, while the decoder uses the same label embedding to help reconstruct the original image based on class-specific characteristics.

- We implement a reparameterization trick to sample latent variables from the predicted Gaussian distribution defined by (mean) and $\log(^2)$.

- We define a combined loss function that adds a KL divergence penalty to encourage continuous latent structure while

25

maintaining good reconstruction quality.

- Finally, we train the network end-to-end and demonstrate how to sample specific digit classes from the learned conditional VAE.

Python Code Snippet

```python
import torch
import torch.nn as nn
import torch.optim as optim
import torch.nn.functional as F
from torchvision import datasets, transforms
from torch.utils.data import DataLoader
import matplotlib.pyplot as plt
import numpy as np
import os


# ---------------------------------------------------------------
# 1) Define the Conditional VAE architecture
# ---------------------------------------------------------------
class ConditionalVAE(nn.Module):
    """
    A conditional Variational Autoencoder for MNIST-like images.
    The encoder and decoder each receive an embedding of the class
    ↪ label.
    """
    def __init__(self, label_dim=10, embedding_dim=10,
    ↪ latent_dim=20, hidden_dim=400):
        super(ConditionalVAE, self).__init__()
        # Label embedding layer
        self.label_emb = nn.Embedding(num_embeddings=label_dim,
        ↪ embedding_dim=embedding_dim)

        # Encoder layers
        # Input is the flattened image (28*28=784) + label embedding
        self.fc_enc = nn.Sequential(
            nn.Linear(784 + embedding_dim, hidden_dim),
            nn.ReLU(True),
            nn.Linear(hidden_dim, hidden_dim),
            nn.ReLU(True),
        )
        self.fc_mu = nn.Linear(hidden_dim, latent_dim)
        self.fc_logvar = nn.Linear(hidden_dim, latent_dim)

        # Decoder layers
        # Input is latent_dim + label embedding
        self.fc_dec = nn.Sequential(
            nn.Linear(latent_dim + embedding_dim, hidden_dim),
            nn.ReLU(True),
```

26

```python
            nn.Linear(hidden_dim, hidden_dim),
            nn.ReLU(True),
            nn.Linear(hidden_dim, 784),   # output is 28*28
        )

        self.latent_dim = latent_dim

    def encode(self, x, labels):
        # Flatten image to [batch, 784]
        x = x.view(x.size(0), -1)
        # Look up label embedding
        label_embed = self.label_emb(labels)
        # Concatenate image + label embedding
        enc_input = torch.cat([x, label_embed], dim=1)

        h = self.fc_enc(enc_input)
        mu = self.fc_mu(h)
        logvar = self.fc_logvar(h)
        return mu, logvar

    def reparameterize(self, mu, logvar):
        """
        Reparameterization trick: z = mu + sigma * epsilon
        """
        std = torch.exp(0.5 * logvar)
        eps = torch.randn_like(std)
        return mu + eps * std

    def decode(self, z, labels):
        # Get label embedding
        label_embed = self.label_emb(labels)
        # Concatenate latent vector + label embedding
        dec_input = torch.cat([z, label_embed], dim=1)
        x_recon = self.fc_dec(dec_input)
        # Output 784 -> reshape to image
        x_recon = x_recon.view(-1, 1, 28, 28)
        return x_recon

    def forward(self, x, labels):
        mu, logvar = self.encode(x, labels)
        z = self.reparameterize(mu, logvar)
        x_recon = self.decode(z, labels)
        return x_recon, mu, logvar

# ----------------------------------------------------------------
# 2) Define the loss function
# ----------------------------------------------------------------
def vae_loss_function(recon_x, x, mu, logvar):
    """
    Computes the standard VAE loss with reconstruction + KL
    ↪   divergence.
    Uses binary cross-entropy for reconstruction.
    """
```

```python
    # Flatten inputs and outputs for reconstruction error
    recon_x_flat = recon_x.view(recon_x.size(0), -1)
    x_flat = x.view(x.size(0), -1)
    recon_loss = F.binary_cross_entropy_with_logits(recon_x_flat,
    ↪   x_flat, reduction='sum')

    # KL divergence
    kld = -0.5 * torch.sum(1 + logvar - mu.pow(2) - logvar.exp())
    return recon_loss + kld, recon_loss, kld

# ---------------------------------------------------------------
# 3) Training routine
# ---------------------------------------------------------------
def train_one_epoch(model, dataloader, optimizer, device):
    model.train()
    total_loss = 0.0
    for images, labels in dataloader:
        images = images.to(device)
        labels = labels.to(device)

        optimizer.zero_grad()
        recon_x, mu, logvar = model(images, labels)
        loss, recon_loss, kld = vae_loss_function(recon_x, images,
        ↪   mu, logvar)
        loss.backward()
        optimizer.step()

        total_loss += loss.item()

    return total_loss / len(dataloader)

# ---------------------------------------------------------------
# 4) Evaluation routine
# ---------------------------------------------------------------
def evaluate_model(model, dataloader, device):
    model.eval()
    total_loss = 0.0
    with torch.no_grad():
        for images, labels in dataloader:
            images = images.to(device)
            labels = labels.to(device)
            recon_x, mu, logvar = model(images, labels)
            loss, _, _ = vae_loss_function(recon_x, images, mu,
            ↪   logvar)
            total_loss += loss.item()
    return total_loss / len(dataloader)

# ---------------------------------------------------------------
# 5) Function to sample from the conditional VAE
# ---------------------------------------------------------------
def sample_for_label(model, label, device, n_samples=8):
    """
    Generates n_samples images for a given numeric label (0-9).
```

```
    """
    model.eval()
    with torch.no_grad():
        # Sample latent vectors from standard normal
        z = torch.randn(n_samples, model.latent_dim).to(device)
        # Make repeated label
        labels = torch.tensor([label]*n_samples,
        ↪  dtype=torch.long).to(device)
        recon = model.decode(z, labels)
        # Convert logits to probabilities
        recon_sigmoid = torch.sigmoid(recon)
    return recon_sigmoid


# -----------------------------------------------------------------
# 6) Main script
# -----------------------------------------------------------------
def main():
    # Hyperparameters
    batch_size = 64
    epochs = 5
    lr = 1e-3
    latent_dim = 20
    hidden_dim = 400
    embedding_dim = 10

    # Check device
    device = torch.device("cuda" if torch.cuda.is_available() else
    ↪  "cpu")

    # Prepare data and DataLoaders (MNIST)
    transform = transforms.Compose([
        transforms.ToTensor()
    ])
    train_data = datasets.MNIST(root='data', train=True,
    ↪  transform=transform, download=True)
    test_data = datasets.MNIST(root='data', train=False,
    ↪  transform=transform, download=True)
    train_loader = DataLoader(train_data, batch_size=batch_size,
    ↪  shuffle=True)
    test_loader = DataLoader(test_data, batch_size=batch_size,
    ↪  shuffle=False)

    # Initialize model, optimizer
    model = ConditionalVAE(label_dim=10,
    ↪  embedding_dim=embedding_dim,
                           latent_dim=latent_dim,
                           ↪  hidden_dim=hidden_dim).to(device)
    optimizer = optim.Adam(model.parameters(), lr=lr)

    # Train loop
    os.makedirs("results", exist_ok=True)
    for epoch in range(epochs):
```

```
train_loss = train_one_epoch(model, train_loader, optimizer,
 ↪ device)
test_loss = evaluate_model(model, test_loader, device)

print(f"Epoch [{epoch+1}/{epochs}] - Train Loss:
 ↪ {train_loss:.2f}, Test Loss: {test_loss:.2f}")

# Sampling demonstration
if (epoch+1) % 1 == 0:  # sample each epoch
    # Pick a random label
    random_label = np.random.randint(0, 10)
    gen_images = sample_for_label(model, random_label,
 ↪ device, n_samples=16)
    # Plot and save
    grid_img = torch.cat([img for img in gen_images.cpu()],
 ↪ dim=2)
    plt.figure(figsize=(8,2))
    plt.axis('off')
    plt.title(f"Samples for label {random_label}")
    plt.imshow(grid_img.squeeze().numpy(), cmap='gray')

 ↪ plt.savefig(f"results/epoch_{epoch+1}_label_{random_label}.png")
    plt.close()

if __name__ == "__main__":
    main()
```

Key Implementation Details:

- **Label Embedding:** We use nn.Embedding in the ConditionalVAE
  to transform numeric labels into dense vectors before concate-
  nating them with image features.

- **Encoder and Decoder:** The encoder (encode) merges the
  flattened image with the label embedding, producing mean
  (mu) and log-variance (logvar). The decoder (decode) also
  takes a label embedding, ensuring the generator knows which
  class to reconstruct.

- **Reparameterization Trick:** The function reparameterize
  samples latent representations z using and ^{2}, enabling gradient flow through the stochastic node.

- **Loss Function:** The vae_loss_function combines binary
  cross-entropy reconstruction term and a KL divergence penalty
  to regularize the latent space.

30

- **Conditional Sampling:** By passing a chosen class label to `sample_for_label`, the decoder can synthesize new images specific to that label, demonstrating class-controlled generation.

Chapter 5

VAE for Anomaly Detection in Time Series

In this chapter, we move into time-series data and showcase how a VAE can detect unusual patterns. We prepare sequence data, design an LSTM-based encoder-decoder, and train the VAE to learn normal sequences. We then monitor reconstruction errors to detect anomalies when the observed data deviates from learned patterns. By carefully implementing the training loop, batch processing, and anomaly scoring, you'll gain practical experience applying VAEs to real-world temporal data.

Python Code Snippet

```python
import torch
import torch.nn as nn
import torch.optim as optim
import numpy as np
from torch.utils.data import Dataset, DataLoader
import random
import matplotlib.pyplot as plt


# -------------------------------------------------------------
# 1) Synthetic dataset creation for demonstration
# -------------------------------------------------------------
def generate_synthetic_timeseries(num_samples=2000, seq_len=30,
    anomaly_ratio=0.1):
```

```python
    """
    Generate a synthetic time series. The 'normal' component is a
    ↪  combination
    of sine waves. Some sequences are artificially made 'anomalous'
    ↪  by adding
    random spikes.
    """
    t = np.linspace(0, 4*np.pi, num_samples)
    # A baseline normal signal
    data = 0.5*np.sin(t) + 0.3*np.cos(2*t)

    # Create random anomalies in a fraction of the data
    num_anomalies = int(num_samples * anomaly_ratio)
    anomaly_indices = np.random.choice(num_samples, num_anomalies,
    ↪  replace=False)
    data[anomaly_indices] += np.random.normal(0, 3.0,
    ↪  size=num_anomalies)

    # Build sequences of length seq_len
    sequences = []
    labels = []

    # Label = 0 for normal window, 1 for any window containing an
    ↪  anomaly
    for i in range(num_samples - seq_len):
        seq = data[i : i + seq_len]
        if np.any(np.isin(range(i, i + seq_len), anomaly_indices)):
            label = 1
        else:
            label = 0
        sequences.append(seq)
        labels.append(label)

    sequences = np.array(sequences, dtype=np.float32)
    labels = np.array(labels, dtype=np.int64)
    return sequences, labels

class TimeSeriesDataset(Dataset):
    """
    A custom dataset that stores time-series sequences (features)
    ↪  and labels.
    """
    def __init__(self, sequences, labels):
        super().__init__()
        self.sequences = sequences
        self.labels = labels

    def __len__(self):
        return len(self.sequences)

    def __getitem__(self, idx):
        seq = self.sequences[idx]
        label = self.labels[idx]
```

```python
        return seq, label

# -----------------------------------------------------------------
# 2) LSTM-based VAE model
# -----------------------------------------------------------------
class LSTMVAE(nn.Module):
    """
    LSTM-based Variational Autoencoder for time-series
    ↪   reconstruction.
    Encodes a sequence into a latent vector (mu, logvar), then
    ↪   decodes
    to reconstruct the sequence.
    """
    def __init__(self, input_dim=1, hidden_dim=32, latent_dim=16,
    ↪   num_layers=1):
        """
        input_dim: dimensionality of each time step in the sequence
        hidden_dim: hidden dimension for LSTM
        latent_dim: dimension of the latent representation
        num_layers: LSTM layers
        """
        super(LSTMVAE, self).__init__()

        self.input_dim = input_dim
        self.hidden_dim = hidden_dim
        self.latent_dim = latent_dim

        # Encoder LSTM
        self.encoder_lstm = nn.LSTM(input_dim, hidden_dim,
        ↪   num_layers=num_layers, batch_first=True)

        # Project LSTM hidden state to mu and logvar
        self.mu_lin = nn.Linear(hidden_dim, latent_dim)
        self.logvar_lin = nn.Linear(hidden_dim, latent_dim)

        # Decoder LSTM
        self.decoder_lstm = nn.LSTM(input_dim, hidden_dim,
        ↪   num_layers=num_layers, batch_first=True)

        # Project hidden state back to original feature dimension
        self.output_lin = nn.Linear(hidden_dim, input_dim)

    def encode(self, x):
        """
        Encode the input sequence into mu and logvar of latent
        ↪   distribution.
        x shape: (batch, seq_len, input_dim)
        """
        # Pass through encoder LSTM
        _, (h_n, _) = self.encoder_lstm(x)

        # h_n shape: (num_layers, batch, hidden_dim)
        # We take the last layer's hidden state
```

34

```python
        h_n = h_n[-1, :, :]   # shape: (batch, hidden_dim)

        mu = self.mu_lin(h_n)
        logvar = self.logvar_lin(h_n)
        return mu, logvar

    def reparameterize(self, mu, logvar):
        """
        Reparameterization trick: z = mu + sigma * epsilon
        """
        std = torch.exp(0.5 * logvar)
        eps = torch.randn_like(std)
        return mu + eps * std

    def decode(self, z, seq_len):
        """
        Decode the latent vector z into a sequence of length
        ↪  seq_len.
        We replicate z across the sequence or feed zero inputs to
        ↪  LSTM
        and use z as an initial hidden state, for example.
        Here, we feed a zero input while initializing hidden state
        ↪  with z.
        """
        batch_size = z.size(0)

        # Initialize hidden and cell states using z
        # We map latent dimension -> hidden_dim
        h_0 = z.unsqueeze(0)   # shape: (1, batch, latent_dim)
        h_0 = torch.tanh(h_0)   # optional nonlinearity
        h_0 = nn.Linear(self.latent_dim, self.hidden_dim)(h_0)

        c_0 = torch.zeros_like(h_0)

        # Provide zero-vector as input to the decoder LSTM
        decoder_input = torch.zeros(batch_size, seq_len,
        ↪  self.input_dim, device=z.device)

        out, _ = self.decoder_lstm(decoder_input, (h_0, c_0))
        # out shape: (batch, seq_len, hidden_dim)

        # Map each hidden state to the reconstructed feature
        recon = self.output_lin(out)   # shape: (batch, seq_len,
        ↪  input_dim)
        return recon

    def forward(self, x):
        """
        Full forward pass: encode -> reparameterize -> decode
        x shape: (batch, seq_len, input_dim)
        """
        mu, logvar = self.encode(x)
        z = self.reparameterize(mu, logvar)
```

35

```
        seq_len = x.size(1)
        recon = self.decode(z, seq_len)
        return recon, mu, logvar


# -------------------------------------------------------------
# 3) Loss function
# -------------------------------------------------------------
def vae_loss_function(recon_x, x, mu, logvar):
    """
    Compute the VAE loss = reconstruction loss + KL divergence.
    We'll use MSE as reconstruction term for time-series.
    """
    recon_loss = nn.MSELoss()(recon_x, x)
    # KL divergence
    # KL = -0.5 * sum(1 + logvar - mu^2 - exp(logvar))
    kld = -0.5 * torch.mean(1 + logvar - mu.pow(2) - logvar.exp())
    return recon_loss + kld, recon_loss, kld


# -------------------------------------------------------------
# 4) Training and evaluation
# -------------------------------------------------------------
def train_epoch(model, dataloader, optimizer, device):
    model.train()
    total_loss = 0
    total_recon_loss = 0
    total_kld = 0

    for batch_data, _ in dataloader:
        # batch_data shape: (batch, seq_len)
        # Expand to (batch, seq_len, 1) if we're using input_dim=1
        batch_data = batch_data.unsqueeze(-1).to(device)

        optimizer.zero_grad()
        recon, mu, logvar = model(batch_data)

        loss, recon_loss, kld = vae_loss_function(recon, batch_data,
        ↪  mu, logvar)
        loss.backward()
        optimizer.step()

        total_loss += loss.item()
        total_recon_loss += recon_loss.item()
        total_kld += kld.item()

    return total_loss / len(dataloader), total_recon_loss /
    ↪  len(dataloader), total_kld / len(dataloader)

def evaluate_model(model, dataloader, device):
    model.eval()
    total_loss = 0
    total_recon_loss = 0
    total_kld = 0
    with torch.no_grad():
```

```
        for batch_data, _ in dataloader:
            batch_data = batch_data.unsqueeze(-1).to(device)
            recon, mu, logvar = model(batch_data)
            loss, recon_loss, kld = vae_loss_function(recon,
            ↪  batch_data, mu, logvar)

            total_loss += loss.item()
            total_recon_loss += recon_loss.item()
            total_kld += kld.item()

    return total_loss / len(dataloader), total_recon_loss /
    ↪  len(dataloader), total_kld / len(dataloader)

def reconstruct_sequences(model, dataloader, device):
    """
    Reconstruct all sequences in the dataloader and return
    reconstruction errors for each sequence.
    """
    model.eval()
    errors = []
    labels_list = []

    with torch.no_grad():
        for batch_data, batch_labels in dataloader:
            batch_data = batch_data.unsqueeze(-1).to(device)
            recon, _, _ = model(batch_data)
            recon_error = torch.mean((recon - batch_data)**2,
            ↪  dim=(1,2))
            errors.append(recon_error.cpu().numpy())
            labels_list.append(batch_labels.numpy())

    errors = np.concatenate(errors, axis=0)
    labels_list = np.concatenate(labels_list, axis=0)
    return errors, labels_list

# ---------------------------------------------------------------
# 5) Main script to demonstrate training, evaluation, anomaly
↪  detection
# ---------------------------------------------------------------
def main():
    random.seed(42)
    np.random.seed(42)
    torch.manual_seed(42)

    device = torch.device("cuda" if torch.cuda.is_available() else
    ↪  "cpu")

    # Generate synthetic data
    sequences, labels = generate_synthetic_timeseries(
        num_samples=2000, seq_len=30, anomaly_ratio=0.1
    )

    # Split data into train (normal only) and test (mixed)
```

```python
# We assume the first part is mostly normal; test set includes
↪    anomalies.
train_size = 1400
val_size = 200
test_size = len(sequences) - (train_size + val_size)

# Indices for train/val/test
# We'll heuristically take the first portion as "normal."
# In a real scenario, you'd have truly normal data for training
↪    the VAE.
train_indices = np.where(labels[:train_size] == 0)[0]  # normal
↪    only from the first segment
train_sequences = sequences[train_indices]
train_labels = labels[train_indices]

val_indices = range(train_size, train_size + val_size)
test_indices = range(train_size + val_size, train_size +
↪    val_size + test_size)

# Build dataset objects
train_dataset = TimeSeriesDataset(train_sequences, train_labels)
val_dataset = TimeSeriesDataset(sequences[val_indices],
↪    labels[val_indices])
test_dataset = TimeSeriesDataset(sequences[test_indices],
↪    labels[test_indices])

# DataLoaders
train_loader = DataLoader(train_dataset, batch_size=32,
↪    shuffle=True)
val_loader = DataLoader(val_dataset, batch_size=32,
↪    shuffle=False)
test_loader = DataLoader(test_dataset, batch_size=32,
↪    shuffle=False)

# Create model
model = LSTMVAE(input_dim=1, hidden_dim=32, latent_dim=16,
↪    num_layers=1).to(device)

# Optimizer
optimizer = optim.Adam(model.parameters(), lr=1e-3)

# Training loop
epochs = 20
for epoch in range(epochs):
    train_loss, train_recon, train_kld = train_epoch(model,
↪        train_loader, optimizer, device)
    val_loss, val_recon, val_kld = evaluate_model(model,
↪        val_loader, device)

    print(f"Epoch [{epoch+1}/{epochs}] "
          f"Train Loss: {train_loss:.4f} (Recon:
↪        {train_recon:.4f}, KLD: {train_kld:.4f}) "
```

```python
        f"Val Loss: {val_loss:.4f} (Recon: {val_recon:.4f},
        ↪   KLD: {val_kld:.4f})")

    # After training, compute reconstruction errors on test set
    test_errors, test_labels = reconstruct_sequences(model,
    ↪   test_loader, device)

    # We pick a threshold based on training or validation
    ↪   distribution
    # For simplicity, we can guess a threshold from the val set as
    ↪   mean + 3*std
    val_errors, val_labels = reconstruct_sequences(model,
    ↪   val_loader, device)
    threshold = np.mean(val_errors) + 3.0 * np.std(val_errors)

    # Predict anomalies where reconstruction error > threshold
    pred_anomalies = (test_errors > threshold).astype(int)
    true_anomalies = test_labels

    # Evaluate anomaly detection with a simple accuracy measure
    accuracy = np.mean(pred_anomalies == true_anomalies)
    print(f"Anomaly detection accuracy (test set):
    ↪   {accuracy*100:.2f}%")

    # Example plot of reconstruction error distribution
    plt.figure(figsize=(6,4))
    plt.hist(test_errors, bins=50, alpha=0.7, label='Test
    ↪   Reconstruction Errors')
    plt.axvline(threshold, color='red', linestyle='--',
    ↪   label='Threshold')
    plt.title("Reconstruction Error Distribution on Test Set")
    plt.xlabel("Error")
    plt.ylabel("Count")
    plt.legend()
    plt.show()

if __name__ == "__main__":
    main()
```

Key Implementation Details:

- **Data Preparation:** We created a synthetic time series composed of sinusoidal data plus injected spikes. The dataset is split into training, validation, and test subsets, with training data containing mostly normal sequences.

- **LSTM VAE Architecture:** The LSTMVAE uses an LSTM-based encoder to produce mu and logvar, then performs the reparameterization trick in reparameterize, and decodes

39

the latent state through a second LSTM-based decoder.

- **VAE Loss Function:** The total loss combines mean-squared error reconstruction loss and a KL divergence term, as implemented in `vae_loss_function`.

- **Training Loop:** Each epoch calls `train_epoch`, which runs forward passes, computes losses, and backpropagates. We also use `evaluate_model` for validation.

- **Anomaly Scoring:** We compute reconstruction errors for each sequence using `reconstruct_sequences`. If errors exceed a threshold derived from validation statistics, we flag the sequence as anomalous.

- **Complete Pipeline:** The `main` function orchestrates data generation, model initialization, training, threshold selection, and final anomaly detection evaluation in a concise workflow.

Chapter 6

VAE for 3D Data Generation

- This chapter explores how VAEs can be extended to 3D data representations, such as point clouds or voxel grids.

- We discuss data loading and preprocessing steps for 3D models, adapting the encoder to learn latent distributions from these representations, and constructing a matching decoder to regenerate 3D shapes.

- The chapter covers strategies for training stability, memory management, and using CUDA for potentially large 3D datasets.

- By the end, you will have a pipeline that demonstrates generative modeling of three-dimensional objects.

Python Code Snippet

```python
import torch
import torch.nn as nn
import torch.optim as optim
import numpy as np
from torch.utils.data import Dataset, DataLoader
import random

# -----------------------------------------------------------
# 1) Synthetic dataset that generates random 3D voxel shapes
# -----------------------------------------------------------
```

```python
class SyntheticShapes3DDataset(Dataset):
    """
    A simple dataset of random 3D volumes. Each sample is a binary
    ↪   3D voxel
    with a randomly placed sphere or solid shape. The shapes are
    ↪   stored as
    tensors of size [1, depth, height, width].
    """
    def __init__(self, n_samples=1000, shape_size=32):
        super().__init__()
        self.n_samples = n_samples
        self.shape_size = shape_size
        self.data = self._generate_data(n_samples, shape_size)

    def _generate_data(self, n_samples, shape_size):
        """
        Generate random 3D volumes with spheres.
        """
        all_data = []
        for _ in range(n_samples):
            volume = np.zeros((shape_size, shape_size, shape_size),
            ↪   dtype=np.float32)
            # Randomly pick a center and radius
            center_x = random.randint(5, shape_size - 5)
            center_y = random.randint(5, shape_size - 5)
            center_z = random.randint(5, shape_size - 5)
            radius = random.randint(3, 6)
            # Fill volume with a sphere
            for x in range(shape_size):
                for y in range(shape_size):
                    for z in range(shape_size):
                        dist_sq = (x - center_x)**2 + (y -
                        ↪   center_y)**2 + (z - center_z)**2
                        if dist_sq <= radius**2:
                            volume[x, y, z] = 1.0
            all_data.append(volume)
        return np.array(all_data)

    def __len__(self):
        return self.n_samples

    def __getitem__(self, idx):
        volume = self.data[idx]
        # Convert to [channels, D, H, W] and float32
        volume = torch.tensor(volume).unsqueeze(0)
        return volume

# ----------------------------------------------------------------
# 2) Define a Variational Autoencoder for 3D data
# ----------------------------------------------------------------
class VAE3D(nn.Module):
    """
```

```python
A simple 3D VAE with Conv3d layers for encoder and
↪   ConvTranspose3d for decoder,
producing latent mean (mu) and log-variance (logvar) for a
↪   reparameterization trick.
"""
def __init__(self, latent_dim=64, base_channels=32):
    super(VAE3D, self).__init__()
    self.latent_dim = latent_dim

    # Encoder: 3D Convolutional layers
    self.enc_conv1 = nn.Conv3d(1, base_channels, kernel_size=4,
    ↪   stride=2, padding=1)
    self.enc_conv2 = nn.Conv3d(base_channels, base_channels*2,
    ↪   kernel_size=4, stride=2, padding=1)
    self.enc_conv3 = nn.Conv3d(base_channels*2, base_channels*4,
    ↪   kernel_size=4, stride=2, padding=1)

    # Flatten -> linear for mu and logvar
    # size after 3 downsamples with kernel=4,stride=2 for
    ↪   shape_size=32: 32/(2*2*2)=4
    # so we get base_channels*4 x 4 x 4 x 4 features
    self.flat_dim = base_channels*4 * 4 * 4 * 4
    self.enc_fc_mu = nn.Linear(self.flat_dim, latent_dim)
    self.enc_fc_logvar = nn.Linear(self.flat_dim, latent_dim)

    # Decoder: project from latent -> unflatten ->
    ↪   ConvTranspose3d
    self.dec_fc = nn.Linear(latent_dim, self.flat_dim)
    self.dec_conv1 = nn.ConvTranspose3d(base_channels*4,
    ↪   base_channels*2, kernel_size=4, stride=2, padding=1)
    self.dec_conv2 = nn.ConvTranspose3d(base_channels*2,
    ↪   base_channels, kernel_size=4, stride=2, padding=1)
    self.dec_conv3 = nn.ConvTranspose3d(base_channels, 1,
    ↪   kernel_size=4, stride=2, padding=1)

    self.relu = nn.ReLU()
    self.sigmoid = nn.Sigmoid()

def encode(self, x):
    """
    Encode 3D input to latent parameters mu and logvar.
    """
    h = self.relu(self.enc_conv1(x))
    h = self.relu(self.enc_conv2(h))
    h = self.relu(self.enc_conv3(h))
    # Flatten
    h = h.view(-1, self.flat_dim)
    mu = self.enc_fc_mu(h)
    logvar = self.enc_fc_logvar(h)
    return mu, logvar

def reparameterize(self, mu, logvar):
    """
```

```python
    Reparameterization trick to sample from N(mu, sigma^2).
    """
    std = torch.exp(0.5 * logvar)
    eps = torch.randn_like(std)
    return mu + eps * std

def decode(self, z):
    """
    Decode latent vector z to reconstruct the 3D volume.
    """
    h = self.relu(self.dec_fc(z))
    # Unflatten
    h = h.view(-1, 128, 4, 4, 4)   # base_channels*4 = 128
    h = self.relu(self.dec_conv1(h))
    h = self.relu(self.dec_conv2(h))
    h = self.dec_conv3(h)
    # We use sigmoid to ensure values range between [0,1]
    return self.sigmoid(h)

def forward(self, x):
    """
    Full forward pass: encode -> reparam -> decode.
    """
    mu, logvar = self.encode(x)
    z = self.reparameterize(mu, logvar)
    x_recon = self.decode(z)
    return x_recon, mu, logvar


# ----------------------------------------------------------------
# 3) Define the VAE loss function
# ----------------------------------------------------------------
def vae_loss_function(recon_x, x, mu, logvar):
    """
    Standard VAE loss = reconstruction loss + KL divergence
    """
    # MSE or BCE can be used; we use MSE for voxel data
    recon_loss = nn.MSELoss(reduction='sum')(recon_x, x)

    # KL divergence
    # KLD = -0.5 * sum(1 + logvar - mu^2 - exp(logvar))
    kld = -0.5 * torch.sum(1 + logvar - mu.pow(2) - logvar.exp())

    return (recon_loss + kld) / x.size(0)


# ----------------------------------------------------------------
# 4) Training routine for one epoch
# ----------------------------------------------------------------
def train_one_epoch(model, dataloader, optimizer, device):
    """
    Train the VAE for one epoch, returning the average loss.
    """
    model.train()
    total_loss = 0
```

```python
    for batch in dataloader:
        batch = batch.to(device)
        optimizer.zero_grad()
        recon_batch, mu, logvar = model(batch)
        loss = vae_loss_function(recon_batch, batch, mu, logvar)
        loss.backward()
        optimizer.step()
        total_loss += loss.item()
    return total_loss / len(dataloader)


# ----------------------------------------------------------------
# 5) Validation routine
# ----------------------------------------------------------------
def validate_model(model, dataloader, device):
    """
    Evaluate the VAE on the validation dataset, returning the
    ↪   average loss.
    """
    model.eval()
    total_loss = 0
    with torch.no_grad():
        for batch in dataloader:
            batch = batch.to(device)
            recon_batch, mu, logvar = model(batch)
            loss = vae_loss_function(recon_batch, batch, mu, logvar)
            total_loss += loss.item()
    return total_loss / len(dataloader)


# ----------------------------------------------------------------
# 6) Function to generate new samples from random latent vectors
# ----------------------------------------------------------------
def generate_samples(model, num_samples, device):
    """
    Generate new 3D samples by sampling random latents from a normal
    ↪   distribution.
    """
    model.eval()
    z = torch.randn(num_samples, model.latent_dim).to(device)
    with torch.no_grad():
        samples = model.decode(z)
    return samples


# ----------------------------------------------------------------
# 7) Main script for data loading, model creation, and training
# ----------------------------------------------------------------
def main():
    # Basic settings
    device = torch.device("cuda" if torch.cuda.is_available() else
    ↪   "cpu")
    torch.manual_seed(42)
    random.seed(42)
    np.random.seed(42)
```

```
# Create synthetic dataset
train_dataset = SyntheticShapes3DDataset(n_samples=800,
↪  shape_size=32)
val_dataset  = SyntheticShapes3DDataset(n_samples=200,
↪  shape_size=32)

train_loader = DataLoader(train_dataset, batch_size=8,
↪  shuffle=True)
val_loader  = DataLoader(val_dataset, batch_size=8,
↪  shuffle=False)

# Initialize VAE model
model = VAE3D(latent_dim=64, base_channels=32).to(device)
optimizer = optim.Adam(model.parameters(), lr=1e-3)

# Training loop
epochs = 5
for epoch in range(epochs):
    train_loss = train_one_epoch(model, train_loader, optimizer,
    ↪  device)
    val_loss = validate_model(model, val_loader, device)
    print(f"Epoch [{epoch+1}/{epochs}] - Train Loss:
    ↪  {train_loss:.4f}, Val Loss: {val_loss:.4f}")

# Generate and display shape of random samples
with torch.no_grad():
    new_samples = generate_samples(model, num_samples=2,
    ↪  device=device)
print(f"Generated sample shape: {new_samples.shape}")

# Indicate end of training
print("VAE 3D training complete. Sample generation done.")

if __name__ == "__main__":
    main()
```

Key Implementation Details:

- **Dataset Generation:** In SyntheticShapes3DDataset, we create simple 3D volumes ($32 \times 32 \times 32$) containing random spheres. This simulates basic 3D shapes that we can feed into the model.

- **VAE Architecture:** VAE3D includes a 3D convolutional encoder producing *mu* and *logvar*, a reparameterize function (reparameterization trick), and a 3D convolutional decoder to reconstruct volumes from latent codes.

- **Loss Function:** In vae_loss_function, we combine the

reconstruction term (MSE) and KL divergence to guide the encoder towards learning a smooth latent distribution.

- **Training Routine:** Each epoch in `train_one_epoch` involves forward passing a batch through the network, computing the VAE loss, performing backpropagation, and updating weights.

- **Sampling New 3D Shapes:** `generate_samples` demonstrates how to draw random latent vectors and decode them to produce entirely new 3D volumes, illustrating the generative potential of VAEs for 3D data.

Chapter 7

VAE for Text Generation

Here, we shift focus to natural language processing by training a Variational Autoencoder (VAE) on text data. This involves tokenizing sentences, creating embeddings, and using LSTM-based encoders and decoders to represent sequences. We train the model to reconstruct sentences while learning a smooth latent space. To handle the discrete nature of text, we apply the reparameterization trick and explore stable training setups. This chapter covers details like padding, masking, and text sampling from the probabilistic latent space.

- We load or create a dataset of text sentences.

- Each sentence is converted to a list of token IDs (e.g., word indices).

- We define and apply padding/masking to handle variable sentence lengths.

- An LSTM-based encoder outputs mean and log-variance for the latent distribution.

- A reparameterization step samples from this distribution to get latent vectors.

- An LSTM-based decoder reconstructs sentences from latent vectors, trained via a combination of reconstruction loss (cross-entropy) and KL divergence.

- The resulting latent space can then be sampled to produce novel text.

Python Code Snippet

```python
import torch
import torch.nn as nn
import torch.optim as optim
import torch.nn.functional as F
from torch.utils.data import Dataset, DataLoader
import numpy as np
import random


# -----------------------------------------------------------------
# 1) Set random seed for reproducibility
# -----------------------------------------------------------------
def set_seed(seed=42):
    random.seed(seed)
    np.random.seed(seed)
    torch.manual_seed(seed)
    if torch.cuda.is_available():
        torch.cuda.manual_seed_all(seed)


# -----------------------------------------------------------------
# 2) Example text dataset and vocabulary building
# -----------------------------------------------------------------
class ToyTextDataset(Dataset):
    """
    A simple toy dataset for demonstration.
    Each data sample is a sentence converted to a list of token
     ↳   indices.
    We'll handle <PAD>, <SOS>, and <EOS> tokens to denote padding,
    start-of-sentence, and end-of-sentence.
    """
    def __init__(self, sentences, word2idx, max_length=10):
        super().__init__()
        self.sentences = sentences
        self.word2idx = word2idx
        self.max_length = max_length
        self.sos_idx = self.word2idx["<SOS>"]
        self.eos_idx = self.word2idx["<EOS>"]
        self.pad_idx = self.word2idx["<PAD>"]
        self.data = self._encode_sentences()

    def _encode_sentences(self):
        encoded = []
        for s in self.sentences:
            tokens = s.lower().split()  # naive tokenization
            token_ids = [self.word2idx.get(t,
             ↳   self.word2idx["<UNK>"]) for t in tokens]
```

```python
        # Insert <SOS> and <EOS>
        token_ids = [self.sos_idx] + token_ids + [self.eos_idx]
        # Pad or truncate to max_length
        token_ids = token_ids[:self.max_length]
        if len(token_ids) < self.max_length:
            token_ids += [self.pad_idx] * (self.max_length -
            ↪  len(token_ids))

        encoded.append(token_ids)
    return encoded

    def __getitem__(self, idx):
        return torch.tensor(self.data[idx], dtype=torch.long)

    def __len__(self):
        return len(self.data)

def build_vocab(sentences, vocab_size=50):
    """
    Build a naive vocabulary from a list of sentences.
    We'll keep this minimal; in practice you'd use a proper
    ↪  tokenizer.
    """
    # Count word frequencies
    freq = {}
    for s in sentences:
        for w in s.lower().split():
            freq[w] = freq.get(w, 0) + 1

    # Sort by frequency
    sorted_words = sorted(freq.keys(), key=lambda x: freq[x],
    ↪  reverse=True)
    # Keep top 'vocab_size' words + special tokens
    sorted_words = sorted_words[: vocab_size - 4]  # minus special
    ↪  tokens
    word2idx = {
        "<PAD>": 0,
        "<UNK>": 1,
        "<SOS>": 2,
        "<EOS>": 3,
    }
    idx2word = {}
    idx = 4
    for w in sorted_words:
        word2idx[w] = idx
        idx += 1

    # Build reverse mapping
    idx2word = {v: k for k, v in word2idx.items()}
    return word2idx, idx2word

# --------------------------------------------------------------
```

50

```
# 3) Define the VAE model (LSTM-based encoder and decoder)
# ------------------------------------------------------------
class LSTMEncoder(nn.Module):
    """
    LSTM-based encoder that produces mean and logvar for the latent
    ↪  space.
    """
    def __init__(self, vocab_size, embed_dim, hidden_dim,
    ↪  latent_dim, pad_idx):
        super().__init__()
        self.embedding = nn.Embedding(vocab_size, embed_dim,
        ↪  padding_idx=pad_idx)
        self.lstm = nn.LSTM(embed_dim, hidden_dim, batch_first=True)
        self.hidden_dim = hidden_dim
        self.latent_dim = latent_dim
        # Convert LSTM output (hidden_dim) to latent distribution
        self.fc_mean = nn.Linear(hidden_dim, latent_dim)
        self.fc_logvar = nn.Linear(hidden_dim, latent_dim)

    def forward(self, x):
        """
        x shape: (batch_size, seq_len)
        """
        embedded = self.embedding(x)  # (batch_size, seq_len,
        ↪  embed_dim)
        _, (h, _) = self.lstm(embedded)  # h shape: (1, batch_size,
        ↪  hidden_dim)
        h = h.squeeze(0)  # (batch_size, hidden_dim)
        mean = self.fc_mean(h)
        logvar = self.fc_logvar(h)
        return mean, logvar

class LSTMDecoder(nn.Module):
    """
    LSTM-based decoder that reconstructs the sentence from a sampled
    ↪  latent vector.
    """
    def __init__(self, vocab_size, embed_dim, hidden_dim,
    ↪  latent_dim, pad_idx):
        super().__init__()
        self.embedding = nn.Embedding(vocab_size, embed_dim,
        ↪  padding_idx=pad_idx)
        self.lstm = nn.LSTM(embed_dim + latent_dim, hidden_dim,
        ↪  batch_first=True)
        self.output_fc = nn.Linear(hidden_dim, vocab_size)
        self.latent_dim = latent_dim

    def forward(self, z, x, hidden=None):
        """
        z shape: (batch_size, latent_dim)
        x shape: (batch_size, seq_len) - teacher forcing inputs
        """
        batch_size, seq_len = x.size()
```

```python
        embedded = self.embedding(x)  # (batch_size, seq_len,
        ↪   embed_dim)

        # Repeat latent z across seq_len dimension, then concat
        z = z.unsqueeze(1).repeat(1, seq_len, 1)  # (batch_size,
        ↪   seq_len, latent_dim)
        lstm_input = torch.cat([embedded, z], dim=2)  # (batch_size,
        ↪   seq_len, embed_dim+latent_dim)

        out, hidden = self.lstm(lstm_input, hidden)
        logits = self.output_fc(out)  # (batch_size, seq_len,
        ↪   vocab_size)
        return logits, hidden


class TextVAE(nn.Module):
    """
    Full text VAE combining the LSTM encoder and decoder with
    the reparameterization trick and a standard VAE forward pass.
    """
    def __init__(self, vocab_size, embed_dim, hidden_dim,
    ↪   latent_dim, pad_idx):
        super().__init__()
        self.encoder = LSTMEncoder(vocab_size, embed_dim,
        ↪   hidden_dim, latent_dim, pad_idx)
        self.decoder = LSTMDecoder(vocab_size, embed_dim,
        ↪   hidden_dim, latent_dim, pad_idx)

    def reparameterize(self, mean, logvar):
        """
        Reparameterization trick to sample: z = mean + eps *
        ↪   exp(0.5*logvar)
        """
        std = torch.exp(0.5 * logvar)
        eps = torch.randn_like(std)
        return mean + eps * std

    def forward(self, x):
        """
        Return the logits for reconstruction, plus mean and logvar
        ↪   for KL.
        """
        mean, logvar = self.encoder(x)
        z = self.reparameterize(mean, logvar)
        logits, _ = self.decoder(z, x)
        return logits, mean, logvar


# --------------------------------------------------------------
# 4) Loss functions: reconstruction + KL divergence
# --------------------------------------------------------------
def sequence_cross_entropy_loss(logits, targets, pad_idx):
    """
    Compute cross-entropy (token by token) ignoring <PAD> tokens.
    logits: (batch_size, seq_len, vocab_size)
```

```
    targets: (batch_size, seq_len)
    """
    batch_size, seq_len, vocab_size = logits.size()
    logits_2d = logits.view(-1, vocab_size)   # (batch_size*seq_len,
    ↪   vocab_size)
    targets_1d = targets.view(-1)             #
    ↪   (batch_size*seq_len)

    # We can mask out the pad_idx tokens
    loss = F.cross_entropy(logits_2d, targets_1d,
    ↪   ignore_index=pad_idx)
    return loss


def kl_divergence_loss(mean, logvar):
    """
    KL divergence between N(mean, exp(logvar)) and N(0,1).
    Using formula: KL = -0.5 * sum(1 + logvar - mean^2 -
    ↪   exp(logvar))
    """
    kl = -0.5 * torch.sum(1 + logvar - mean.pow(2) - logvar.exp(),
    ↪   dim=1)
    return kl.mean()


# -------------------------------------------------------------
# 5) Training and sampling routines
# -------------------------------------------------------------
def train_one_epoch(model, optimizer, dataloader, pad_idx, device,
↪   beta=1.0):
    """
    Train model for one epoch on entire dataloader.
    'beta' is a hyperparameter to scale the KL term
    (useful for beta-VAE style or warm-up).
    """
    model.train()
    epoch_loss = 0.0
    for x_batch in dataloader:
        x_batch = x_batch.to(device)
        optimizer.zero_grad()

        logits, mean, logvar = model(x_batch)

        # Reconstruction loss
        recon_loss = sequence_cross_entropy_loss(logits, x_batch,
        ↪   pad_idx)
        # KL divergence
        kl_loss = kl_divergence_loss(mean, logvar)

        loss = recon_loss + beta * kl_loss
        loss.backward()
        optimizer.step()

        epoch_loss += loss.item()
    return epoch_loss / len(dataloader)
```

```python
def evaluate_model(model, dataloader, pad_idx, device, beta=1.0):
    model.eval()
    epoch_loss = 0.0
    with torch.no_grad():
        for x_batch in dataloader:
            x_batch = x_batch.to(device)
            logits, mean, logvar = model(x_batch)
            recon_loss = sequence_cross_entropy_loss(logits,
            ↪ x_batch, pad_idx)
            kl_loss = kl_divergence_loss(mean, logvar)
            loss = recon_loss + beta * kl_loss
            epoch_loss += loss.item()
    return epoch_loss / len(dataloader)

def sample_sentences(model, idx2word, max_length=10, device="cpu",
↪ num_samples=5):
    """
    Sample new sentences from the VAE by sampling z ~ N(0,I).
    We'll use greedy decoding for simplicity.
    """
    model.eval()
    sampled_sentences = []
    with torch.no_grad():
        for _ in range(num_samples):
            # Sample from Standard Gaussian in latent space
            z = torch.randn((1, model.encoder.latent_dim),
            ↪ device=device)

            # We start with <SOS> token
            sos_idx = 2
            current_input = torch.tensor([[sos_idx]], device=device)
            hidden = None
            generated_tokens = [sos_idx]

            for _ in range(max_length - 1):
                logits, hidden = model.decoder(z, current_input,
                ↪ hidden=hidden)
                # logits shape: (1, seq_len, vocab_size)
                next_token_dist = logits[:, -1, :]  # last time
                ↪ step
                next_token = torch.argmax(next_token_dist, dim=-1)
                ↪ # greedy
                generated_tokens.append(next_token.item())
                current_input = torch.cat([current_input,
                ↪ next_token.unsqueeze(0)], dim=1)

            # Convert token IDs to words
            sentence_words = []
            for token_id in generated_tokens:
                word = idx2word.get(token_id, "<UNK>")
                if word == "<EOS>":
                    break
```

```python
            if word not in ["<SOS>", "<PAD>"]:
                sentence_words.append(word)

        sampled_sentences.append(" ".join(sentence_words))
    return sampled_sentences

# ----------------------------------------------------------------
# 6) Main script: define dataset, build model, and train
# ----------------------------------------------------------------
def main():
    set_seed(42)
    device = torch.device("cuda" if torch.cuda.is_available() else
    ↪   "cpu")

    # Example toy sentences
    sentences = [
        "i love deep learning",
        "this is a simple example",
        "pytorch is quite flexible",
        "deep learning with lstms",
        "variational autoencoders are interesting",
        "hello world",
        "text generation is cool",
        "train the model on sentences",
        "make sure we handle pad",
        "just a few example lines"
    ]

    # Build vocabulary
    vocab_size = 30  # limit for demonstration
    word2idx, idx2word = build_vocab(sentences,
    ↪   vocab_size=vocab_size)
    pad_idx = word2idx["<PAD>"]

    # Prepare dataset & dataloader
    dataset = ToyTextDataset(sentences, word2idx, max_length=8)
    dataloader = DataLoader(dataset, batch_size=4, shuffle=True)

    # Instantiate the VAE
    embed_dim = 16
    hidden_dim = 32
    latent_dim = 16
    model = TextVAE(
        vocab_size=len(word2idx),
        embed_dim=embed_dim,
        hidden_dim=hidden_dim,
        latent_dim=latent_dim,
        pad_idx=pad_idx
    ).to(device)

    optimizer = optim.Adam(model.parameters(), lr=1e-3)

    # Training loop
```

```
epochs = 10
for epoch in range(1, epochs + 1):
    train_loss = train_one_epoch(model, optimizer, dataloader,
    ↪  pad_idx, device, beta=1.0)
    val_loss = evaluate_model(model, dataloader, pad_idx,
    ↪  device, beta=1.0)

    print(f"Epoch [{epoch}/{epochs}] - Train Loss:
    ↪  {train_loss:.4f}, Val Loss: {val_loss:.4f}")

    # Generate some samples after each epoch
    samples = sample_sentences(model, idx2word, max_length=8,
    ↪  device=device, num_samples=3)
    print("Sampled sentences:", samples)

    print("Training complete!")

if __name__ == "__main__":
    main()
```

Key Implementation Details:

- **Encoder-Decoder Architecture:** We employ two LSTM networks. The first (encoder) outputs mean and log-variance (logvar) for the latent distribution. The second (decoder) reconstructs sentences from sampled latent vectors.

- **Reparameterization Trick:** The network learns mean () and log-variance ($\log^2$). We sample $z = + \cdot \exp(0.5 \cdot \log^2)$ to enable gradient-based optimization through sampling.

- **VAE Loss Function:** The total loss is composed of a cross-entropy term to reconstruct each token, plus the KL divergence between the learned distribution and the standard normal prior.

- **Padding and Masking:** We designate <PAD> tokens for sentences shorter than the maximum sequence length. Cross-entropy loss ignores these <PAD> regions using the argument ignore_index.

- **Sampling Procedure:** After training, we generate new sentences by sampling latent vectors from N(0, I). The decoder then unfolds the sentence token by token (greedy decoding here), illustrating how latent space sampling can yield new text.

- **Extensions:** While this example uses a small LSTM-based model and naive data, you can adapt the framework for larger corpora, more sophisticated tokenization (e.g., BPE), and deeper networks (e.g., Transformer encoders/decoders).

Chapter 8

VAE for Semi-Supervised Learning

We take advantage of the expressive capabilities of VAEs to handle partially labeled datasets. By combining labeled and unlabeled data, the encoder learns representative latent features while a classification head is trained on available labels. Implementation details include creating a multi-objective loss function that balances label prediction with the VAE's reconstruction and KL terms. The chapter emphasizes data loader design, supervised loss weighting, and explains how this approach can improve classifier performance with limited labels.

- First, we create a custom dataset that randomly discards labels for a fraction of samples, simulating a partially labeled scenario.

- We construct an encoder-decoder architecture for the VAE and add a classification head that predicts class labels when available.

- We minimize a combination of reconstruction error, KL divergence, and classification cross-entropy for labeled instances.

- Through this multi-loss design, we leverage both labeled and unlabeled data to learn a meaningful latent structure that improves classification with limited labels.

Python Code Snippet

```python
import torch
import torch.nn as nn
import torch.optim as optim
from torch.utils.data import DataLoader
import torchvision
import torchvision.transforms as transforms
import random
import numpy as np
import matplotlib.pyplot as plt
import os


# ----------------------------------------------------------------
# 1) Configuration & Utilities
# ----------------------------------------------------------------

def set_seed(seed=42):
    """
    Set random seed for reproducibility.
    """
    random.seed(seed)
    np.random.seed(seed)
    torch.manual_seed(seed)
    if torch.cuda.is_available():
        torch.cuda.manual_seed_all(seed)


class PartiallyLabeledMNIST(torchvision.datasets.MNIST):
    """
    Custom MNIST dataset that randomly appears unlabeled for a given
    ↪  fraction.
    Unlabeled samples have their labels replaced with -1.
    """
    def __init__(self, root, train=True, transform=None,
    ↪  download=True, fraction_labeled=0.1, seed=42):
        super(PartiallyLabeledMNIST, self).__init__(root=root,
        ↪  train=train,

                                          ↪  transform=transform,
                                          ↪  download=download)
        set_seed(seed)
        num_samples = len(self.data)
        labeled_count = int(fraction_labeled * num_samples)
        # Shuffle indices and pick a subset as labeled
        all_indices = np.arange(num_samples)
        np.random.shuffle(all_indices)
        labeled_indices = set(all_indices[:labeled_count])
        # create mask
        self.label_mask = np.zeros(num_samples, dtype=bool)
        self.label_mask[list(labeled_indices)] = True
```

```python
    def __getitem__(self, index):
        img, target = super(PartiallyLabeledMNIST,
        ↪ self).__getitem__(index)
        # If this sample is unlabeled, set the label to -1
        if not self.label_mask[index]:
            target = -1
        return img, target


# ----------------------------------------------------------------
# 2) Model Definition: Encoder, Decoder, Classifier, and
↪ SemiSuperVAE
# ----------------------------------------------------------------

class Encoder(nn.Module):
    """
    Simple MLP-based encoder that outputs mu and logvar.
    """
    def __init__(self, input_dim=784, hidden_dim=512,
    ↪ latent_dim=20):
        super(Encoder, self).__init__()
        self.fc1 = nn.Linear(input_dim, hidden_dim)
        self.fc2 = nn.Linear(hidden_dim, hidden_dim)
        self.fc_mu = nn.Linear(hidden_dim, latent_dim)
        self.fc_logvar = nn.Linear(hidden_dim, latent_dim)
        self.relu = nn.ReLU(inplace=True)

    def forward(self, x):
        # Flatten input
        x = x.view(x.size(0), -1)
        h = self.relu(self.fc1(x))
        h = self.relu(self.fc2(h))
        mu = self.fc_mu(h)
        logvar = self.fc_logvar(h)
        return mu, logvar


class Decoder(nn.Module):
    """
    Simple MLP-based decoder that reconstructs from latent z.
    """
    def __init__(self, latent_dim=20, hidden_dim=512,
    ↪ output_dim=784):
        super(Decoder, self).__init__()
        self.fc1 = nn.Linear(latent_dim, hidden_dim)
        self.fc2 = nn.Linear(hidden_dim, hidden_dim)
        self.fc3 = nn.Linear(hidden_dim, output_dim)
        self.relu = nn.ReLU(inplace=True)
        self.sigmoid = nn.Sigmoid()

    def forward(self, z):
        h = self.relu(self.fc1(z))
        h = self.relu(self.fc2(h))
```

60

```python
        x_recon = self.sigmoid(self.fc3(h))
        # Reshape to match MNIST image dimensions (1 x 28 x 28)
        x_recon = x_recon.view(z.size(0), 1, 28, 28)
        return x_recon


class ClassifierHead(nn.Module):
    """
    Classification head that receives the latent vector z.
    """
    def __init__(self, latent_dim=20, num_classes=10,
    ↪   hidden_dim=256):
        super(ClassifierHead, self).__init__()
        self.fc1 = nn.Linear(latent_dim, hidden_dim)
        self.fc2 = nn.Linear(hidden_dim, num_classes)
        self.relu = nn.ReLU(inplace=True)

    def forward(self, z):
        h = self.relu(self.fc1(z))
        logits = self.fc2(h)
        return logits


class SemiSuperVAE(nn.Module):
    """
    Semi-supervised VAE that includes:
    - encoder (returns mu, logvar)
    - decoder (reconstructs)
    - classifier head (predicts label)
    """
    def __init__(self, latent_dim=20):
        super(SemiSuperVAE, self).__init__()
        self.encoder = Encoder(latent_dim=latent_dim)
        self.decoder = Decoder(latent_dim=latent_dim)
        self.classifier = ClassifierHead(latent_dim=latent_dim)

    def reparameterize(self, mu, logvar):
        std = torch.exp(0.5 * logvar)
        eps = torch.randn_like(std)
        return mu + eps * std

    def forward(self, x):
        mu, logvar = self.encoder(x)
        z = self.reparameterize(mu, logvar)
        x_recon = self.decoder(z)
        logits = self.classifier(z)
        return x_recon, mu, logvar, logits


# --------------------------------------------------------------
# 3) Loss Functions
# --------------------------------------------------------------
```

```python
def vae_loss_function(x, x_recon, mu, logvar):
    """
    Reconstruction + KL divergence losses.
    Using BCE for reconstruction, summation over all pixels.
    """
    bce = nn.functional.binary_cross_entropy(
        x_recon.view(x.size(0), -1),
        x.view(x.size(0), -1),
        reduction='sum'
    )
    # KL divergence
    kl = -0.5 * torch.sum(1 + logvar - mu.pow(2) - logvar.exp())
    return bce + kl


def classification_loss_function(logits, labels):
    """
    Classification cross-entropy for labeled samples only.
    We ignore masked (unlabeled) samples with label = -1.
    """
    # Filter valid indices
    valid_indices = (labels >= 0)
    if valid_indices.sum() == 0:
        return torch.tensor(0.0, device=labels.device)
    valid_labels = labels[valid_indices]
    valid_logits = logits[valid_indices]
    return nn.functional.cross_entropy(valid_logits, valid_labels)


# ----------------------------------------------------------------
# 4) Training and Evaluation
# ----------------------------------------------------------------

def train_one_epoch(model, optimizer, dataloader, device,
    alpha=1.0):
    """
    A single training epoch.
    The parameter alpha controls the weight of the classification
        loss.
    """
    model.train()
    epoch_loss = 0.0
    for x, y in dataloader:
        x, y = x.to(device), y.to(device)
        optimizer.zero_grad()
        x_recon, mu, logvar, logits = model(x)

        # Compute VAE loss
        vae_loss = vae_loss_function(x, x_recon, mu, logvar)
        # Compute classification loss
        cls_loss = classification_loss_function(logits, y)
        # Combine
        loss = vae_loss + alpha * cls_loss
```

```python
            loss.backward()
            optimizer.step()

            epoch_loss += loss.item()
        return epoch_loss / len(dataloader)


def evaluate_classification_accuracy(model, dataloader, device):
    """
    Evaluate classification accuracy on labeled data.
    Ignores unlabeled samples (label = -1).
    """
    model.eval()
    correct = 0
    total = 0
    with torch.no_grad():
        for x, y in dataloader:
            x, y = x.to(device), y.to(device)
            # Only evaluate labeled samples
            valid_indices = (y >= 0)
            if valid_indices.sum() == 0:
                continue
            valid_x = x[valid_indices]
            valid_y = y[valid_indices]

            # Forward pass
            _, _, _, logits = model(valid_x)
            pred = logits.argmax(dim=1)
            correct += (pred == valid_y).sum().item()
            total += valid_y.size(0)
    if total == 0:
        return 0.0
    return correct / total


def reconstruct_samples(model, dataloader, device,
    save_path="reconstructions.png"):
    """
    Visual check: reconstruct a few samples from the test set.
    """
    model.eval()
    os.makedirs("results", exist_ok=True)
    with torch.no_grad():
        data_iter = iter(dataloader)
        x, _ = next(data_iter)
        x = x.to(device)
        x_recon, _, _, _ = model(x)
        # Move both to CPU for plotting
        x = x.cpu()
        x_recon = x_recon.cpu()

        fig, axes = plt.subplots(nrows=2, ncols=8, figsize=(12, 3))
        for i in range(8):
```

```python
            # Original
            axes[0, i].imshow(x[i].squeeze(), cmap='gray')
            axes[0, i].axis('off')
            # Reconstruction
            axes[1, i].imshow(x_recon[i].squeeze(), cmap='gray')
            axes[1, i].axis('off')
        plt.savefig(os.path.join("results", save_path))
        plt.close()


# -------------------------------------------------------------
# 5) Main Script
# -------------------------------------------------------------

def main():
    set_seed(42)
    device = torch.device("cuda" if torch.cuda.is_available() else
    ↪    "cpu")

    # Define transforms
    transform = transforms.Compose([
        transforms.ToTensor()
    ])

    # Create partially labeled MNIST dataset
    train_dataset = PartiallyLabeledMNIST(
        root="data",
        train=True,
        transform=transform,
        download=True,
        fraction_labeled=0.1,   # Only 10% labeled
        seed=42
    )
    test_dataset = PartiallyLabeledMNIST(
        root="data",
        train=False,
        transform=transform,
        download=True,
        fraction_labeled=1.0,   # For testing, keep all labels
        seed=999   # Different seed
    )

    train_loader = DataLoader(train_dataset, batch_size=64,
    ↪    shuffle=True)
    test_loader = DataLoader(test_dataset, batch_size=64,
    ↪    shuffle=False)

    # Initialize model
    model = SemiSuperVAE(latent_dim=20).to(device)
    # Define optimizer
    optimizer = optim.Adam(model.parameters(), lr=1e-3)

    # Training parameters
```

64

```
epochs = 5
alpha = 0.1  # weight for classification loss

for epoch in range(epochs):
    train_loss = train_one_epoch(model, optimizer, train_loader,
    ↪    device, alpha=alpha)
    # Evaluate classification accuracy on test set (labeled)
    test_acc = evaluate_classification_accuracy(model,
    ↪    test_loader, device)

    print(f"Epoch [{epoch+1}/{epochs}] - Loss: {train_loss:.4f},
    ↪    Test Acc: {test_acc*100:.2f}%")
    # Reconstruct a few samples
    reconstruct_samples(model, test_loader, device,
    ↪    save_path=f"recons_epoch_{epoch+1}.png")

    print("Training complete! Reconstruction images saved in
    ↪    'results' folder.")


if __name__ == "__main__":
    main()
```

Key Implementation Details:

- **Dataset:** In `PartiallyLabeledMNIST`, we randomly replace up to 90

- **VAE Architecture:** We define a straightforward MLP `Encoder` and `Decoder`, using `ReLU` activations. The encoder outputs both and $\log^2$ for reparameterization.

- **Classifier Head:** The `ClassifierHead` is attached to the encoder's latent space. It is only trained on labeled samples (where label -1).

- **Training Objective:** For every batch, we compute the total loss as the sum of VAE loss (`vae_loss_function`) and a scaled classification cross-entropy (`classification_loss_function`) for labeled data points. The `alpha` parameter balances these terms.

- **Evaluation:** We measure classification accuracy on a fully labeled test set, ignoring entries with label = -1 in `evaluate_classification_accuracy`.

65

- **Reconstruction Samples:** We visualize and save original digits and their reconstructions using `reconstruct_samples`, allowing us to inspect the VAE's reconstruction quality.

Chapter 9

Beta-VAE for Disentangled Representation

- Disentangling latent factors is critical in interpretability. This chapter details how to modify the VAE objective with a hyperparameter to emphasize the KL divergence term, encouraging more factorized latent representations.

- We discuss how to alter your PyTorch or TensorFlow code to incorporate , tune it for appropriate trade-offs between reconstruction quality and disentanglement, and assess which factors are learned.

- Practical tips are provided for selecting architectures that naturally encourage independent latent dimensions.

Python Code Snippet

```python
import torch
import torch.nn as nn
import torch.optim as optim
import torch.nn.functional as F
from torchvision import datasets, transforms
from torch.utils.data import DataLoader
import numpy as np
import random
import os
```

```python
#
↪ -------------------------------------------------------------------
# 1) Set random seed for reproducibility
#
↪ -------------------------------------------------------------------
def set_seed(seed=42):
    random.seed(seed)
    np.random.seed(seed)
    torch.manual_seed(seed)
    if torch.cuda.is_available():
        torch.cuda.manual_seed_all(seed)


#
↪ -------------------------------------------------------------------
# 2) Define the Beta-VAE model
#
↪ -------------------------------------------------------------------
class BetaVAE(nn.Module):
    """
    A Beta Variational Autoencoder for learning disentangled
    ↪ representations.
    Encodes an input to latent parameters (mu, logvar) and decodes
    ↪ samples
    back to reconstruction. The beta parameter scales the KL
    ↪ divergence term.
    """
    def __init__(self, latent_dim=10):
        super(BetaVAE, self).__init__()
        self.latent_dim = latent_dim

        # Encoder: 784 -> 400 -> 20 (mu/logvar for latent_dim=10)
        self.fc1 = nn.Linear(784, 400)
        self.fc2_mu = nn.Linear(400, latent_dim)
        self.fc2_logvar = nn.Linear(400, latent_dim)

        # Decoder: 10 -> 400 -> 784
        self.fc3 = nn.Linear(latent_dim, 400)
        self.fc4 = nn.Linear(400, 784)

    def encode(self, x):
        """
        Encoder that outputs the parameters of the latent
        ↪ distribution.
        """
        h = F.relu(self.fc1(x))
        mu = self.fc2_mu(h)
        logvar = self.fc2_logvar(h)
        return mu, logvar

    def reparameterize(self, mu, logvar):
        """
        Reparameterization trick: z = mu + sigma * eps
```

68

```python
        """
        std = torch.exp(0.5 * logvar)
        eps = torch.randn_like(std)
        return mu + eps * std

    def decode(self, z):
        """
        Decode latent variable z to reconstruct the input.
        """
        h = F.relu(self.fc3(z))
        x_recon = torch.sigmoid(self.fc4(h))
        return x_recon

    def forward(self, x):
        mu, logvar = self.encode(x)
        z = self.reparameterize(mu, logvar)
        recon = self.decode(z)
        return recon, mu, logvar


#
↪    --------------------------------------------------------------------
# 3) Define the Beta-VAE loss function
#
↪    --------------------------------------------------------------------
def beta_vae_loss(recon_x, x, mu, logvar, beta=4.0):
    """
    Combines the reconstruction loss with beta-scaled KL divergence.
    recon_x: reconstructed data
    x: original data
    mu, logvar: latent distribution parameters
    beta: weight for KL term
    """
    # We use binary cross-entropy for reconstruction
    # 'reduction=sum' to sum over all pixels
    BCE = F.binary_cross_entropy(recon_x, x, reduction='sum')

    # KL Divergence
    # KLD = -0.5 * sum(1 + logvar - mu^2 - exp(logvar))
    KLD = -0.5 * torch.sum(1 + logvar - mu.pow(2) - logvar.exp())

    return BCE + beta * KLD


#
↪    --------------------------------------------------------------------
# 4) Training routine
#
↪    --------------------------------------------------------------------
def train_epoch(model, dataloader, optimizer, device, beta=4.0):
    model.train()
    train_loss = 0
    for data, _ in dataloader:
        # Flatten MNIST images into a 784-vector
        data = data.view(-1, 784).to(device)
```

```python
        optimizer.zero_grad()
        recon, mu, logvar = model(data)
        loss = beta_vae_loss(recon, data, mu, logvar, beta)
        loss.backward()
        optimizer.step()

        train_loss += loss.item()
    return train_loss / len(dataloader.dataset)


# ↪ ---------------------------------------------------------------
# 5) Testing routine
# ↪ ---------------------------------------------------------------
def test_epoch(model, dataloader, device, beta=4.0):
    model.eval()
    test_loss = 0
    with torch.no_grad():
        for data, _ in dataloader:
            data = data.view(-1, 784).to(device)
            recon, mu, logvar = model(data)
            loss = beta_vae_loss(recon, data, mu, logvar, beta)
            test_loss += loss.item()
    return test_loss / len(dataloader.dataset)


# ↪ ---------------------------------------------------------------
# 6) Utility function to save reconstructed examples
# ↪ ---------------------------------------------------------------
def save_reconstructed_images(model, data, epoch, device,
↪   results_dir='results'):
    model.eval()
    # Encode -> reparam -> decode
    recon, _, _ = model(data)
    recon = recon.view(-1, 1, 28, 28).cpu().data

    os.makedirs(results_dir, exist_ok=True)
    from torchvision.utils import save_image
    save_image(recon, f"{results_dir}/recon_epoch_{epoch}.png")


# ↪ ---------------------------------------------------------------
# 7) Main function
# ↪ ---------------------------------------------------------------
def main():
    set_seed(42)
    device = torch.device('cuda' if torch.cuda.is_available() else
    ↪   'cpu')

    # Hyperparameters
```

```python
    batch_size = 128
    epochs = 5
    latent_dim = 10
    beta = 4.0
    learning_rate = 1e-3

    # Prepare MNIST Data
    transform = transforms.Compose([
        transforms.ToTensor(),
    ])
    train_dataset = datasets.MNIST(root='./data', train=True,
    ↪   download=True, transform=transform)
    test_dataset = datasets.MNIST(root='./data', train=False,
    ↪   download=True, transform=transform)

    train_loader = DataLoader(train_dataset, batch_size=batch_size,
    ↪   shuffle=True)
    test_loader = DataLoader(test_dataset, batch_size=batch_size,
    ↪   shuffle=False)

    # Initialize BetaVAE
    model = BetaVAE(latent_dim=latent_dim).to(device)
    optimizer = optim.Adam(model.parameters(), lr=learning_rate)

    # Training Loop
    for epoch in range(1, epochs + 1):
        train_loss = train_epoch(model, train_loader, optimizer,
        ↪   device, beta=beta)
        test_loss = test_epoch(model, test_loader, device,
        ↪   beta=beta)
        print(f"Epoch [{epoch}/{epochs}] - Train Loss:
        ↪   {train_loss:.4f}, Test Loss: {test_loss:.4f}")

        # Save a small batch of reconstructed images
        sample_data, _ = next(iter(test_loader))
        sample_data = sample_data[:8].view(-1, 784).to(device)
        save_reconstructed_images(model, sample_data, epoch, device,
        ↪   results_dir='results_beta_vae')

    print("Training complete. Reconstructed images are saved in
    ↪   'results_beta_vae' directory.")

if __name__ == "__main__":
    main()
```

Key Implementation Details:

- **Forward Pass:** We call encode to obtain (, log²), then sample z via the **reparameterize** function. Finally, we invoke decode to obtain the reconstruction layer.

- **Beta Hyperparameter:** In `beta_vae_loss`, the KL term is scaled by , encouraging more factorization and disentanglement in the latent space.

- **Loss Computation:** The reconstruction loss is computed with binary cross-entropy. We add times the KL divergence, producing a trade-off between reconstructive fidelity and latent disentanglement.

- **Training Loop:** Each epoch calls `train_epoch` on the training set and `test_epoch` on the validation set, printing out the average ELBO plus -weighted KL cost.

- **Reconstructed Images:** After each epoch, the script saves reconstructed samples, enabling quick visualization of model performance and disentanglement progress.

Chapter 10

VAE-GAN for High-Fidelity Image Synthesis

Combining VAE with Generative Adversarial Networks can yield higher-quality outcomes. In this chapter, we design a joint architecture: a VAE that encodes and decodes images, and a discriminator that distinguishes between real and generated samples. Construction involves writing separate training loops for the generator (decoder) and the discriminator, modifying the reconstruction loss with adversarial feedback, and balancing the KL term. You will learn how to properly implement stable training techniques with multiple optimizers and avoid typical GAN pitfalls.

- First, we build a `VAE` that encodes input images into a latent distribution via an encoder network. We reparameterize to sample latent vectors and pass them into a decoder, producing reconstructed images.

- Next, we add a `Discriminator` network that tries to distinguish between real images from the dataset and reconstructed (or sampled) images from the VAE.

- We update the `Discriminator` to correctly classify real vs. fake, and then update the `VAE` using a combination of reconstruction, KL divergence, and adversarial terms so that it not only reconstructs effectively but also tries to fool the `Discriminator`.

Python Code Snippet

```python
import torch
import torch.nn as nn
import torch.optim as optim
import torch.nn.functional as F
from torch.utils.data import DataLoader
import torchvision
import torchvision.transforms as transforms
import numpy as np
import os


# -----------------------------------------------------------------
# 1) Define the Variational Autoencoder
# -----------------------------------------------------------------
class VAE(nn.Module):
    """
    A simple MLP-based VAE for 28x28-dimensional MNIST images.
    Encoder: 784 -> 400 -> (mu, logvar) each dimension = latent_dim
    Decoder: latent_dim -> 400 -> 784
    """
    def __init__(self, latent_dim=20):
        super(VAE, self).__init__()
        self.fc1 = nn.Linear(784, 400)
        self.fc_mu = nn.Linear(400, latent_dim)
        self.fc_logvar = nn.Linear(400, latent_dim)
        self.fc2 = nn.Linear(latent_dim, 400)
        self.fc3 = nn.Linear(400, 784)
        self.latent_dim = latent_dim

    def encode(self, x):
        # Flatten input : B x 1 x 28 x 28 -> B x 784
        x = x.view(-1, 784)
        h = F.relu(self.fc1(x))
        mu = self.fc_mu(h)
        logvar = self.fc_logvar(h)
        return mu, logvar

    def reparameterize(self, mu, logvar):
        # reparameterization trick
        std = torch.exp(0.5 * logvar)
        eps = torch.randn_like(std)
        return mu + eps * std

    def decode(self, z):
        h = F.relu(self.fc2(z))
        x_recon = torch.sigmoid(self.fc3(h))
        # Reshape back to image
        x_recon = x_recon.view(-1, 1, 28, 28)
        return x_recon

    def forward(self, x):
```

74

```python
        mu, logvar = self.encode(x)
        z = self.reparameterize(mu, logvar)
        x_recon = self.decode(z)
        return x_recon, mu, logvar


# ----------------------------------------------------------------
# 2) Define the Discriminator
# ----------------------------------------------------------------
class Discriminator(nn.Module):
    """
    A simple MLP discriminator that distinguishes
    between real and fake 28x28 images.
    """

    def __init__(self):
        super(Discriminator, self).__init__()
        self.fc1 = nn.Linear(784, 256)
        self.fc2 = nn.Linear(256, 64)
        self.fc3 = nn.Linear(64, 1)

    def forward(self, x):
        # Flatten input
        x = x.view(-1, 784)
        x = F.leaky_relu(self.fc1(x), 0.2)
        x = F.leaky_relu(self.fc2(x), 0.2)
        x = self.fc3(x)  # no activation, logits
        return x


# ----------------------------------------------------------------
# 3) Loss Functions
# ----------------------------------------------------------------
def vae_loss(x_recon, x, mu, logvar):
    """
    Computes the standard VAE loss = Reconstruction + KL divergence.
    We'll use BCE for reconstruction.
    """
    recon_bce = F.binary_cross_entropy(
        x_recon, x, reduction='sum'
    )
    # KL divergence
    kld = -0.5 * torch.sum(1 + logvar - mu.pow(2) - logvar.exp())
    return recon_bce + kld, recon_bce, kld


def discriminator_loss(d_real_pred, d_fake_pred):
    """
    Discriminator wants to maximize log(D(real)) + log(1 - D(fake)).
    We'll implement it with a BCE loss.
    """
    real_labels = torch.ones_like(d_real_pred)
    fake_labels = torch.zeros_like(d_fake_pred)

    d_real_loss = F.binary_cross_entropy_with_logits(d_real_pred,
    ↪   real_labels)
```

75

```python
    d_fake_loss = F.binary_cross_entropy_with_logits(d_fake_pred,
    ↪    fake_labels)

    return d_real_loss + d_fake_loss

def generator_loss(d_fake_pred):
    """
    Generator tries to fool the Discriminator, so we want
    to maximize log(D(fake)) or minimize log(1 - D(fake)).
    With BCE, we treat our fake images as 'real' = 1.
    """
    gen_labels = torch.ones_like(d_fake_pred)
    return F.binary_cross_entropy_with_logits(d_fake_pred,
    ↪    gen_labels)

# ---------------------------------------------------------------
# 4) Training routine per epoch
# ---------------------------------------------------------------
def train_one_epoch(vae, disc, vae_optimizer, disc_optimizer,
↪    dataloader, device):
    vae.train()
    disc.train()
    total_vae_loss = 0.0
    total_disc_loss = 0.0

    for real_imgs, _ in dataloader:
        real_imgs = real_imgs.to(device)

        # -------------------------
        # 1. Update Discriminator
        # -------------------------
        disc_optimizer.zero_grad()

        # Real images
        d_real_pred = disc(real_imgs)

        # Generate reconstructed images via VAE
        x_recon, mu, logvar = vae(real_imgs)
        d_fake_pred = disc(x_recon.detach())

        # Discriminator loss
        d_loss = discriminator_loss(d_real_pred, d_fake_pred)
        d_loss.backward()
        disc_optimizer.step()

        # -------------------------
        # 2. Update VAE (Generator)
        # -------------------------
        vae_optimizer.zero_grad()

        # Recompute fake preds for updated weights
        d_fake_pred = disc(x_recon)
```

```python
    # VAE loss = recon + KL + generator adversarial
    vae_total_loss, recon_bce, kld = vae_loss(x_recon,
    ↪   real_imgs, mu, logvar)
    adv_loss = generator_loss(d_fake_pred)
    # Combine them (balance factor can be tweaked if desired)
    total_g_loss = vae_total_loss + 0.1 * adv_loss

    total_g_loss.backward()
    vae_optimizer.step()

    total_vae_loss += vae_total_loss.item()
    total_disc_loss += d_loss.item()

    return total_vae_loss / len(dataloader), total_disc_loss /
    ↪   len(dataloader)

# ------------------------------------------------------------
# 5) Utility for saving samples
# ------------------------------------------------------------
def save_samples(vae, epoch, device, folder="samples"):
    """
    Saves a grid of reconstructed and random-sampled images.
    """
    os.makedirs(folder, exist_ok=True)
    vae.eval()
    with torch.no_grad():
        # Example real batch
        fixed_noise = torch.randn(16, vae.latent_dim).to(device)
        # Generate from random z
        fake_images = vae.decode(fixed_noise)

        fake_images = fake_images.cpu()
        grid = torchvision.utils.make_grid(fake_images, nrow=4)
        torchvision.utils.save_image(grid,
        ↪   f"{folder}/random_epoch_{epoch}.png")

# ------------------------------------------------------------
# 6) Main function: load data, init models, train
# ------------------------------------------------------------
def main():
    # Hyperparameters
    device = torch.device("cuda" if torch.cuda.is_available() else
    ↪   "cpu")
    batch_size = 64
    latent_dim = 20
    epochs = 5
    lr_vae = 1e-3
    lr_disc = 1e-3

    # MNIST dataset
    transform = transforms.Compose([
        transforms.ToTensor()
    ])
```

```
train_dataset = torchvision.datasets.MNIST(
    root="data", train=True, download=True, transform=transform
)
train_loader = DataLoader(train_dataset, batch_size=batch_size,
↪  shuffle=True)

# Initialize models
vae = VAE(latent_dim=latent_dim).to(device)
disc = Discriminator().to(device)

# Optimizers
vae_optimizer = optim.Adam(vae.parameters(), lr=lr_vae)
disc_optimizer = optim.Adam(disc.parameters(), lr=lr_disc)

# Training loop
for epoch in range(epochs):
    vae_loss_val, disc_loss_val = train_one_epoch(
        vae, disc, vae_optimizer, disc_optimizer, train_loader,
        ↪  device
    )
    print(f"Epoch [{epoch+1}/{epochs}] | "
          f"VAE Loss: {vae_loss_val:.4f} | Disc Loss:
          ↪  {disc_loss_val:.4f}")

    # Save sample images for inspection
    save_samples(vae, epoch+1, device)

print("Training complete. Sample images saved in 'samples'
↪  folder.")

if __name__ == "__main__":
    main()
```

Key Implementation Details:

- **VAE Structure:** Our VAE class includes a fully connected
  encoder (encode) producing μ and $\log \sigma^2$, a reparameterize
  step, and a fully connected decoder (decode). The reparameterization trick ensures gradients flow from the decoder back
  to the encoder during training.

- **Discriminator Network:** The Discriminator is an MLP
  that outputs a single logit, indicating whether an image is
  real or fake.

- **Loss Functions:** vae_loss combines binary cross-entropy
  for reconstruction and KL divergence. discriminator_loss

and `generator_loss` handle the adversarial aspect: real vs. fake classification.

- **Training Loop Workflow:** Within `train_one_epoch`, we first train the `Discriminator` by classifying real images and the VAE's reconstructed images. Then, we train the `VAE` to minimize reconstruction error, KL divergence, and the adversarial loss (generator loss) that tries to fool the `Discriminator`.

- **Sampling:** `save_samples` shows how to generate and save new images from random latent vectors, illustrating the VAE's generative capacity.

- **Balance of Terms:** A small coefficient (e.g., 0.1) multiplies the adversarial part of the VAE loss. Adjusting this hyperparameter can shift emphasis between pure VAE reconstruction quality and fooling the `Discriminator` for higher realism.

Chapter 11

VAE for Music Generation

Music data presents a unique challenge due to its temporal and harmonic structure. In this chapter, we preprocess MIDI files or audio signals into a sequence representation, and implement an RNN-based encoder-decoder with a VAE objective. We cover data augmentation techniques, modeling multiple instruments, and sampling strategies for generating new musical phrases. The chapter offers practical guidance on hyperparameter tuning and performance considerations for large MIDI corpuses.

- We begin by reading or synthesizing MIDI sequences, optionally applying data augmentation (e.g., random transposition).

- Next, we build an RNN-based encoder that produces mean and log-variance vectors for the latent distribution.

- We implement the reparameterization trick to sample from the latent space.

- A recurrent decoder reconstructs the music sequences from latent codes, potentially handling multiple instruments through an auxiliary embedding.

- We then train this model using the VAE objective, balancing reconstruction quality with a Kullback–Leibler (KL) divergence term.

- Finally, we generate new tracks by sampling from the learned latent space, providing novel musical phrases.

Python Code Snippet

```python
import torch
import torch.nn as nn
import torch.optim as optim
from torch.utils.data import Dataset, DataLoader
import random
import numpy as np


# ----------------------------------------------------------------
# 1) Set random seed for reproducibility
# ----------------------------------------------------------------
def set_seed(seed=42):
    random.seed(seed)
    np.random.seed(seed)
    torch.manual_seed(seed)
    if torch.cuda.is_available():
        torch.cuda.manual_seed_all(seed)


# ----------------------------------------------------------------
# 2) Simple data augmentation function for transposition
# ----------------------------------------------------------------
def random_transpose(sequence, max_steps=2):
    """
    Randomly transpose a sequence of note pitches by up to max_steps
    ↪ semitones.
    This is a placeholder for demonstration purposes.
    sequence: list of note indices (0..127).
    """
    transpose_amount = random.randint(-max_steps, max_steps)
    # Clip notes to a valid MIDI range [0, 127]
    new_seq = [max(0, min(127, note + transpose_amount)) for note in
    ↪ sequence]
    return new_seq


# ----------------------------------------------------------------
# 3) Synthetic Music Dataset with multiple instruments
# ----------------------------------------------------------------
class MusicDataset(Dataset):
    """
    A placeholder dataset that yields random sequences of notes
    ↪ (0..127),
    along with an instrument class ID to illustrate multi-instrument
    ↪ handling.
    In a real scenario, you would parse MIDI files and create
    ↪ sequences.
    """
```

```python
    def __init__(self, num_sequences=1000, seq_length=32,
    ↪ num_instruments=4, apply_augmentation=True):
        super().__init__()
        self.num_sequences = num_sequences
        self.seq_length = seq_length
        self.num_instruments = num_instruments
        self.apply_augmentation = apply_augmentation

        # Each sequence is random integers in [0..127], each
        ↪ instrument is in [0..num_instruments-1]
        self.data = []
        for _ in range(num_sequences):
            notes = [random.randint(0, 127) for _ in
            ↪ range(seq_length)]
            instr_id = random.randint(0, num_instruments - 1)
            self.data.append((notes, instr_id))

    def __len__(self):
        return self.num_sequences

    def __getitem__(self, idx):
        notes, instr_id = self.data[idx]

        # Optional data augmentation via random transposition
        if self.apply_augmentation:
            notes = random_transpose(notes, max_steps=2)

        # Convert to tensors
        notes_tensor = torch.tensor(notes, dtype=torch.long)
        instr_id_tensor = torch.tensor(instr_id, dtype=torch.long)
        return notes_tensor, instr_id_tensor

# ----------------------------------------------------------------
# 4) Collate function to handle variable batch construction
# ----------------------------------------------------------------
def music_collate_fn(batch):
    """
    Batch is a list of (notes_tensor, instr_id_tensor).
    We'll simply stack them into larger tensors.
    """
    notes_batch = [item[0] for item in batch]
    instr_batch = [item[1] for item in batch]

    notes_batch = torch.stack(notes_batch, dim=0)
    instr_batch = torch.stack(instr_batch, dim=0)
    return notes_batch, instr_batch

# ----------------------------------------------------------------
# 5) RNN-based VAE with LSTM encoder-decoder
# ----------------------------------------------------------------
class MusicVAE(nn.Module):
    """
```

```python
    RNN-based VAE that encodes a sequence of note events into a
    ↪   latent distribution,
    and decodes from that distribution to reconstruct the original
    ↪   note sequence.
    Incorporates an optional instrument embedding for
    ↪   multi-instrument scenarios.
    """
    def __init__(
        self,
        vocab_size=128,
        embed_dim=64,
        rnn_hidden=128,
        latent_dim=32,
        num_instruments=4
    ):
        super(MusicVAE, self).__init__()
        self.vocab_size = vocab_size
        self.embed_dim = embed_dim
        self.rnn_hidden = rnn_hidden
        self.latent_dim = latent_dim
        self.num_instruments = num_instruments

        # Note embedding and instrument embedding
        self.note_embed = nn.Embedding(vocab_size, embed_dim)
        self.instrument_embed = nn.Embedding(num_instruments,
        ↪   embed_dim)

        # LSTM encoder that outputs final hidden state
        self.encoder_rnn = nn.LSTM(input_size=embed_dim * 2,
        ↪   hidden_size=rnn_hidden, batch_first=True)

        # Layers to produce mean and log variance for the latent
        ↪   variable
        self.fc_mu = nn.Linear(rnn_hidden, latent_dim)
        self.fc_logvar = nn.Linear(rnn_hidden, latent_dim)

        # Decoder LSTM
        self.decoder_rnn = nn.LSTM(input_size=embed_dim +
        ↪   latent_dim, hidden_size=rnn_hidden, batch_first=True)
        self.fc_out = nn.Linear(rnn_hidden, vocab_size)

    def encode(self, notes, instr_ids):
        """
        Encode input sequences into latent distribution parameters.
        notes: [batch, seq_length]
        instr_ids: [batch]
        """
        batch_size, seq_length = notes.shape

        # [batch, seq_length, embed_dim]
        note_embeddings = self.note_embed(notes)

        # [batch, embed_dim]
```

83

```python
        instrument_embeddings = self.instrument_embed(instr_ids)
        # Expand instrument embeddings to have shape [batch,
        ↪ seq_length, embed_dim]
        instrument_embeddings_expanded =
        ↪ instrument_embeddings.unsqueeze(1).repeat(1, seq_length,
        ↪ 1)

        # Combine note + instrument embeddings along last dimension
        rnn_input = torch.cat([note_embeddings,
        ↪ instrument_embeddings_expanded], dim=2)

        # LSTM encoder
        _, (h_n, _) = self.encoder_rnn(rnn_input)
        # h_n: [1, batch, rnn_hidden]

        # Hidden state => mu and logvar
        h_n = h_n.squeeze(0)   # [batch, rnn_hidden]
        mu = self.fc_mu(h_n)   # [batch, latent_dim]
        logvar = self.fc_logvar(h_n)   # [batch, latent_dim]
        return mu, logvar

    def reparameterize(self, mu, logvar):
        """
        Reparameterization trick to sample latent vector z from
        ↪ N(mu, sigma^2).
        """
        std = torch.exp(0.5 * logvar)
        eps = torch.randn_like(std)
        return mu + eps * std

    def decode(self, z, notes, instr_ids, teacher_forcing=True):
        """
        Decode a latent vector z back into a sequence.
        Optionally use teacher forcing for training.
        z: [batch, latent_dim]
        notes: [batch, seq_length]
        instr_ids: [batch]
        """
        batch_size, seq_length = notes.shape

        # We'll feed the note embeddings step by step to the LSTM
        # while concatenating the latent code z to each input token.
        z_expanded = z.unsqueeze(1).repeat(1, seq_length, 1)   #
        ↪ [batch, seq_length, latent_dim]
        instrument_embeddings =
        ↪ self.instrument_embed(instr_ids).unsqueeze(1).repeat(1,
        ↪ seq_length, 1)

        # Start with a hidden state of zeros
        h_state = torch.zeros(1, batch_size, self.rnn_hidden,
        ↪ device=z.device)
        c_state = torch.zeros(1, batch_size, self.rnn_hidden,
        ↪ device=z.device)
```

84

```
        outputs = []
        prev_note = notes[:, 0]   # first token in each sequence
        for t in range(seq_length):
            if t == 0 or teacher_forcing:
                current_embed = self.note_embed(notes[:, t])
            else:
                # use the token from the last step's output if not
                ↪   teacher forcing
                current_embed = self.note_embed(prev_note)

            # Combine current note embedding, instrument embedding
            ↪   (one step), and z
            combined_input = torch.cat(
                [current_embed, instrument_embeddings[:, t, :],
                ↪   z_expanded[:, t, :]],
                dim=1
            ).unsqueeze(1)   # [batch, 1, embed_dim + embed_dim +
            ↪   latent_dim]

            # Pass into the decoder LSTM for one step
            out, (h_state, c_state) =
            ↪   self.decoder_rnn(combined_input, (h_state, c_state))
            # out: [batch, 1, rnn_hidden]

            # Compute logits
            logits = self.fc_out(out.squeeze(1))   # [batch,
            ↪   vocab_size]
            outputs.append(logits)

            # Next note's predicted ID
            prev_note = torch.argmax(logits, dim=1)

        # Stack outputs along the time dimension
        outputs = torch.stack(outputs, dim=1)   # [batch, seq_length,
        ↪   vocab_size]
        return outputs

    def forward(self, notes, instr_ids, teacher_forcing=True):
        """
        Full forward pass for training.
        1) Encode to get mu, logvar
        2) Reparameterize to sample z
        3) Decode to get logits
        """
        mu, logvar = self.encode(notes, instr_ids)
        z = self.reparameterize(mu, logvar)
        logits = self.decode(z, notes, instr_ids,
        ↪   teacher_forcing=teacher_forcing)
        return logits, mu, logvar

# --------------------------------------------------------------------
# 6) Define the loss function (ELBO)
```

```python
# -------------------------------------------------------------
def vae_loss_function(logits, targets, mu, logvar):
    """
    Compute the VAE loss = reconstruction loss + KL divergence.

    logits: [batch, seq_length, vocab_size]
    targets: [batch, seq_length]
    mu, logvar: latent distribution params

    Returns scalar loss.
    """
    # Reconstruction loss (cross entropy)
    recon_loss = nn.functional.cross_entropy(
        logits.permute(0, 2, 1),  # => [batch, vocab_size,
        ↪   seq_length]
        targets,
        reduction='mean'
    )

    # KL divergence
    # KL = -0.5 * sum(1 + logvar - mu^2 - exp(logvar))
    kl = -0.5 * torch.sum(1 + logvar - mu.pow(2) - logvar.exp(),
        ↪   dim=1)
    kl = torch.mean(kl)  # average over batch

    return recon_loss + kl

# -------------------------------------------------------------
# 7) Training and evaluation routines
# -------------------------------------------------------------
def train_one_epoch(model, dataloader, optimizer, device):
    model.train()
    total_loss = 0
    for notes, instr_ids in dataloader:
        notes = notes.to(device)
        instr_ids = instr_ids.to(device)

        optimizer.zero_grad()
        logits, mu, logvar = model(notes, instr_ids,
        ↪   teacher_forcing=True)
        loss = vae_loss_function(logits, notes, mu, logvar)
        loss.backward()
        optimizer.step()

        total_loss += loss.item()

    return total_loss / len(dataloader)

def evaluate_model(model, dataloader, device):
    model.eval()
    total_loss = 0
    with torch.no_grad():
        for notes, instr_ids in dataloader:
```

```
            notes = notes.to(device)
            instr_ids = instr_ids.to(device)

            logits, mu, logvar = model(notes, instr_ids,
            ↪  teacher_forcing=False)
            loss = vae_loss_function(logits, notes, mu, logvar)
            total_loss += loss.item()
    return total_loss / len(dataloader)

# ---------------------------------------------------------------
# 8) Generating new musical phrases
# ---------------------------------------------------------------
def generate_music(model, start_notes, instr_id, max_steps=32,
↪  device='cpu'):
    """
    Generate a new musical phrase by sampling from the learned
    ↪  latent space.
    We feed the start_notes to warm up the decoder, then predict
    ↪  subsequent tokens.
    """
    model.eval()
    # Expand batch dimension
    start_notes = torch.tensor(start_notes, dtype=torch.long,
    ↪  device=device).unsqueeze(0)
    instr_id = torch.tensor([instr_id], dtype=torch.long,
    ↪  device=device)

    with torch.no_grad():
        # Encode
        mu, logvar = model.encode(start_notes, instr_id)
        z = model.reparameterize(mu, logvar)

        # We'll decode step by step, starting with 'start_notes'
        batch_size, seq_length = start_notes.shape
        h_state = torch.zeros(1, batch_size, model.rnn_hidden,
        ↪  device=device)
        c_state = torch.zeros(1, batch_size, model.rnn_hidden,
        ↪  device=device)

        # Use the entire 'start_notes' as a warm-up (teacher
        ↪  forcing) for the first part
        outputs = []
        prev_note = start_notes[:, 0]

        for t in range(max_steps):
            if t < seq_length:
                current_embed = model.note_embed(start_notes[:, t])
            else:
                # Now generate new tokens from the predicted
                ↪  distribution
                current_embed = model.note_embed(prev_note)

            # Instrument embedding repeated
```

87

```python
        instr_embed_step = model.instrument_embed(instr_id)
        combined_input = torch.cat([current_embed,
        ↪  instr_embed_step, z], dim=1).unsqueeze(1)

        out, (h_state, c_state) =
        ↪  model.decoder_rnn(combined_input, (h_state,
        ↪  c_state))
        logits = model.fc_out(out.squeeze(1))  # [batch,
        ↪  vocab_size]
        outputs.append(logits)

        prev_note = torch.argmax(logits, dim=1)

    # Convert all predicted tokens
    outputs = torch.stack(outputs, dim=1)  # [batch, max_steps,
    ↪  vocab_size]
    predicted_notes = torch.argmax(outputs, dim=2)  # [batch,
    ↪  max_steps]

    return predicted_notes.squeeze(0).cpu().numpy().tolist()

# --------------------------------------------------------------
# 9) Main script to tie everything together
# --------------------------------------------------------------
def main():
    set_seed(42)
    device = torch.device("cuda" if torch.cuda.is_available() else
    ↪  "cpu")

    # Create dataset and dataloader
    train_dataset = MusicDataset(num_sequences=2000, seq_length=32,
    ↪  num_instruments=4, apply_augmentation=True)
    test_dataset = MusicDataset(num_sequences=500, seq_length=32,
    ↪  num_instruments=4, apply_augmentation=False)

    train_loader = DataLoader(train_dataset, batch_size=32,
    ↪  shuffle=True, collate_fn=music_collate_fn)
    test_loader = DataLoader(test_dataset, batch_size=32,
    ↪  shuffle=False, collate_fn=music_collate_fn)

    # Initialize the VAE model
    model = MusicVAE(
        vocab_size=128,
        embed_dim=64,
        rnn_hidden=128,
        latent_dim=32,
        num_instruments=4
    ).to(device)

    # Define optimizer
    optimizer = optim.Adam(model.parameters(), lr=1e-3)

    # Training loop
```

```
epochs = 5
for epoch in range(epochs):
    train_loss = train_one_epoch(model, train_loader, optimizer,
    ↪  device)
    val_loss = evaluate_model(model, test_loader, device)
    print(f"Epoch [{epoch+1}/{epochs}] - Train Loss:
    ↪  {train_loss:.4f}, Val Loss: {val_loss:.4f}")

# Generate a sample after training
start_notes = [60, 62, 64, 65, 67]  # C-D-E-F-G as a simple
↪  warm-up
instrument_id = 1
generated_sequence = generate_music(model, start_notes,
↪  instrument_id, max_steps=32, device=device)
print("Generated sequence:", generated_sequence)

if __name__ == "__main__":
    main()
```

Key Implementation Details:

- **RNN Encoder and Decoder:** Our model uses LSTM layers to handle temporal dependencies in note sequences. The encoder outputs a final hidden state which is projected into `mu` and `logvar`.

- **Reparameterization Trick:** The function `reparameterize` computes $z = +$ (where $N(0, I)$) ensuring backpropagation through random sampling.

- **Instrument Embedding:** Each instrument ID is embedded and concatenated with note embeddings, allowing the model to differentiate multiple instruments.

- **Data Augmentation:** We apply a simplistic random transposition of pitches to simulate key changes, expanding the variety of training data.

- **VAE Loss:** The ELBO includes cross-entropy reconstruction loss plus the KL divergence that enforces a smooth latent distribution.

- **Generation Loop:** The `generate_music` function exemplifies how to move from a latent vector z back to musical tokens, enabling novel phrases to be synthesized from the learned latent space.

- **Performance Tips:** In practice, larger hidden dimensions and more robust data loading for real MIDI files will be beneficial. Techniques such as teacher forcing ratio scheduling and advanced data augmentations can help stabilize training for large corpuses.

Chapter 12

VAE for Speech Synthesis

Similar to music generation, speech synthesis involves temporal data with complex patterns. We design a Variational Autoencoder (VAE) that can process mel-spectrograms or raw audio waveforms, using either 1D convolutions or recurrent layers. The encoder learns a latent representation of the speech signal, and the decoder reconstructs it into waveforms or spectrograms. By the end, you will have a working prototype for generating new speech samples. The process typically involves:

- **Data Preparation:** Converting raw audio into mel-spectrograms (or using waveforms directly) for input to the VAE.

- **Encoder:** Using 1D convolutions (or RNNs) to create a compact latent representation, parametrized by μ and $\log \sigma^2$.

- **Reparameterization Trick:** Sampling $z = \mu + \sigma \times \epsilon$ so that gradients pass through stochastic nodes.

- **Decoder:** Reconstructing spectrograms (or raw waveforms) from the latent variable z.

- **Loss Function:** Combining reconstruction loss (e.g., L1 or MSE between input and output) with the KL divergence between the approximate posterior $q_\phi(z|x)$ and the prior $p(z)$.

- **Training and Generation:** Optimizing VAE parameters on a dataset of speech (optionally across multiple speakers), then sampling random z to generate new speech segments or manipulate timbre.

Python Code Snippet

```python
import os
import glob
import random
import torch
import torchaudio
import torchaudio.transforms as T
import torch.nn as nn
import torch.optim as optim
from torch.utils.data import Dataset, DataLoader


# ----------------------------------------------------------------
# 1) SpeechDataset to load audio files and return mel-spectrograms
# ----------------------------------------------------------------
class SpeechDataset(Dataset):
    """
    A dataset that loads .wav files from a directory,
    converts them to mel-spectrograms, and optionally
    applies truncation/padding for a fixed length.
    """
    def __init__(self, folder_path, n_mels=80, segment_length=128):
        super().__init__()
        self.file_list = glob.glob(os.path.join(folder_path,
        ↪   '*.wav'))
        self.mel_transform = T.MelSpectrogram(
            sample_rate=16000, n_fft=1024, hop_length=256,
            ↪   n_mels=n_mels
        )
        self.segment_length = segment_length
        self.n_mels = n_mels

    def __len__(self):
        return len(self.file_list)

    def __getitem__(self, idx):
        wav_path = self.file_list[idx]
        waveform, sr = torchaudio.load(wav_path)
        # Resample to 16kHz if needed
        if sr != 16000:
            resampler = T.Resample(sr, 16000)
            waveform = resampler(waveform)

        # Convert to single channel if multiple channels
        waveform = waveform.mean(dim=0, keepdim=True)

        # Create mel-spectrogram
```

```python
        mel_spec = self.mel_transform(waveform)
        # mel_spec shape: (n_mels, time)

        # Optional: handle random crop or padding to fixed
        ↪  segment_length
        if mel_spec.size(1) >= self.segment_length:
            # Randomly crop
            start = random.randint(0, mel_spec.size(1) -
            ↪  self.segment_length)
            mel_spec = mel_spec[:, start:start+self.segment_length]
        else:
            # Pad to segment_length
            pad_amount = self.segment_length - mel_spec.size(1)
            mel_spec = nn.functional.pad(mel_spec, (0, pad_amount),
            ↪  'constant', 0.0)

        # For VAE, we'll treat this as 2D input [n_mels,
        ↪  segment_length]
        # Expand to (1, n_mels, segment_length) so it can be
        ↪  interpreted like a "1D image"
        mel_spec = mel_spec.unsqueeze(0)

        return mel_spec


# ------------------------------------------------------------
# 2) AudioVAE model: 1D convolutional VAE for mel-spectrograms
# ------------------------------------------------------------
class AudioVAE(nn.Module):
    """
    Variational Autoencoder for mel-spectrogram segments.
    The encoder learns mu, logvar. The decoder reconstructs
    the mel-spectrogram from latent z.
    """
    def __init__(self,
                 in_channels=1,
                 n_mels=80,
                 segment_length=128,
                 latent_dim=32,
                 hidden_channels=64):
        super(AudioVAE, self).__init__()

        self.n_mels = n_mels
        self.segment_length = segment_length
        self.latent_dim = latent_dim

        # Encoder: 1D conv layers (treat n_mels as "channel"
        ↪  dimension)
        self.encoder = nn.Sequential(
            nn.Conv2d(in_channels, hidden_channels, kernel_size=3,
            ↪  stride=2, padding=1),
            nn.ReLU(),
            nn.Conv2d(hidden_channels, hidden_channels*2,
            ↪  kernel_size=3, stride=2, padding=1),
```

```python
        nn.ReLU(),
        nn.Conv2d(hidden_channels*2, hidden_channels*4,
        ↪  kernel_size=3, stride=2, padding=1),
        nn.ReLU(),
    )

    # Determine downsampled feature map size for fully-connected
    ↪  layers
    # Input shape: (B, 1, n_mels, segment_length)
    # After 3 conv strided layers, freq and time dims are
    ↪  reduced by factor 8
    freq_reduced = n_mels // 8
    time_reduced = segment_length // 8
    enc_out_dim = hidden_channels*4 * freq_reduced *
    ↪  time_reduced

    # Mu and logvar heads
    self.fc_mu = nn.Linear(enc_out_dim, latent_dim)
    self.fc_logvar = nn.Linear(enc_out_dim, latent_dim)

    # Decoder FC
    self.fc_decode = nn.Linear(latent_dim, enc_out_dim)

    # Decoder: transposed conv to reconstruct
    self.decoder = nn.Sequential(
        nn.ConvTranspose2d(hidden_channels*4, hidden_channels*2,
        ↪  kernel_size=4, stride=2, padding=1),
        nn.ReLU(),
        nn.ConvTranspose2d(hidden_channels*2, hidden_channels,
        ↪  kernel_size=4, stride=2, padding=1),
        nn.ReLU(),
        nn.ConvTranspose2d(hidden_channels, in_channels,
        ↪  kernel_size=4, stride=2, padding=1),
        nn.Sigmoid()  # or use no activation for unbounded
        ↪  reconstruction
    )

def encode(self, x):
    """
    Encodes the input mel-spectrogram into a latent
    ↪  distribution.
    """
    enc_feats = self.encoder(x)
    # Flatten
    enc_feats = enc_feats.view(enc_feats.size(0), -1)
    mu = self.fc_mu(enc_feats)
    logvar = self.fc_logvar(enc_feats)
    return mu, logvar

def reparameterize(self, mu, logvar):
    """
    Reparameterization trick to sample z.
    """
```

```python
        std = torch.exp(0.5 * logvar)
        eps = torch.randn_like(std)
        return mu + eps * std

    def decode(self, z):
        """
        Decodes latent z into a mel-spectrogram.
        """
        d = self.fc_decode(z)
        # Reshape back to conv feature map
        batch_size = d.size(0)
        freq_reduced = self.n_mels // 8
        time_reduced = self.segment_length // 8
        d = d.view(batch_size, -1, freq_reduced, time_reduced)
        recon = self.decoder(d)  # shape: (B, 1, n_mels,
        ↪ segment_length) after upsampling
        return recon

    def forward(self, x):
        """
        Full forward pass: encode -> reparameterize -> decode
        """
        mu, logvar = self.encode(x)
        z = self.reparameterize(mu, logvar)
        recon = self.decode(z)
        return recon, mu, logvar


# ----------------------------------------------------------------
# 3) VAE loss function: Reconstruction + KL Divergence
# ----------------------------------------------------------------
def vae_loss_function(recon, x, mu, logvar):
    """
    Standard VAE loss: reconstruction term + KL term
    """
    recon_loss = nn.functional.mse_loss(recon, x, reduction='sum')
    # KL divergence
    kl_loss = -0.5 * torch.sum(1 + logvar - mu.pow(2) -
    ↪ logvar.exp())
    return recon_loss + kl_loss, recon_loss, kl_loss


# ----------------------------------------------------------------
# 4) Training loop for the AudioVAE
# ----------------------------------------------------------------
def train_vae(model, dataloader, optimizer, device):
    model.train()
    total_loss = 0.0
    total_recon = 0.0
    total_kl = 0.0

    for batch_idx, mel_segments in enumerate(dataloader):
        mel_segments = mel_segments.to(device)
        optimizer.zero_grad()
```

```python
        recon, mu, logvar = model(mel_segments)
        loss, r_loss, kl_loss = vae_loss_function(recon,
        ↪  mel_segments, mu, logvar)

        loss.backward()
        optimizer.step()

        total_loss += loss.item()
        total_recon += r_loss.item()
        total_kl += kl_loss.item()

    avg_loss = total_loss / len(dataloader.dataset)
    avg_recon = total_recon / len(dataloader.dataset)
    avg_kl = total_kl / len(dataloader.dataset)
    return avg_loss, avg_recon, avg_kl

@torch.no_grad()
def evaluate_vae(model, dataloader, device):
    model.eval()
    total_loss = 0.0
    total_recon = 0.0
    total_kl = 0.0

    for mel_segments in dataloader:
        mel_segments = mel_segments.to(device)

        recon, mu, logvar = model(mel_segments)
        loss, r_loss, kl_loss = vae_loss_function(recon,
        ↪  mel_segments, mu, logvar)

        total_loss += loss.item()
        total_recon += r_loss.item()
        total_kl += kl_loss.item()

    avg_loss = total_loss / len(dataloader.dataset)
    avg_recon = total_recon / len(dataloader.dataset)
    avg_kl = total_kl / len(dataloader.dataset)
    return avg_loss, avg_recon, avg_kl

# ---------------------------------------------------------------
# 5) Generation: sample random z and decode to new mel
# ---------------------------------------------------------------
@torch.no_grad()
def generate_audio(model, num_samples, device):
    model.eval()
    # Sample from a standard normal distribution
    z = torch.randn(num_samples, model.latent_dim).to(device)
    # Decode
    generated_mels = model.decode(z)
    # generated_mels shape: (B, 1, n_mels, segment_length)
    # Additional step: one could invert mel-spectrogram to wave,
    ↪  e.g., with Griffin-Lim
    return generated_mels
```

96

```
# ---------------------------------------------------------------
# 6) Main function: set up dataset, model, train, evaluate, generate
# ---------------------------------------------------------------
def main():
    device = torch.device("cuda" if torch.cuda.is_available() else
    ↪  "cpu")

    # Paths and hyperparameters
    train_folder = "path_to_train_data"   # Update with actual folder
    test_folder = "path_to_test_data"     # Update with actual folder
    batch_size = 8
    epochs = 5
    latent_dim = 32

    # Prepare datasets
    train_dataset = SpeechDataset(train_folder, n_mels=80,
    ↪  segment_length=128)
    test_dataset = SpeechDataset(test_folder, n_mels=80,
    ↪  segment_length=128)

    train_loader = DataLoader(train_dataset, batch_size=batch_size,
    ↪  shuffle=True, drop_last=True)
    test_loader = DataLoader(test_dataset, batch_size=batch_size,
    ↪  shuffle=False, drop_last=True)

    # Initialize model, optimizer
    model = AudioVAE(
        in_channels=1,
        n_mels=80,
        segment_length=128,
        latent_dim=latent_dim,
        hidden_channels=64
    ).to(device)

    optimizer = optim.Adam(model.parameters(), lr=1e-3)

    # Training loop
    for epoch in range(1, epochs+1):
        train_loss, train_recon, train_kl = train_vae(model,
        ↪  train_loader, optimizer, device)
        val_loss, val_recon, val_kl = evaluate_vae(model,
        ↪  test_loader, device)

        print(f"Epoch [{epoch}/{epochs}] | "
              f"Train Loss: {train_loss:.4f} (Recon
              ↪  {train_recon:.4f}, KL {train_kl:.4f}) | "
              f"Val Loss: {val_loss:.4f} (Recon {val_recon:.4f}, KL
              ↪  {val_kl:.4f})")

    # Generate new samples
    num_samples_to_generate = 4
```

```
generated_mels = generate_audio(model, num_samples_to_generate,
↪  device)

# (Optional) Save or invert mel-spectrogram to wave
# for idx, gen_mel in enumerate(generated_mels):
#     # Invert mel if desired using ref:
↪  torchaudio.functional.griffinlim
#     # ...
#     pass

print("Finished training. Generated mel-spectrograms of size:",
↪  generated_mels.shape)

if __name__ == "__main__":
    main()
```

Key Implementation Details:

- **Dataset Preparation:** `SpeechDataset` reads .wav files, down-samples to 16kHz, then converts them to mel-spectrograms using `MelSpectrogram`. A fixed segment length allows batching and convolution.

- **Encoder & Decoder:** The encoder downsamples the spectrogram through strided 2D convolutions, producing μ and $\log \sigma^2$. The decoder upsamples using transposed convolutions to reconstruct.

- **Reparameterization Trick:** `model.reparameterize(mu, logvar)` samples from the latent space while allowing gradients to flow.

- **VAE Loss:** The `vae_loss_function` sums the reconstruction error (MSE) and the KL divergence between approximate posterior $q\_\phi(z|x)$ and the prior $p(z)$.

- **Training Loop:** `train_vae` iterates over the dataset, computing gradients and optimizing. `evaluate_vae` measures validation loss.

- **Generation:** `generate_audio` samples random latent vectors and decodes to new mel-spectrogram segments. Actual audio can be reconstructed by applying a spectral inversion method such as Griffin-Lim or a neural vocoder.

98

- **Scalability:** The latent dimension can be adjusted to control the level of timbre detail. Batch size and model depth can be increased for larger datasets and more complex audio patterns.

Chapter 13

FactorVAE for Factorized Representations

Building on disentanglement, FactorVAE uses a separate discriminator to enforce independence within the latent space more strongly. In this chapter, we integrate that additional discriminator into the standard VAE training loop, showing how to penalize correlations among latent units. We'll discuss details like the total correlation metric, balancing multiple losses, and diagnosing latent factor separation. Implementation snippets demonstrate constructing the factor discriminator, updating the main network, and analyzing emergent latent semantics.

Python Code Snippet

```python
import os
import torch
import torch.nn as nn
import torch.nn.functional as F
import torchvision
import torchvision.transforms as T
from torch.utils.data import DataLoader
from torch.optim import Adam
import numpy as np
import random
import matplotlib.pyplot as plt
```

```python
# ------------------------------------------------------------------
# 1) Set random seed for reproducibility
# ------------------------------------------------------------------
def set_seed(seed=42):
    random.seed(seed)
    np.random.seed(seed)
    torch.manual_seed(seed)
    if torch.cuda.is_available():
        torch.cuda.manual_seed_all(seed)


# ------------------------------------------------------------------
# 2) Define the VAE (Encoder + Decoder)
# ------------------------------------------------------------------
class Encoder(nn.Module):
    """
    Encoder network that outputs the mean and log variance of the
    ↳   latent distribution.
    """
    def __init__(self, z_dim=10):
        super(Encoder, self).__init__()
        self.z_dim = z_dim
        self.net = nn.Sequential(
            nn.Linear(28*28, 512),
            nn.ReLU(),
            nn.Linear(512, 256),
            nn.ReLU()
        )
        self.mu = nn.Linear(256, z_dim)
        self.logvar = nn.Linear(256, z_dim)

    def forward(self, x):
        # x : [B, 1, 28, 28]
        x = x.view(x.size(0), -1)    # flatten
        h = self.net(x)              # [B, 256]
        mu = self.mu(h)              # [B, z_dim]
        logvar = self.logvar(h)      # [B, z_dim]
        return mu, logvar

class Decoder(nn.Module):
    """
    Decoder network that reconstructs images from latent vectors.
    """
    def __init__(self, z_dim=10):
        super(Decoder, self).__init__()
        self.z_dim = z_dim
        self.net = nn.Sequential(
            nn.Linear(z_dim, 256),
            nn.ReLU(),
            nn.Linear(256, 512),
            nn.ReLU(),
            nn.Linear(512, 28*28),
            nn.Sigmoid()
```

```python
        )

    def forward(self, z):
        # z : [B, z_dim]
        h = self.net(z)           # [B, 28*28]
        recon = h.view(h.size(0), 1, 28, 28)   # [B, 1, 28, 28]
        return recon

class FactorVAE(nn.Module):
    """
    The main FactorVAE module that combines the Encoder and Decoder.
    It provides a forward pass that returns the reconstruction, mu,
    ↪ logvar, and latent sample.
    """
    def __init__(self, z_dim=10):
        super(FactorVAE, self).__init__()
        self.encoder = Encoder(z_dim=z_dim)
        self.decoder = Decoder(z_dim=z_dim)

    def reparameterize(self, mu, logvar):
        std = torch.exp(0.5 * logvar)
        eps = torch.randn_like(std)
        return mu + eps * std

    def forward(self, x):
        mu, logvar = self.encoder(x)
        z = self.reparameterize(mu, logvar)
        recon = self.decoder(z)
        return recon, mu, logvar, z

# ------------------------------------------------------------
# 3) Factor Discriminator for total correlation
# ------------------------------------------------------------
class FactorDiscriminator(nn.Module):
    """
    A simple MLP-based discriminator that distinguishes between
    latent samples from the joint distribution vs. the factorized
    ↪ (permuted) distribution.
    """
    def __init__(self, z_dim=10, hidden_dim=256):
        super(FactorDiscriminator, self).__init__()
        self.net = nn.Sequential(
            nn.Linear(z_dim, hidden_dim),
            nn.ReLU(),
            nn.Linear(hidden_dim, hidden_dim),
            nn.ReLU(),
            nn.Linear(hidden_dim, 1),
            nn.Sigmoid()
        )

    def forward(self, z):
        # z : [B, z_dim]
        return self.net(z).squeeze(-1)   # [B]
```

```python
def permute_dims(z):
    """
    For each dimension of z, shuffle across the batch dimension
    to create an artificial 'factorized' sample from the product of
    ↪   marginals.
    """
    B, dim = z.size()
    z_perm = []
    for i in range(dim):
        idx = torch.randperm(B, device=z.device)
        z_perm.append(z[:, i][idx])
    z_perm = torch.stack(z_perm, dim=1)
    return z_perm


# -------------------------------------------------------------
# 4) Loss functions
# -------------------------------------------------------------
def reconstruction_loss(recon, x):
    # Using binary cross-entropy per pixel
    return F.binary_cross_entropy(recon, x, reduction='sum') /
    ↪   x.size(0)


def kl_divergence(mu, logvar):
    # Standard formula for KL divergence
    return 0.5 * torch.sum(mu.pow(2) + logvar.exp() - logvar - 1) /
    ↪   mu.size(0)


# -------------------------------------------------------------
# 5) Training Step Utilities
# -------------------------------------------------------------
def train_factor_vae_step(vae, disc, x, vae_opt, disc_opt,
↪   gamma=10.0):
    """
    Performs one training step for FactorVAE:
    1) Forward pass VAE -> get z, recon
    2) Permute z -> z_perm
    3) Train Discriminator on z vs. z_perm
    4) Compute FactorVAE objective (reconstruction + KL - gamma *
    ↪   total_correlation)
    5) Update VAE
    6) Update Discriminator
    """
    # ============= VAE Forward =============
    recon, mu, logvar, z = vae(x)

    # ============= Permute z =============
    z_perm = permute_dims(z.detach())  # detach to avoid interfering
    ↪   with VAE gradients

    # ============= Discriminator forward =============
    D_z = disc(z.detach())          # Probability for real latents
    D_z_perm = disc(z_perm)         # Probability for permuted latents
```

```python
    # ============= Discriminator Loss =============
    # We want disc to classify z as 1 and z_perm as 0
    disc_loss = -0.5 * (torch.log(D_z + 1e-12).mean() + torch.log(1.
    ↪    - D_z_perm + 1e-12).mean())

    # ============= VAE Loss =============
    rec_loss = reconstruction_loss(recon, x)
    kl_loss = kl_divergence(mu, logvar)

    # Approximate total correlation = E[log(D(z))] -
    ↪    E[log(1-D(z_perm))]
    # But in practice, only D_z is used for the VAE gradient
    ↪    (FactorVAE paper),
    # we can keep a simplified approach:
    tc_estimate = (torch.log(D_z + 1e-12)).mean() - (torch.log(1. -
    ↪    D_z_perm + 1e-12)).mean()

    factor_vae_loss = rec_loss + kl_loss - gamma * tc_estimate

    # ============= Backprop VAE =============
    vae_opt.zero_grad()
    factor_vae_loss.backward(retain_graph=True)   # retain_graph to
    ↪    allow disc update
    vae_opt.step()

    # ============= Backprop Discriminator =============
    disc_opt.zero_grad()
    disc_loss.backward()
    disc_opt.step()

    return factor_vae_loss.item(), rec_loss.item(), kl_loss.item(),
    ↪    disc_loss.item()

# ----------------------------------------------------------------
# 6) Main training loop
# ----------------------------------------------------------------
def main():
    set_seed(42)
    device = torch.device("cuda" if torch.cuda.is_available() else
    ↪    "cpu")

    # Hyperparameters
    z_dim = 10
    batch_size = 64
    epochs = 5
    gamma = 10.0
    lr_vae = 1e-3
    lr_disc = 1e-3

    # ============= Data Loading (MNIST) =============
    transform = T.Compose([
        T.ToTensor()
```

104

```python
])
train_dataset = torchvision.datasets.MNIST(root='data',
↪   train=True, download=True, transform=transform)
train_loader = DataLoader(train_dataset, batch_size=batch_size,
↪   shuffle=True)

# ============== Initialize models ==============
vae = FactorVAE(z_dim=z_dim).to(device)
disc = FactorDiscriminator(z_dim=z_dim).to(device)

vae_opt = Adam(vae.parameters(), lr=lr_vae)
disc_opt = Adam(disc.parameters(), lr=lr_disc)

# ============== Training ==============
for epoch in range(epochs):
    vae.train()
    disc.train()
    total_vae_loss = 0.0
    total_rec_loss = 0.0
    total_kl_loss = 0.0
    total_disc_loss = 0.0

    for i, (imgs, _) in enumerate(train_loader):
        imgs = imgs.to(device)
        vae_loss_val, rec_loss_val, kl_loss_val, disc_loss_val =
        ↪   train_factor_vae_step(
            vae, disc, imgs, vae_opt, disc_opt, gamma
        )

        total_vae_loss += vae_loss_val
        total_rec_loss += rec_loss_val
        total_kl_loss += kl_loss_val
        total_disc_loss += disc_loss_val

    avg_vae_loss = total_vae_loss / len(train_loader)
    avg_rec_loss = total_rec_loss / len(train_loader)
    avg_kl_loss = total_kl_loss / len(train_loader)
    avg_disc_loss = total_disc_loss / len(train_loader)

    print(f"Epoch [{epoch+1}/{epochs}] "
        f"VAE Loss: {avg_vae_loss:.4f} | "
        f"Recon: {avg_rec_loss:.4f} | KL: {avg_kl_loss:.4f} |
        ↪   Disc: {avg_disc_loss:.4f}")

    # Generate some samples at the end of each epoch
    sample_and_save(vae, device, epoch)

print("Training complete! Check the 'factor_vae_results' folder
↪   for generated samples.")

# ----------------------------------------------------------------
# 7) Sampling function
# ----------------------------------------------------------------
```

```python
def sample_and_save(vae, device, epoch=0, num_samples=16):
    """
    Draw random samples from the learned latent space and save a
    ↪  grid of images.
    """
    vae.eval()
    with torch.no_grad():
        z = torch.randn(num_samples, vae.encoder.z_dim).to(device)
        generated = vae.decoder(z)
        save_image_grid(generated, epoch, num_samples)

def save_image_grid(img_tensor, epoch, num_samples):
    """
    Utility to save a grid of generated images to disk.
    """
    # img_tensor: [B, 1, 28, 28], range [0,1] if the decoder uses
    ↪  Sigmoid
    grid = torchvision.utils.make_grid(img_tensor, nrow=4)
    npimg = grid.cpu().numpy()
    os.makedirs("factor_vae_results", exist_ok=True)

    plt.figure(figsize=(4,4))
    plt.axis("off")
    plt.imshow(np.transpose(npimg, (1, 2, 0)),
    ↪  interpolation='nearest')
    plt.savefig(f"factor_vae_results/epoch_{epoch}.png")
    plt.close()

# ----------------------------------------------------------------
# 8) Run the script
# ----------------------------------------------------------------
if __name__ == "__main__":
    main()
```

Key Implementation Details:

- **VAE Architecture:** The FactorVAE uses a standard encoder-decoder setup where the encoder produces a mean and log-variance, and the reparameterization trick generates latent samples. The decoder then reconstructs the input from those latent samples.

- **Discriminator for Total Correlation:** A separate MLP-based discriminator distinguishes between real latent vectors and permuted ones, helping the model reduce dependencies among latent dimensions.

- **FactorVAE Objective:** Apart from the standard recon-

106

struction and KL divergence terms, we subtract a term proportional to the total correlation (approximated by comparing the discriminator's output on real vs. permuted latents).

- **Permutation Function:** The function `permute_dims` shuffles each latent dimension across the batch, simulating samples from a factorized distribution and allowing the discriminator to learn a robust separation.

- **Training Pipeline:** Each iteration updates both the VAE and the discriminator. After forward passes, the discriminator's parameters are updated to classify real vs. permuted latents, while the VAE's parameters are updated to minimize reconstruction error, KL divergence, and the total correlation penalty. This leads to a disentangled, factorized latent space.

Chapter 14

CycleVAE for Image Translation

We adapt the idea of cycle consistency to VAEs for tasks like unpaired image-to-image translation. This involves designing two VAEs (one per domain) and forcing an image translated to the other domain and back to remain consistent. You will learn to write a custom training procedure that updates each VAE and includes cross-domain reconstruction losses. Key implementation steps include building domain-specific encoders and decoders, balancing cycle loss, and applying suitable normalization layers for stable training.

- For each domain (A and B), construct a VAE composed of an encoder and decoder.

- Use the reparameterization trick to learn a latent distribution for each domain.

- Translate an image from domain A to domain B using A's encoder + B's decoder and back again to measure cycle consistency.

- Repeat the same approach in reverse (B → A → B).

- Combine the losses for individual VAE reconstruction, KL regularization, as well as cross-domain/cycle reconstruction.

- Train end-to-end using these combined objectives to ensure domain translation while preserving image identity.

Python Code Snippet

```python
import torch
import torch.nn as nn
import torch.optim as optim
import torch.nn.functional as F
from torch.utils.data import Dataset, DataLoader
import numpy as np
import random


# ---------------------------
# 1) Utility functions
# ---------------------------
def set_seed(seed=42):
    random.seed(seed)
    np.random.seed(seed)
    torch.manual_seed(seed)
    if torch.cuda.is_available():
        torch.cuda.manual_seed_all(seed)

def reparameterize(mu, logvar):
    """
    Uses the reparameterization trick:
    z = mu + std * epsilon, where epsilon ~ N(0, I)
    """
    std = torch.exp(0.5 * logvar)
    eps = torch.randn_like(std)
    return mu + eps * std

# ---------------------------
# 2) Dummy datasets
# ---------------------------
class RandomDomainADataset(Dataset):
    """
    A placeholder dataset for domain A that returns random images.
    Ideally, you would load real data from domain A in a real
    ↪ project.
    """
    def __init__(self, length=1000, shape=(1, 28, 28)):
        super().__init__()
        self.length = length
        self.shape = shape

    def __len__(self):
        return self.length

    def __getitem__(self, idx):
        # Random 'images' in [-1, 1]
        data = (torch.rand(self.shape) * 2.) - 1.
        return data, 0  # no labels in this toy example

class RandomDomainBDataset(Dataset):
```

109

```python
    """
    A placeholder dataset for domain B that returns random images.
    """
    def __init__(self, length=1000, shape=(3, 28, 28)):
        super().__init__()
        self.length = length
        self.shape = shape

    def __len__(self):
        return self.length

    def __getitem__(self, idx):
        # Random 'images' in [-1, 1] with 3 channels for
        ↪  demonstration
        data = (torch.rand(self.shape) * 2.) - 1.
        return data, 0


# ---------------------------
# 3) Encoder/Decoder modules
# ---------------------------
class ConvEncoder(nn.Module):
    """
    A simple convolutional encoder for a VAE. Outputs mu and logvar.
    Uses BatchNorm for stability.
    """
    def __init__(self, in_channels=1, latent_dim=16,
    ↪  hidden_dims=(32, 64)):
        super().__init__()
        layers = []
        channels = in_channels
        for h_dim in hidden_dims:
            layers.append(
                nn.Sequential(
                    nn.Conv2d(channels, h_dim, kernel_size=4,
                    ↪  stride=2, padding=1),
                    nn.BatchNorm2d(h_dim),
                    nn.ReLU(inplace=True),
                )
            )
            channels = h_dim
        self.conv = nn.Sequential(*layers)
        # Compute the final output size or define a fixed linear
        ↪  layer
        self.flatten = nn.Flatten()

        # We'll assume the feature map is 7x7 if input is 28x28
        ↪  (after 2 conv reductions).
        out_size = hidden_dims[-1] * 7 * 7
        self.fc_mu = nn.Linear(out_size, latent_dim)
        self.fc_logvar = nn.Linear(out_size, latent_dim)

    def forward(self, x):
        x = self.conv(x)
```

110

```python
        x = self.flatten(x)
        mu = self.fc_mu(x)
        logvar = self.fc_logvar(x)
        return mu, logvar


class ConvDecoder(nn.Module):
    """
    A simple convolutional decoder that mirrors the ConvEncoder
    ↪    architecture.
    """
    def __init__(self, out_channels=1, latent_dim=16,
    ↪    hidden_dims=(64, 32)):
        super().__init__()
        # Mirror the size used in the encoder
        self.latent_dim = latent_dim
        self.hidden_dims = hidden_dims
        self.fc = nn.Linear(latent_dim, hidden_dims[0] * 7 * 7)

        layers = []
        # Build in reverse
        for i in range(len(hidden_dims) - 1):
            layers.append(
                nn.Sequential(
                    nn.ConvTranspose2d(hidden_dims[i],
                    ↪    hidden_dims[i+1],
                                        kernel_size=4, stride=2,
                                        ↪    padding=1),
                    nn.BatchNorm2d(hidden_dims[i+1]),
                    nn.ReLU(inplace=True),
                )
            )
        # Final layer to get the desired out_channels (with
        ↪    stride=2)
        layers.append(
            nn.Sequential(
                nn.ConvTranspose2d(hidden_dims[-1], out_channels,
                                    kernel_size=4, stride=2,
                                    ↪    padding=1),
                nn.Tanh()   # output in [-1,1]
            )
        )
        self.deconv = nn.Sequential(*layers)

    def forward(self, z):
        x = self.fc(z)
        # Reshape for conv transpose: (batch, hidden_dims[0], 7, 7)
        x = x.view(-1, self.hidden_dims[0], 7, 7)
        x = self.deconv(x)
        return x


# ----------------------------
# 4) VAE model for a single domain
# ----------------------------
```

```python
class VAE(nn.Module):
    """
    Variational Autoencoder combining an encoder and decoder.
    """
    def __init__(self, in_channels=1, out_channels=1,
    ↪  latent_dim=16):
        super().__init__()
        self.encoder = ConvEncoder(in_channels=in_channels,
        ↪  latent_dim=latent_dim)
        self.decoder = ConvDecoder(out_channels=out_channels,
        ↪  latent_dim=latent_dim)

    def forward(self, x):
        mu, logvar = self.encoder(x)
        z = reparameterize(mu, logvar)
        recon = self.decoder(z)
        return recon, mu, logvar

# ----------------------------
# 5) CycleVAE container with two distinct VAEs for domains A and B
# ----------------------------
class CycleVAE(nn.Module):
    """
    Holds two separate VAEs, one for domain A and one for domain B.
    """
    def __init__(self, vaeA, vaeB):
        super().__init__()
        self.vaeA = vaeA
        self.vaeB = vaeB

    def forward_AtoA(self, xA):
        """
        Reconstruct domain A image with A's VAE.
        """
        reconA, muA, logvarA = self.vaeA(xA)
        return reconA, muA, logvarA

    def forward_BtoB(self, xB):
        """
        Reconstruct domain B image with B's VAE.
        """
        reconB, muB, logvarB = self.vaeB(xB)
        return reconB, muB, logvarB

    def forward_AtoB(self, xA):
        """
        Translate from domain A to domain B using A's encoder and
        ↪  B's decoder.
        """
        muA, logvarA = self.vaeA.encoder(xA)
        zA = reparameterize(muA, logvarA)
        reconB = self.vaeB.decoder(zA)
        return reconB, muA, logvarA
```

```python
    def forward_BtoA(self, xB):
        """
        Translate from domain B to domain A using B's encoder and
        ↪  A's decoder.
        """
        muB, logvarB = self.vaeB.encoder(xB)
        zB = reparameterize(muB, logvarB)
        reconA = self.vaeA.decoder(zB)
        return reconA, muB, logvarB


# ----------------------------
# 6) Loss functions
# ----------------------------
def kl_divergence(mu, logvar):
    """
    KL divergence between q(z|x) and p(z).
    We'll sum across latent dimension, then mean over batch.
    """
    kld = -0.5 * torch.sum(1 + logvar - mu.pow(2) - logvar.exp(),
    ↪  dim=1)
    return kld.mean()


def reconstruction_loss(x, x_recon, loss_type='mse'):
    """
    Compare x and x_recon under either MSE or L1.
    """
    if loss_type == 'mse':
        return F.mse_loss(x_recon, x, reduction='mean')
    elif loss_type == 'l1':
        return F.l1_loss(x_recon, x, reduction='mean')
    else:
        raise ValueError("Unsupported reconstruction loss type.")


def cycle_vae_loss(cycle_vae, xA, xB, lambda_cycle=10.0):
    """
    Compute the total loss for the cycle approach, combining:
    1) VAE reconstruction for domain A
    2) VAE reconstruction for domain B
    3) KL regularization for A and B
    4) Cross-domain translation + cycle reconstruction
    """
    # 1) Domain A self-recon
    reconA, muA, logvarA = cycle_vae.forward_AtoA(xA)
    lossA_rec = reconstruction_loss(xA, reconA)
    lossA_kl = kl_divergence(muA, logvarA)

    # 2) Domain B self-recon
    reconB, muB, logvarB = cycle_vae.forward_BtoB(xB)
    lossB_rec = reconstruction_loss(xB, reconB)
    lossB_kl = kl_divergence(muB, logvarB)

    # 3) A -> B -> A cycle recon
```

113

```python
A_to_B, muA_x, logvarA_x = cycle_vae.forward_AtoB(xA)
# Then pass this A->B output back into domain B's encoder =>
↪  domain B's latents => domain A's decoder
# But we want to cycle back to A, so: A->B image is the "B
↪  image". We'll do: forward_BtoA(A_to_B).
Aback, muB_x, logvarB_x = cycle_vae.forward_BtoA(A_to_B)
lossA_cycle = reconstruction_loss(xA, Aback)

# 4) B -> A -> B cycle recon
B_to_A, muB_y, logvarB_y = cycle_vae.forward_BtoA(xB)
Bback, muA_y, logvarA_y = cycle_vae.forward_AtoB(B_to_A)
lossB_cycle = reconstruction_loss(xB, Bback)

# Sum up all losses
loss_vae = (lossA_rec + lossB_rec) + (lossA_kl + lossB_kl)
loss_cycle = (lossA_cycle + lossB_cycle) * lambda_cycle

total_loss = loss_vae + loss_cycle
return total_loss

# ----------------------------
# 7) Training routine
# ----------------------------
def train_cycle_vae(cycle_vae, loaderA, loaderB, optimizer, device,
↪  lambda_cycle=10.0):
    cycle_vae.train()
    total_loss = 0.0
    # We'll zip both loaders so we get pairs of samples (A, B).
    for (xA, _), (xB, _) in zip(loaderA, loaderB):
        xA = xA.to(device)
        xB = xB.to(device)
        optimizer.zero_grad()
        loss = cycle_vae_loss(cycle_vae, xA, xB,
        ↪  lambda_cycle=lambda_cycle)
        loss.backward()
        optimizer.step()
        total_loss += loss.item()

    return total_loss / min(len(loaderA), len(loaderB))

# ----------------------------
# 8) Main script
# ----------------------------
def main():
    set_seed(42)
    device = torch.device("cuda" if torch.cuda.is_available() else
    ↪  "cpu")

    # Dummy data for demonstration:
    datasetA = RandomDomainADataset(length=500, shape=(1,28,28))
    datasetB = RandomDomainBDataset(length=500, shape=(3,28,28))

    loaderA = DataLoader(datasetA, batch_size=16, shuffle=True)
```

```
    loaderB = DataLoader(datasetB, batch_size=16, shuffle=True)

    # Instantiate VAEs for domain A and domain B
    vaeA = VAE(in_channels=1, out_channels=1,
    ↪  latent_dim=16).to(device)
    vaeB = VAE(in_channels=3, out_channels=3,
    ↪  latent_dim=16).to(device)

    cycle_vae = CycleVAE(vaeA, vaeB).to(device)

    # Optimizer
    optimizer = optim.Adam(cycle_vae.parameters(), lr=1e-3)

    # Training loop
    epochs = 5
    for epoch in range(epochs):
        loss_val = train_cycle_vae(cycle_vae, loaderA, loaderB,
        ↪  optimizer, device, lambda_cycle=10.0)
        print(f"Epoch [{epoch+1}/{epochs}] - Loss: {loss_val:.4f}")

    print("Training complete. The cycle-VAEs have been trained on
    ↪  random data!")

if __name__ == "__main__":
    main()
```

Key Implementation Details:

- **Two Distinct VAEs:** Each domain has its own encoder and
  decoder. For domain A, we use (EncoderA + DecoderA); for
  domain B, we use (EncoderB + DecoderB).

- **Reparameterization Trick:** In each domain's encoder, we
  generate a latent distribution (μ, $\log \sigma^2$), then sample z via
  `reparameterize(mu, logvar)`.

- **Cycle Consistency:** We translate from domain A $\rightarrow$ B $\rightarrow$
  A and from domain B $\rightarrow$ A $\rightarrow$ B and measure reconstruction
  loss on the "cycled" images.

- **KL Divergence:** Each domain's encoder is penalized by
  the KL term to encourage the latent space to follow a normal
  prior.

- **Cross-Domain Loss:** The cycle consistency loss is scaled
  by a hyperparameter (λ_cycle) which balances the strength
  of domain translation vs. self-reconstruction.

- **Normalization Layers:** We include `BatchNorm2d` in both the encoder and decoder to stabilize training, but alternatives like instance normalization are also commonly used for image-to-image tasks.

- **End-to-End Pipeline:** The `main` function synthesizes the random dataset creation and training loop. In practice, you would replace the toy dataset with real domain-specific images for unpaired image-to-image translation.

Chapter 15

VAE for Graph Generation

In this chapter, we handle structured data in the form of graph representations. We create an encoder that converts graph adjacency matrices (or node features) into latent codes, and a decoder that reconstructs or samples new graphs. The implementation details involve using graph neural networks like GCNs or GraphSAGE. We explore potential data formats, handle varying graph sizes, and address issues of node ordering. By the end, you'll be able to generate synthetic graphs for tasks such as molecular design or social network analysis.

Python Code Snippet

```
import torch
import torch.nn as nn
import torch.optim as optim
import torch.nn.functional as F
import random

from torch_geometric.data import Data
from torch_geometric.loader import DataLoader
from torch_geometric.nn import GCNConv, global_mean_pool
from torch_geometric.utils import to_dense_adj, dense_to_sparse

# ------------------------------------------------------------
# 1) Simple Synthetic Graph Dataset
# ------------------------------------------------------------
class SyntheticGraphDataset(torch.utils.data.Dataset):
```

```python
"""
Synthetic dataset of random graphs with a fixed number of nodes.
Each graph is represented as a PyG Data object, storing:
  - node features (all ones in this demo)
  - edge_index for connectivity
  - adjacency matrix (dense) for reconstruction
"""
def __init__(self, num_graphs=1000, num_nodes=8, p=0.3,
↪   seed=42):
    super().__init__()
    random.seed(seed)
    torch.manual_seed(seed)

    self.num_graphs = num_graphs
    self.num_nodes = num_nodes
    self.p = p
    self.graphs = []
    self._generate_graphs()

def _generate_graphs(self):
    """
    Uses an Erdős-Rényi model to create random graphs with a
    ↪   given edge probability p.
    """
    for _ in range(self.num_graphs):
        # Generate a random adjacency matrix
        # Symmetric adjacency for an undirected graph
        adj = (torch.rand(self.num_nodes, self.num_nodes) <
        ↪   self.p).int()
        adj = torch.triu(adj, diagonal=1)  # keep upper
        ↪   triangular
        adj = adj + adj.T  # make symmetric

        # Node features: a simple example with '1' for all nodes
        x = torch.ones((self.num_nodes, 1), dtype=torch.float)

        # Convert adjacency to edge_index
        edge_index = dense_to_sparse(adj)[0]

        data = Data(x=x, edge_index=edge_index)
        data.adj = adj.float()  # store dense adjacency for
        ↪   reconstruction
        self.graphs.append(data)

def __len__(self):
    return self.num_graphs

def __getitem__(self, idx):
    return self.graphs[idx]

# ------------------------------------------------------------
# 2) GCN-based Encoder for VAE
# ------------------------------------------------------------
```

118

```python
class GraphEncoder(nn.Module):
    """
    A simple GCN-based encoder that outputs mu and logvar for the
    ↪ latent distribution.
    """
    def __init__(self, in_channels, hidden_dim, latent_dim):
        super(GraphEncoder, self).__init__()
        self.conv1 = GCNConv(in_channels, hidden_dim)
        self.conv2 = GCNConv(hidden_dim, hidden_dim)
        self.lin_mu = nn.Linear(hidden_dim, latent_dim)
        self.lin_logvar = nn.Linear(hidden_dim, latent_dim)

    def forward(self, x, edge_index, batch):
        # Two-layer GCN
        x = self.conv1(x, edge_index)
        x = F.relu(x)
        x = self.conv2(x, edge_index)
        x = F.relu(x)

        # Global pooling
        x = global_mean_pool(x, batch)

        # Produce mu and logvar
        mu = self.lin_mu(x)
        logvar = self.lin_logvar(x)
        return mu, logvar


# ------------------------------------------------------------
# 3) MLP-based Decoder that reconstructs adjacency
# ------------------------------------------------------------
class GraphDecoder(nn.Module):
    """
    Given a latent vector z, produce a (num_nodes x num_nodes)
    ↪ adjacency matrix.
    We'll flatten the upper triangle of the adjacency and use a
    ↪ simple MLP that
    outputs logits for each pair.
    """
    def __init__(self, latent_dim, hidden_dim, num_nodes):
        super(GraphDecoder, self).__init__()
        self.num_nodes = num_nodes
        self.lin1 = nn.Linear(latent_dim, hidden_dim)
        self.lin2 = nn.Linear(hidden_dim, hidden_dim)
        self.lin3 = nn.Linear(hidden_dim, (num_nodes * (num_nodes +
        ↪ 1)) // 2)

    def forward(self, z):
        z = F.relu(self.lin1(z))
        z = F.relu(self.lin2(z))
        # Output logits for the upper-triangular entries (including
        ↪ diagonal)
        logits_flat = self.lin3(z)
        return logits_flat
```

119

```python
def reconstruct_adjacency(self, logits_flat):
    """
    Convert the flat upper-triangle (including diagonal) logits
    into a full adjacency matrix. We'll apply a sigmoid to get
    ↪ probabilities.
    """
    batch_size = logits_flat.size(0)
    A = []
    idx = 0
    for b in range(batch_size):
        # For each graph in the batch
        upper_tri_flat = logits_flat[b]
        # We'll build a full adjacency in dense form
        mat = torch.zeros(self.num_nodes, self.num_nodes,
        ↪ device=upper_tri_flat.device)

        # We'll fill the upper triangle first
        u = 0
        for row in range(self.num_nodes):
            for col in range(row, self.num_nodes):
                mat[row, col] = upper_tri_flat[u]
                u += 1
        # Symmetrize
        mat = mat + mat.T - torch.diag(torch.diag(mat))
        A.append(mat.unsqueeze(0))

    A = torch.cat(A, dim=0)
    return A


# -----------------------------------------------------------
# 4) Reparameterization function
# -----------------------------------------------------------
def reparameterize(mu, logvar):
    std = torch.exp(0.5 * logvar)
    eps = torch.randn_like(std)
    return mu + eps * std


# -----------------------------------------------------------
# 5) Full GraphVAE architecture
# -----------------------------------------------------------
class GraphVAE(nn.Module):
    """
    Graph VAE model combining GraphEncoder and GraphDecoder.
    """
    def __init__(self, in_channels, hidden_dim, latent_dim,
    ↪ num_nodes):
        super(GraphVAE, self).__init__()
        self.encoder = GraphEncoder(in_channels, hidden_dim,
        ↪ latent_dim)
        self.decoder = GraphDecoder(latent_dim, hidden_dim,
        ↪ num_nodes)
        self.num_nodes = num_nodes
```

```python
    def forward(self, x, edge_index, batch):
        # Encode to get mu and logvar
        mu, logvar = self.encoder(x, edge_index, batch)
        # Reparameterize
        z = reparameterize(mu, logvar)
        # Decode
        logits_flat = self.decoder(z)
        return logits_flat, mu, logvar


# ------------------------------------------------------------
# 6) Training and evaluation loops
# ------------------------------------------------------------
def train_vae(model, dataloader, optimizer, device):
    model.train()
    total_loss = 0.0

    for data in dataloader:
        data = data.to(device)
        # If using a PyG DataLoader with multiple graphs, we have:
        x, edge_index, batch = data.x, data.edge_index, data.batch

        optimizer.zero_grad()
        logits_flat, mu, logvar = model(x, edge_index, batch)

        # Reconstruct adjacency
        # Real adjacency
        A_real = to_dense_adj(edge_index, batch,
        ↪   max_num_nodes=model.num_nodes)
        # A_real shape: [batch_size, num_nodes, num_nodes]
        # Flatten the upper triangle
        upper_mask = torch.triu(torch.ones(model.num_nodes,
        ↪   model.num_nodes), diagonal=0).bool()
        A_real_flat = A_real[:, upper_mask]

        # Predicted adjacency (logits)
        recon_loss = F.binary_cross_entropy_with_logits(logits_flat,
        ↪   A_real_flat)

        # KL divergence
        kld = -0.5 * torch.mean(1 + logvar - mu.pow(2) -
        ↪   logvar.exp())
        loss = recon_loss + kld

        loss.backward()
        optimizer.step()

        total_loss += loss.item()

    return total_loss / len(dataloader)

def test_vae(model, dataloader, device):
    model.eval()
```

```
    total_loss = 0.0
    with torch.no_grad():
        for data in dataloader:
            data = data.to(device)
            x, edge_index, batch = data.x, data.edge_index,
            ↪   data.batch

            logits_flat, mu, logvar = model(x, edge_index, batch)

            A_real = to_dense_adj(edge_index, batch,
            ↪   max_num_nodes=model.num_nodes)
            upper_mask = torch.triu(torch.ones(model.num_nodes,
            ↪   model.num_nodes), diagonal=0).bool()
            A_real_flat = A_real[:, upper_mask]

            recon_loss =
            ↪   F.binary_cross_entropy_with_logits(logits_flat,
            ↪   A_real_flat)
            kld = -0.5 * torch.mean(1 + logvar - mu.pow(2) -
            ↪   logvar.exp())
            loss = recon_loss + kld

            total_loss += loss.item()

    return total_loss / len(dataloader)

# ---------------------------------------------------------------
# 7) Sampling function
# ---------------------------------------------------------------
def sample_graphs(model, num_samples, device, threshold=0.5):
    """
    Sample new graphs from the prior (z ~ N(0, I)) and reconstruct
    ↪   adjacency matrices.
    """
    model.eval()
    with torch.no_grad():
        # z ~ N(0,1)
        z = torch.randn(num_samples,
        ↪   model.encoder.lin_mu.out_features, device=device)
        logits_flat = model.decoder(z)
        # Convert logits to adjacency
        adjacency_logits =
        ↪   model.decoder.reconstruct_adjacency(logits_flat)
        adjacency_probs = torch.sigmoid(adjacency_logits)

        # Binarize with a threshold
        sampled_adjacencies = (adjacency_probs > threshold).float()
        return sampled_adjacencies

# ---------------------------------------------------------------
# 8) Main function to tie everything together
# ---------------------------------------------------------------
def main():
```

```
device = torch.device("cuda" if torch.cuda.is_available() else
↪   "cpu")
# Create synthetic dataset
dataset = SyntheticGraphDataset(num_graphs=500, num_nodes=8,
↪   p=0.3, seed=42)

# Split train/test
train_size = int(0.8 * len(dataset))
test_size = len(dataset) - train_size
train_dataset, test_dataset =
↪   torch.utils.data.random_split(dataset, [train_size,
↪   test_size])

train_loader = DataLoader(train_dataset, batch_size=16,
↪   shuffle=True)
test_loader = DataLoader(test_dataset, batch_size=16,
↪   shuffle=False)

# Hyperparameters
in_channels = 1      # node feature dimension
hidden_dim = 32
latent_dim = 16
num_nodes = 8

model = GraphVAE(in_channels, hidden_dim, latent_dim,
↪   num_nodes).to(device)
optimizer = optim.Adam(model.parameters(), lr=1e-3)

epochs = 10
for epoch in range(1, epochs+1):
    train_loss = train_vae(model, train_loader, optimizer,
↪       device)
    test_loss = test_vae(model, test_loader, device)
    print(f"Epoch [{epoch}/{epochs}] - Train Loss:
↪       {train_loss:.4f}, Test Loss: {test_loss:.4f}")

# Sample new graphs
sampled_adjs = sample_graphs(model, num_samples=3,
↪   device=device, threshold=0.5)
print("Sampled adjacency matrices (thresholded at 0.5):")
for i, adj in enumerate(sampled_adjs):
    print(f"Sample {i+1}:\n{adj.cpu().numpy()}")

if __name__ == "__main__":
    main()
```

Key Implementation Details:

- **Graph Encoding:** We implement `GraphEncoder` using two
  GCN layers and a global mean pooling step to extract a single

123

feature vector per graph. This vector is then transformed into `mu` and `logvar`.

- **Latent Sampling:** The `reparameterize` function ensures gradients can flow through the random node sampling by transforming `mu` and `logvar` into a latent variable.

- **Decoding Step:** In `GraphDecoder`, we flatten the upper triangle of the adjacency and predict its logits. Full adjacency is reconstructed by symmetrizing.

- **VAE Loss:** We combine the reconstruction term, `recon_loss`, using a binary cross-entropy on the predicted adjacency, together with the KL-divergence `kld`, balancing reconstruction quality and latent space regularization.

- **Graph Sampling:** The `sample_graphs` function draws latent vectors from a standard Gaussian, decodes them into logit matrices, and binarizes with a threshold. In practice, you can tune this threshold or apply post-processing to ensure valid graph constraints.

- **Train/Test Workflow:** The `train_vae` and `test_vae` routines illustrate how we optimize and evaluate the model over synthetic random graphs, enabling quick experimentation with VAE-based graph generation.

Chapter 16

Hierarchical VAE for Complex Distributions

We deepen the VAE architecture by adding multiple levels of latents. This hierarchical approach helps in modeling complex distributions like large images or multi-scale data. Implementation requires carefully connecting encoders and decoders across multiple latent layers, and defining multiple KL divergences. We illustrate the training step-by-step, ensuring each latent level is updated correctly. This chapter provides a blueprint for building hierarchical models and monitoring how each layer captures different abstraction levels.

- We define an upper-level latent $\mathbf{z}_2$ drawn from a standard normal prior.

- Conditioned on $\mathbf{z}_2$, we specify a network that provides the prior of the lower-level latent $\mathbf{z}_1$.

- The encoder is split into two stages: first to infer $\mathbf{z}_2$ from $\mathbf{x}$, then to infer $\mathbf{z}_1$ from both $\mathbf{x}$ and $\mathbf{z}_2$.

- The decoder reconstructs $\mathbf{x}$ from $\mathbf{z}_1$.

- We accumulate two KL terms:
  $\mathrm{KL}(q(\mathbf{z}_2|\mathbf{x})\|p(\mathbf{z}_2))$ and $\mathrm{KL}(q(\mathbf{z}_1|\mathbf{x},\mathbf{z}_2)\|p(\mathbf{z}_1|\mathbf{z}_2))$.

Python Code Snippet

```python
import torch
import torch.nn as nn
import torch.optim as optim
from torch.utils.data import DataLoader
import torchvision
import torchvision.transforms as transforms
import torch.nn.functional as F
import math


# ------------------------------------------------------------
# 1) Define utility functions
# ------------------------------------------------------------
def reparameterize(mu, logvar):
    """
    Reparameterization trick to sample z ~ N(mu, exp(logvar)).
    """
    std = torch.exp(0.5 * logvar)
    eps = torch.randn_like(std)
    return mu + eps * std

def kl_divergence_gaussian(mu_q, logvar_q, mu_p, logvar_p):
    """
    KL(N(q|mu_q, logvar_q) || N(p|mu_p, logvar_p))
    logvar_* is the log of the variance, not the standard deviation.
    """
    # Compute element-wise KL
    # kl = 0.5 * [ (_p^2 / _q^2) + (_q - _p)^2 / _q^2 - 1 +
    # ↪  log(_q^2/_p^2) ]
    # but in log form
    var_q = torch.exp(logvar_q)
    var_p = torch.exp(logvar_p)
    kl = 0.5 * (
        (var_q / var_p)
        + (mu_q - mu_p).pow(2) / var_p
        - 1.0
        + (logvar_p - logvar_q)
    )
    return kl.sum(dim=1).mean()


# ------------------------------------------------------------
# 2) Build hierarchical VAE components
# ------------------------------------------------------------
# We'll flatten the image x -> 784 dimension for MNIST.

class EncoderLevel2(nn.Module):
    """
    Encodes x into z2 distribution parameters: (mu2, logvar2).
    """
    def __init__(self, input_dim=784, hidden_dim=512, z2_dim=32):
        super().__init__()
```

```python
        self.fc1 = nn.Linear(input_dim, hidden_dim)
        self.fc2 = nn.Linear(hidden_dim, hidden_dim)
        self.mu = nn.Linear(hidden_dim, z2_dim)
        self.logvar = nn.Linear(hidden_dim, z2_dim)

    def forward(self, x):
        h = F.relu(self.fc1(x))
        h = F.relu(self.fc2(h))
        mu2 = self.mu(h)
        logvar2 = self.logvar(h)
        return mu2, logvar2

class EncoderLevel1(nn.Module):
    """
    Encodes (x, z2) into z1 distribution parameters: (mu1, logvar1).
    """

    def __init__(self, input_dim=784, z2_dim=32, hidden_dim=512,
    ↪  z1_dim=64):
        super().__init__()
        self.fc1 = nn.Linear(input_dim + z2_dim, hidden_dim)
        self.fc2 = nn.Linear(hidden_dim, hidden_dim)
        self.mu = nn.Linear(hidden_dim, z1_dim)
        self.logvar = nn.Linear(hidden_dim, z1_dim)

    def forward(self, x, z2):
        # Concatenate x and z2
        inp = torch.cat([x, z2], dim=1)
        h = F.relu(self.fc1(inp))
        h = F.relu(self.fc2(h))
        mu1 = self.mu(h)
        logvar1 = self.logvar(h)
        return mu1, logvar1

class PriorLevel1(nn.Module):
    """
    Learns the parameters of p(z1|z2): (prior_mu1, prior_logvar1).
    """

    def __init__(self, z2_dim=32, hidden_dim=512, z1_dim=64):
        super().__init__()
        self.fc1 = nn.Linear(z2_dim, hidden_dim)
        self.fc2 = nn.Linear(hidden_dim, hidden_dim)
        self.prior_mu = nn.Linear(hidden_dim, z1_dim)
        self.prior_logvar = nn.Linear(hidden_dim, z1_dim)

    def forward(self, z2):
        h = F.relu(self.fc1(z2))
        h = F.relu(self.fc2(h))
        pmu1 = self.prior_mu(h)
        plogvar1 = self.prior_logvar(h)
        return pmu1, plogvar1

class DecoderLevel1(nn.Module):
    """
```

```
    Decodes z1 into x reconstruction.
    """
    def __init__(self, z1_dim=64, hidden_dim=512, output_dim=784):
        super().__init__()
        self.fc1 = nn.Linear(z1_dim, hidden_dim)
        self.fc2 = nn.Linear(hidden_dim, hidden_dim)
        self.fc3 = nn.Linear(hidden_dim, output_dim)

    def forward(self, z1):
        h = F.relu(self.fc1(z1))
        h = F.relu(self.fc2(h))
        x_recon = torch.sigmoid(self.fc3(h))
        return x_recon


# ----------------------------------------------------------------
# 3) The Hierarchical VAE that ties components together
# ----------------------------------------------------------------
class HierarchicalVAE(nn.Module):
    def __init__(self,
                 input_dim=784,
                 hidden_dim=512,
                 z2_dim=32,
                 z1_dim=64):
        super().__init__()
        # Encoders
        self.encoder2 = EncoderLevel2(input_dim, hidden_dim, z2_dim)
        self.encoder1 = EncoderLevel1(input_dim, z2_dim, hidden_dim,
        ↪    z1_dim)
        # Prior for z1
        self.prior1 = PriorLevel1(z2_dim, hidden_dim, z1_dim)
        # Decoder from z1 -> x
        self.decoder1 = DecoderLevel1(z1_dim, hidden_dim, input_dim)

    def forward(self, x):
        """
        Forward pass returns:
          - reconstructed x
          - kl_z2: KL(q(z2|x) || p(z2))
          - kl_z1: KL(q(z1|x,z2) || p(z1|z2))
        """
        # 1) Flatten input
        x_flat = x.view(x.size(0), -1)

        # 2) Compute q(z2|x)
        mu2, logvar2 = self.encoder2(x_flat)
        z2 = reparameterize(mu2, logvar2)

        # 3) Compute q(z1|x,z2)
        mu1, logvar1 = self.encoder1(x_flat, z2)
        z1 = reparameterize(mu1, logvar1)

        # 4) Prior p(z1|z2)
        pmu1, plogvar1 = self.prior1(z2)
```

```
        # 5) Reconstruct
        x_recon = self.decoder1(z1)

        # 6) KL terms
        # z2 ~ q(z2|x) vs N(0,I)
        kl_z2 = -0.5 * torch.mean(1 + logvar2 - mu2.pow(2) -
        ↪  logvar2.exp())

        # z1 ~ q(z1|x,z2) vs p(z1|z2)
        kl_z1 = kl_divergence_gaussian(mu1, logvar1, pmu1, plogvar1)

        return x_recon, kl_z2, kl_z1


# ----------------------------------------------------------------
# 4) Training/Testing Routines
# ----------------------------------------------------------------
def train_epoch(model, optimizer, dataloader, device):
    model.train()
    running_loss = 0.0
    for x, _ in dataloader:
        x = x.to(device)
        optimizer.zero_grad()
        x_recon, kl_z2, kl_z1 = model(x)

        # Reconstruction loss (BCE)
        x_flat = x.view(x.size(0), -1)
        recon_loss = F.binary_cross_entropy(x_recon, x_flat,
        ↪  reduction='sum') / x.size(0)

        # Combined loss
        loss = recon_loss + kl_z2 + kl_z1
        loss.backward()
        optimizer.step()

        running_loss += loss.item()
    return running_loss / len(dataloader)

def test_epoch(model, dataloader, device):
    model.eval()
    total_loss = 0.0
    with torch.no_grad():
        for x, _ in dataloader:
            x = x.to(device)
            x_recon, kl_z2, kl_z1 = model(x)

            x_flat = x.view(x.size(0), -1)
            recon_loss = F.binary_cross_entropy(x_recon, x_flat,
            ↪  reduction='sum') / x.size(0)

            loss = recon_loss + kl_z2 + kl_z1
            total_loss += loss.item()
    return total_loss / len(dataloader)
```

```
# ---------------------------------------------------------------
# 5) Main function: Load data, train, test
# ---------------------------------------------------------------
def main():
    device = torch.device("cuda" if torch.cuda.is_available() else
    ↪    "cpu")

    # Data: MNIST
    transform = transforms.Compose([
        transforms.ToTensor()
    ])
    train_dataset = torchvision.datasets.MNIST(
        root='./data', train=True, download=True,
        ↪    transform=transform
    )
    test_dataset = torchvision.datasets.MNIST(
        root='./data', train=False, download=True,
        ↪    transform=transform
    )

    train_loader = DataLoader(train_dataset, batch_size=64,
    ↪    shuffle=True)
    test_loader = DataLoader(test_dataset, batch_size=64,
    ↪    shuffle=False)

    # Define the HierarchicalVAE
    model = HierarchicalVAE(input_dim=784, hidden_dim=512,
    ↪    z2_dim=32, z1_dim=64).to(device)
    optimizer = optim.Adam(model.parameters(), lr=1e-3)

    epochs = 5
    for epoch in range(epochs):
        train_loss = train_epoch(model, optimizer, train_loader,
        ↪    device)
        val_loss = test_epoch(model, test_loader, device)
        print(f"Epoch [{epoch+1}/{epochs}] Train Loss:
        ↪    {train_loss:.4f} | Val Loss: {val_loss:.4f}")

    print("Training complete! You can now sample by feeding random
    ↪    z2 -> z1 -> x.")

if __name__ == "__main__":
    main()
```

Key Implementation Details:

- **Multiple Latent Layers:** Two encoders generate z_2 and z_1. The EncoderLevel2 produces the distribution for z_2. Conditioned on z_2 and x, EncoderLevel1 infers z_1.

130

- **Separate KL Terms:** We compute one KL divergence for z_2 against a standard normal prior, and one for z_1 against a learned prior $p(z\_1|z\_2)$. Both terms must be summed.

- **Decoder Reconstruction:** The `DecoderLevel1` maps z_1 back to the data space. Here, we used a fully connected network that outputs a Bernoulli parameter in $[0, 1]$.

- **Training Loop:** Each call to `train_epoch` fetches batches, computes the forward pass, and backpropagates the sum of reconstruction and KL losses.

- **Inference and Sampling:** At inference, `test_epoch` computes the same loss without parameter updates. You can also sample new data by drawing random z_2, then sampling z_1 from $p(z\_1|z\_2)$, and finally decoding z_1 to generate x.

Chapter 17

Multimodal VAE for Cross-Modal Learning

By integrating multiple data modalities—such as images, text, or audio—into a single VAE, we fuse their latent representations for joint learning. This chapter explains how to construct separate encoders for each modality, merge their latent spaces, and design decoders to reconstruct each modality. We handle alignment issues by creating a common latent space and explore partial supervision for missing modalities. Implementation guidelines include data synchronization, specialized loss terms, and bridging the gap between distinct data types.

Python Code Snippet

```
import torch
import torch.nn as nn
import torch.optim as optim
from torch.utils.data import Dataset, DataLoader
import random
import numpy as np

# ------------------------------------------------------------
# 1) Utility for setting reproducible seed
# ------------------------------------------------------------
def set_seed(seed=42):
    random.seed(seed)
    np.random.seed(seed)
    torch.manual_seed(seed)
    if torch.cuda.is_available():
```

```
        torch.cuda.manual_seed_all(seed)

# -----------------------------------------------------------------
# 2) Random dataset that simulates partial availability
#    of image, text, and audio modalities.
#    Each item is (image_tensor, text_tensor, audio_tensor, mask)
#    mask[i] = 1 if modality i is present, else 0
# -----------------------------------------------------------------
class RandomMultimodalDataset(Dataset):
    def __init__(self, length=200):
        super().__init__()
        self.length = length

    def __len__(self):
        return self.length

    def __getitem__(self, idx):
        # Simulate random presence of each modality
        # mask = (image_present, text_present, audio_present)
        mask = [
            random.randint(0, 1),
            random.randint(0, 1),
            random.randint(0, 1)
        ]
        # Avoid the case where all are 0, ensure at least one
        # ↪  modality is present
        while sum(mask) == 0:
            mask = [
                random.randint(0, 1),
                random.randint(0, 1),
                random.randint(0, 1)
            ]

        # If a modality is missing, we store None.
        # Otherwise, we store a random tensor for demonstration.
        # Image shape: (1, 28, 28)
        image = torch.rand(1, 28, 28) if mask[0] == 1 else None

        # Text shape: Let's do a 1D vector of length 10 for
        # ↪  simplicity
        text = torch.rand(10) if mask[1] == 1 else None

        # Audio shape: Let's do a 1D vector of length 50 for
        # ↪  simplicity
        audio = torch.rand(50) if mask[2] == 1 else None

        return (image, text, audio, mask)

# -----------------------------------------------------------------
# 3) Modular Encoders for each modality
#    Each encoder produces mean and logvar of size 'latent_dim'
# -----------------------------------------------------------------
class ImageEncoder(nn.Module):
```

133

```python
    def __init__(self, latent_dim=16):
        super().__init__()
        # A simple MLP that flattens the 1x28x28 image
        self.flatten = nn.Flatten()
        self.net = nn.Sequential(
            nn.Linear(28*28, 128),
            nn.ReLU(),
            nn.Linear(128, 64),
            nn.ReLU()
        )
        self.mu = nn.Linear(64, latent_dim)
        self.logvar = nn.Linear(64, latent_dim)

    def forward(self, x):
        x = self.flatten(x)
        x = self.net(x)
        return self.mu(x), self.logvar(x)

class TextEncoder(nn.Module):
    def __init__(self, latent_dim=16, text_size=10):
        super().__init__()
        self.net = nn.Sequential(
            nn.Linear(text_size, 32),
            nn.ReLU(),
            nn.Linear(32, 32),
            nn.ReLU()
        )
        self.mu = nn.Linear(32, latent_dim)
        self.logvar = nn.Linear(32, latent_dim)

    def forward(self, x):
        x = self.net(x)
        return self.mu(x), self.logvar(x)

class AudioEncoder(nn.Module):
    def __init__(self, latent_dim=16, audio_size=50):
        super().__init__()
        self.net = nn.Sequential(
            nn.Linear(audio_size, 64),
            nn.ReLU(),
            nn.Linear(64, 64),
            nn.ReLU()
        )
        self.mu = nn.Linear(64, latent_dim)
        self.logvar = nn.Linear(64, latent_dim)

    def forward(self, x):
        x = self.net(x)
        return self.mu(x), self.logvar(x)

# -----------------------------------------------------------
# 4) Decoders for each modality
#    Each decoder receives a latent z and reconstructs the modality
```

134

```python
# -----------------------------------------------------------------
class ImageDecoder(nn.Module):
    def __init__(self, latent_dim=16):
        super().__init__()
        self.net = nn.Sequential(
            nn.Linear(latent_dim, 64),
            nn.ReLU(),
            nn.Linear(64, 128),
            nn.ReLU(),
            nn.Linear(128, 28*28),
        )

    def forward(self, z):
        x = self.net(z)
        # Reshape to (1, 28, 28)
        return x.view(-1, 1, 28, 28)

class TextDecoder(nn.Module):
    def __init__(self, latent_dim=16, text_size=10):
        super().__init__()
        self.net = nn.Sequential(
            nn.Linear(latent_dim, 32),
            nn.ReLU(),
            nn.Linear(32, 32),
            nn.ReLU(),
            nn.Linear(32, text_size)
        )

    def forward(self, z):
        return self.net(z)

class AudioDecoder(nn.Module):
    def __init__(self, latent_dim=16, audio_size=50):
        super().__init__()
        self.net = nn.Sequential(
            nn.Linear(latent_dim, 64),
            nn.ReLU(),
            nn.Linear(64, 64),
            nn.ReLU(),
            nn.Linear(64, audio_size)
        )

    def forward(self, z):
        return self.net(z)


# -----------------------------------------------------------------
# 5) Multimodal VAE that wraps encoders, decoders, and
#    merges partial modalities.
# -----------------------------------------------------------------
class MultimodalVAE(nn.Module):
    def __init__(self, latent_dim=16):
        super().__init__()
        self.latent_dim = latent_dim
```

```python
        # Encoders
        self.image_encoder = ImageEncoder(latent_dim)
        self.text_encoder = TextEncoder(latent_dim)
        self.audio_encoder = AudioEncoder(latent_dim)

        # Decoders
        self.image_decoder = ImageDecoder(latent_dim)
        self.text_decoder = TextDecoder(latent_dim)
        self.audio_decoder = AudioDecoder(latent_dim)

    def aggregate_distribution(self, mus, logvars):
        """
        A simplistic aggregator that averages available
        mean and logvar across modalities that are present.
        """
        # Filter out None entries (for missing modalities)
        valid_mus = [m for m in mus if m is not None]
        valid_logvars = [lv for lv in logvars if lv is not None]

        # If no valid modalities, return something safe
        if len(valid_mus) == 0:
            # This scenario generally shouldn't occur if dataset
            ↪   ensures at least 1 present
            dummy_mu = torch.zeros(self.latent_dim,
            ↪   device=mus[0].device)
            dummy_logvar = torch.zeros(self.latent_dim,
            ↪   device=mus[0].device)
            return dummy_mu, dummy_logvar

        mean_agg = torch.stack(valid_mus, dim=0).mean(dim=0)
        logvar_agg = torch.stack(valid_logvars, dim=0).mean(dim=0)
        return mean_agg, logvar_agg

    def reparameterize(self, mu, logvar):
        std = torch.exp(0.5 * logvar)
        eps = torch.randn_like(std)
        return mu + eps * std

    def forward_encoders(self, image, text, audio):
        mu_img, logvar_img = None, None
        mu_txt, logvar_txt = None, None
        mu_aud, logvar_aud = None, None

        if image is not None:
            mu_img, logvar_img = self.image_encoder(image)
        if text is not None:
            mu_txt, logvar_txt = self.text_encoder(text)
        if audio is not None:
            mu_aud, logvar_aud = self.audio_encoder(audio)

        return mu_img, logvar_img, mu_txt, logvar_txt, mu_aud,
        ↪   logvar_aud
```

136

```python
def forward_decoders(self, z):
    # We return all three reconstructions
    recon_image = self.image_decoder(z)
    recon_text = self.text_decoder(z)
    recon_audio = self.audio_decoder(z)
    return recon_image, recon_text, recon_audio

def forward(self, image, text, audio):
    # 1) Encode
    mu_img, logvar_img, mu_txt, logvar_txt, mu_aud, logvar_aud =
    ↪   self.forward_encoders(image, text, audio)

    # 2) Aggregate
    mu_agg, logvar_agg = self.aggregate_distribution([mu_img,
    ↪   mu_txt, mu_aud],

                                                ↪   [logvar_img,
                                                ↪   logvar_txt,
                                                ↪   logvar_aud])

    # 3) Sample
    z = self.reparameterize(mu_agg, logvar_agg)

    # 4) Decode
    recon_image, recon_text, recon_audio =
    ↪   self.forward_decoders(z)

    return (recon_image, recon_text, recon_audio,
            mu_agg, logvar_agg)

# ---------------------------------------------------------------
# 6) Training helpers
# ---------------------------------------------------------------
def vae_loss_function(image, text, audio, recon_image, recon_text,
↪   recon_audio,
                      mu, logvar, mask):
    """
    We compute reconstruction losses for available modalities and
    ↪   sum them,
    then add KL divergence.
    """
    batch_size = 1  # Our dataset yields single samples in this
    ↪   example
    recon_loss = 0.0

    # If image is present, MSE
    if mask[0] == 1 and image is not None:
        recon_loss += torch.nn.functional.mse_loss(recon_image,
        ↪   image)

    # If text is present, MSE
    if mask[1] == 1 and text is not None:
        recon_loss += torch.nn.functional.mse_loss(recon_text, text)
```

```python
    # If audio is present, MSE
    if mask[2] == 1 and audio is not None:
        recon_loss += torch.nn.functional.mse_loss(recon_audio,
        ↪  audio)

    # KL Divergence
    # KL = -0.5 * sum(1 + logvar - mu^2 - exp(logvar))
    kl = -0.5 * torch.sum(1 + logvar - mu.pow(2) - logvar.exp())

    # Note: We might average over batch, but batch_size=1 here
    total_loss = recon_loss + kl
    return total_loss, recon_loss, kl

def train_one_epoch(model, dataloader, optimizer, device):
    model.train()
    total_loss_val = 0.0
    for (image, text, audio, mask) in dataloader:
        # Move data to device if not None
        if image[0] is not None:
            image = image[0].unsqueeze(0).to(device)
        else:
            image = None

        if text[0] is not None:
            text = text[0].unsqueeze(0).to(device)
        else:
            text = None

        if audio[0] is not None:
            audio = audio[0].unsqueeze(0).to(device)
        else:
            audio = None

        mask = mask[0]   # shape is [3]

        # Forward pass
        recon_image, recon_text, recon_audio, mu, logvar =
        ↪  model(image, text, audio)

        # Compute loss
        loss, _, _ = vae_loss_function(image, text, audio,
                                       recon_image, recon_text,
                                       ↪  recon_audio,
                                       mu, logvar, mask)
        optimizer.zero_grad()
        loss.backward()
        optimizer.step()

        total_loss_val += loss.item()

    return total_loss_val / len(dataloader)
```

138

```
# ---------------------------------------------------------------
# 7) Main script
# ---------------------------------------------------------------
def main():
    set_seed(42)
    device = torch.device("cuda" if torch.cuda.is_available() else
    ↪ "cpu")

    # Create dataset and dataloader
    dataset = RandomMultimodalDataset(length=200)
    dataloader = DataLoader(dataset, batch_size=1, shuffle=True)

    # Initialize the model
    model = MultimodalVAE(latent_dim=16).to(device)

    # Optimizer
    optimizer = optim.Adam(model.parameters(), lr=1e-3)

    # Train model
    epochs = 5
    for epoch in range(1, epochs+1):
        avg_loss = train_one_epoch(model, dataloader, optimizer,
        ↪ device)
        print(f"Epoch {epoch}/{epochs}, Loss: {avg_loss:.4f}")

    print("Training complete! Model can now handle partial data and
    ↪ reconstruct multiple modalities.")

if __name__ == "__main__":
    main()
```

Key Implementation Details:

- **Separate Encoders:** Each modal encoder produces a distribution over the latent space (and log ^{2}). Modalities that are absent (None data) are simply skipped.

- **Multimodal Aggregation:** The means and log-variances are averaged for all provided modalities to form a single latent distribution. This ensures a common latent representation for cross-modal learning.

- **Reparameterization Trick:** We sample from the latent distribution using z = + for training stability.

- **Decoders:** Each decoder reconstructs its respective modality from the shared latent code. The training loss sums over available modalities.

- **Partial Supervision:** The mask indicates which modalities are present for each sample. If a modality is missing, it is excluded from both the correlation in the encoder and the reconstruction term in the loss.

- **VAE Objective:** The total loss is the sum of reconstruction losses (only for available modalities) plus the KL divergence, encouraging a smooth latent space for cross-modal generation.

Chapter 18

Sequential VAE for Time Series Forecasting

We apply a recurrent or sequential Variational Autoencoder (VAE) architecture to predict future data points. The encoder maps a window of time series data to a latent distribution, and the decoder reconstructs or forecasts the subsequent values. The following discussion outlines how to:

- Combine RNN modules (e.g., LSTM) with a VAE setup for probabilistic modeling of time series.

- Implement teacher forcing during training, supplying ground truth inputs at each decoder step to stabilize learning.

- Handle variable sequence lengths via padding and masking strategies.

- Incorporate additional features (e.g., external variables) to improve forecasts.

- Use the learned latent representations for estimating uncertainty in future predictions.

Python Code Snippet

```python
import torch
import torch.nn as nn
import torch.optim as optim
import random
import math
import numpy as np
from torch.utils.data import Dataset, DataLoader
import matplotlib.pyplot as plt


# --------------------------------------------------------------
# 1) Synthetic Dataset for Demonstration
# --------------------------------------------------------------
class SyntheticTimeSeriesDataset(Dataset):
    """
    Generates a synthetic time series dataset for demonstration.
    Each sequence is a simple noisy sine wave of random length.
    """
    def __init__(self, num_sequences=1000, max_seq_len=50,
    ↪ min_seq_len=20):
        super().__init__()
        self.data = []
        for _ in range(num_sequences):
            seq_len = random.randint(min_seq_len, max_seq_len)
            t = np.linspace(0, 2 * math.pi, seq_len, endpoint=False)
            amplitude = random.uniform(0.5, 2.0)
            phase = random.uniform(0, 2 * math.pi)
            noise_level = 0.1
            values = amplitude * np.sin(t + phase) + noise_level *
            ↪ np.random.randn(seq_len)
            self.data.append(values.astype(np.float32))

    def __len__(self):
        return len(self.data)

    def __getitem__(self, idx):
        """
        Returns a single time series example.
        We'll turn it into a PyTorch float tensor.
        """
        return torch.tensor(self.data[idx])


def collate_fn(batch):
    """
    Collate function to handle variable-length sequences by padding.
    Returns padded sequences and lengths.
    """
    # batch is a list of tensors, each [seq_len,]
    lengths = [seq.size(0) for seq in batch]
    max_len = max(lengths)
```

```python
    padded_seqs = []
    for seq in batch:
        padded = torch.zeros(max_len, dtype=torch.float32)
        padded[:seq.size(0)] = seq
        padded_seqs.append(padded)
    padded_seqs = torch.stack(padded_seqs, dim=0)  # [B, T]

    # We'll also create a mask to know which elements are valid
    mask = torch.zeros((len(batch), max_len), dtype=torch.bool)
    for i, length in enumerate(lengths):
        mask[i, :length] = True

    return padded_seqs.unsqueeze(-1), mask, lengths


# --------------------------------------------------------------
# 2) Recurrent VAE Architecture
# --------------------------------------------------------------
class RecurrentEncoder(nn.Module):
    """
    RNN-based encoder that reads variable-length sequences
    and outputs a latent distribution (mu, logvar).
    """

    def __init__(self, input_dim=1, hidden_dim=32, latent_dim=16):
        super(RecurrentEncoder, self).__init__()
        self.hidden_dim = hidden_dim
        self.latent_dim = latent_dim

        self.lstm = nn.LSTM(input_dim, hidden_dim, batch_first=True)
        self.mu_layer = nn.Linear(hidden_dim, latent_dim)
        self.logvar_layer = nn.Linear(hidden_dim, latent_dim)

    def forward(self, x, mask):
        """
        x: [B, T, input_dim]
        mask: [B, T] with True for valid timesteps
        """
        # We'll pack the sequence to handle variable length
        lengths = mask.sum(dim=1).cpu()
        packed_x = nn.utils.rnn.pack_padded_sequence(x, lengths,
        ↪   batch_first=True, enforce_sorted=False)

        # Forward pass through LSTM
        _, (h_n, _) = self.lstm(packed_x)

        # h_n has shape [1, B, hidden_dim]
        h_n = h_n.squeeze(0)  # [B, hidden_dim]

        mu = self.mu_layer(h_n)
        logvar = self.logvar_layer(h_n)
        return mu, logvar
```

143

```python
class RecurrentDecoder(nn.Module):
    """
    RNN-based decoder that reconstructs or forecasts from a latent
    ↪   code.
    Teacher forcing is included in forward().
    """
    def __init__(self, input_dim=1, hidden_dim=32, latent_dim=16):
        super(RecurrentDecoder, self).__init__()
        self.hidden_dim = hidden_dim
        self.latent_dim = latent_dim
        self.input_dim = input_dim

        self.lstm = nn.LSTM(input_dim, hidden_dim, batch_first=True)
        self.fc_init = nn.Linear(latent_dim, hidden_dim)
        self.out = nn.Linear(hidden_dim, input_dim)

    def forward(self, z, target_seq, mask,
    ↪   teacher_forcing_ratio=0.5):
        """
        z: [B, latent_dim]
        target_seq: [B, T, input_dim]
        mask: [B, T]
        teacher_forcing_ratio: probability of using ground truth at
        ↪   each step
        Returns: reconstructed sequence of shape [B, T, input_dim]
        """
        batch_size, seq_len, _ = target_seq.shape

        # Initialize hidden state from latent z
        hidden_state = torch.tanh(self.fc_init(z))   # [B,
        ↪   hidden_dim]
        hidden_state = hidden_state.unsqueeze(0)  # [1, B,
        ↪   hidden_dim]
        cell_state = torch.zeros_like(hidden_state)   # [1, B,
        ↪   hidden_dim]

        outputs = []

        # We'll decode step by step
        input_step = torch.zeros(batch_size, 1, self.input_dim,
        ↪   device=z.device)  # [B,1,input_dim]

        for t in range(seq_len):
            # LSTM step
            output, (hidden_state, cell_state) =
            ↪   self.lstm(input_step, (hidden_state, cell_state))
            step_output = self.out(output)   # [B,1,input_dim]
            outputs.append(step_output)

            # Teacher forcing decision
            use_teacher_forcing = (random.random() <
            ↪   teacher_forcing_ratio)
            if t < seq_len - 1:
```

```python
            if use_teacher_forcing:
                # Use ground truth
                input_step = target_seq[:, t+1, :].unsqueeze(1)
            else:
                # Use model output
                input_step = step_output
        else:
            # no next input needed after final step
            pass

    outputs = torch.cat(outputs, dim=1)  # [B, T, input_dim]

    # We might mask out invalid steps if needed
    # (For reconstruction, we'll keep them for now.)
    return outputs


class RecurrentVAE(nn.Module):
    """
    Combines RecurrentEncoder + RecurrentDecoder with
    ↪ reparameterization for a VAE.
    """

    def __init__(self, input_dim=1, hidden_dim=32, latent_dim=16):
        super(RecurrentVAE, self).__init__()
        self.encoder = RecurrentEncoder(input_dim, hidden_dim,
        ↪ latent_dim)
        self.decoder = RecurrentDecoder(input_dim, hidden_dim,
        ↪ latent_dim)

    def reparameterize(self, mu, logvar):
        """
        Reparameterization trick: z = mu + std * epsilon
        """
        std = torch.exp(0.5 * logvar)
        eps = torch.randn_like(std)
        return mu + eps * std

    def forward(self, x, mask, teacher_forcing_ratio=0.5):
        """
        x: [B, T, input_dim], mask: [B, T]
        """
        mu, logvar = self.encoder(x, mask)
        z = self.reparameterize(mu, logvar)
        recon_x = self.decoder(z, x, mask, teacher_forcing_ratio)
        return recon_x, mu, logvar


# ----------------------------------------------------------------
# 3) VAE Loss Function
# ----------------------------------------------------------------
def vae_loss_function(recon_x, x, mu, logvar, mask):
    """
    Standard ELBO loss with MSE reconstruction + KL divergence.
```

145

```
recon_x, x: [B, T, input_dim]
mu, logvar: [B, latent_dim]
mask: [B, T] -> which timesteps are valid
"""
# MSE for reconstruction
# We'll only compute MSE where mask is True
mse = (recon_x - x) ** 2
mse = mse.mean(dim=-1)    # mean over input_dim
mse_masked = mse[mask].mean()   # average over valid timesteps in
↪ the batch

# KL divergence
kld = -0.5 * torch.sum(1 + logvar - mu.pow(2) - logvar.exp(),
↪ dim=1)
kld = kld.mean()   # average over batch

loss = mse_masked + kld
return loss, mse_masked, kld


# -------------------------------------------------------------
# 4) Training, Evaluation, and Forecasting
# -------------------------------------------------------------
def train_one_epoch(model, dataloader, optimizer, device,
↪ teacher_forcing_ratio=0.5):
    model.train()
    total_loss = 0
    for batch in dataloader:
        x, mask, _ = batch
        x = x.to(device)          # [B, T, 1]
        mask = mask.to(device)    # [B, T]

        optimizer.zero_grad()
        recon_x, mu, logvar = model(x, mask, teacher_forcing_ratio)
        loss, _, _ = vae_loss_function(recon_x, x, mu, logvar, mask)
        loss.backward()
        optimizer.step()
        total_loss += loss.item()

    return total_loss / len(dataloader)

def evaluate_model(model, dataloader, device):
    model.eval()
    total_loss = 0
    with torch.no_grad():
        for batch in dataloader:
            x, mask, _ = batch
            x = x.to(device)
            mask = mask.to(device)
            recon_x, mu, logvar = model(x, mask,
            ↪ teacher_forcing_ratio=0.0)  # no forcing at eval
            loss, _, _ = vae_loss_function(recon_x, x, mu, logvar,
            ↪ mask)
```

```
            total_loss += loss.item()
    return total_loss / len(dataloader)

def forecast(model, initial_seq, forecast_horizon, device):
    """
    Use the learned latent representation for future forecasts.
    We'll:
        1) Encode the known sequence to get mu, logvar
        2) Sample from latent (z)
        3) Run decoder for 'forecast_horizon' steps by disabling
        ↪ teacher forcing
    """
    model.eval()
    with torch.no_grad():
        # initial_seq: shape [1, T, 1] ideally
        mask = torch.ones((1, initial_seq.shape[1]),
        ↪ dtype=torch.bool, device=device)
        mu, logvar = model.encoder(initial_seq, mask)
        z = model.reparameterize(mu, logvar)

        # We create a placeholder for the decoder
        # We'll expand time steps to T + forecast_horizon
        # But we'll use the model in "autoregressive" fashion
        outputs = []

        # We'll set hidden state from z
        hidden_state =
        ↪ torch.tanh(model.decoder.fc_init(z)).unsqueeze(0)
        cell_state = torch.zeros_like(hidden_state)

        input_step = initial_seq[:, -1:, :]  # last known value as
        ↪ "seed"
        for _ in range(forecast_horizon):
            output, (hidden_state, cell_state) =
            ↪ model.decoder.lstm(input_step, (hidden_state,
            ↪ cell_state))
            step_output = model.decoder.out(output)
            outputs.append(step_output)
            input_step = step_output  # no teacher forcing
        forecasts = torch.cat(outputs, dim=1)  # [1,
        ↪ forecast_horizon, 1]
        return forecasts.squeeze().cpu().numpy()


# ------------------------------------------------------------------
# 5) Main Script
# ------------------------------------------------------------------
def main():
    device = torch.device("cuda" if torch.cuda.is_available() else
    ↪ "cpu")
    random.seed(42)
    torch.manual_seed(42)
```

```python
# Create synthetic dataset
train_dataset = SyntheticTimeSeriesDataset(num_sequences=800)
val_dataset = SyntheticTimeSeriesDataset(num_sequences=200)

train_loader = DataLoader(train_dataset, batch_size=32,
↪  shuffle=True, collate_fn=collate_fn)
val_loader = DataLoader(val_dataset, batch_size=32,
↪  shuffle=False, collate_fn=collate_fn)

# Initialize model, optimizer
model = RecurrentVAE(input_dim=1, hidden_dim=32,
↪  latent_dim=16).to(device)
optimizer = optim.Adam(model.parameters(), lr=1e-3)

epochs = 10
for epoch in range(1, epochs+1):
    train_loss = train_one_epoch(model, train_loader, optimizer,
    ↪  device, teacher_forcing_ratio=0.6)
    val_loss = evaluate_model(model, val_loader, device)
    print(f"Epoch [{epoch}/{epochs}] | Train Loss:
    ↪  {train_loss:.4f} | Val Loss: {val_loss:.4f}")

# Example forecasting on a new sequence from validation data
example_data = val_dataset[0].unsqueeze(0).to(device)  # shape
↪  [1, T]
forecast_steps = 10
forecast_vals = forecast(model, example_data, forecast_steps,
↪  device=device)

print("Forecasted values:", forecast_vals)

# Plot example
original_seq = example_data.squeeze().cpu().numpy()
t_original = np.arange(len(original_seq))
t_forecast = np.arange(len(original_seq), len(original_seq) +
↪  forecast_steps)

plt.figure(figsize=(8, 4))
plt.plot(t_original, original_seq, label="Original")
plt.plot(t_forecast, forecast_vals, label="Forecast",
↪  marker='o')
plt.legend()
plt.title("Sequential VAE Forecast Example")
plt.show()

if __name__ == "__main__":
    main()
```

Key Implementation Details:

- **Variable-Length Handling:** We use a custom 'collate_fn' to pad sequences and generate a mask, allowing the encoder to process uneven time-series lengths with PyTorch's packing utilities.

- **Recurrent Encoder and Decoder:** The encoder extracts a latent distribution from the final hidden state of an LSTM, while the decoder uses a hidden initialization derived from the latent vector to reconstruct or predict future points.

- **Teacher Forcing:** During training, a probability (e.g., 0.6) governs whether the decoder receives the ground truth input at the next time step or its own previous output, preventing divergence early in training.

- **VAE Loss Components:** The reconstruction error (MSE across valid timesteps) and the KL divergence term jointly encourage the model to learn a smooth latent space and accurate predictions.

- **Forecasting and Uncertainty:** The learned latent space can facilitate sampling multiple z values for diverse future outcomes, providing a measure of uncertainty and potential variability in time-series predictions.

- **Training Loop Integration:** The full pipeline includes data loading, a per-epoch routine for computing the ELBO loss, continuous evaluation, and a simple forecast function to sample from the VAE's latent distribution.

Chapter 19

Disentangled Representation for Style Transfer

We design a VAE to decompose content and style for images, enabling flexible style transfer. The encoder splits latent variables into separate subspaces for content and style, and the decoder recombines them to form synthesized images. Implementation steps involve constructing parallel latent pathways, adjusting the reconstruction loss for separate representations, and applying style matching objectives. By carefully engineering these pathways, you can manipulate style while preserving essential content attributes.

- We first define parallel encoders or an encoder with bifurcated heads that produce two distinct sets of latent variables: one for content and one for style.

- A decoder then fuses these separate vectors (z_content and z_style) back into a unified reconstruction.

- Training uses both a reconstruction objective (on content) and a style-matching objective (on style). KL divergence terms are also included for each latent distribution.

- By isolating distinct style and content pathways, it becomes possible to recombine different style and content elements from separate images.

Python Code Snippet

```python
import torch
import torch.nn as nn
import torch.optim as optim
from torch.utils.data import DataLoader
import torchvision
import torchvision.transforms as transforms
import random
import math
import os

#
↪ --------------------------------------------------------------------
# 1) Define a simple CNN-based encoder that produces shared
↪ features,
#    then splits into separate linear heads for content and style.
#
↪ --------------------------------------------------------------------
class SharedEncoderCNN(nn.Module):
    """
    A small CNN to extract a shared feature map from an image.
    """
    def __init__(self, in_channels=3, feature_dim=128):
        super(SharedEncoderCNN, self).__init__()
        self.conv = nn.Sequential(
            nn.Conv2d(in_channels, 32, kernel_size=4, stride=2,
            ↪ padding=1),  # B, 32, 16, 16 (for 32x32 input)
            nn.ReLU(inplace=True),
            nn.Conv2d(32, 64, kernel_size=4, stride=2, padding=1),
            ↪ # B, 64, 8, 8
            nn.ReLU(inplace=True),
            nn.Conv2d(64, 128, kernel_size=4, stride=2, padding=1),
            ↪ # B, 128, 4, 4
            nn.ReLU(inplace=True),
        )
        self.flatten = nn.Flatten()
        # We'll reduce to 'feature_dim' features for the shared
        ↪ representation
        self.fc = nn.Linear(128 * 4 * 4, feature_dim)

    def forward(self, x):
        x = self.conv(x)
        x = self.flatten(x)
        x = self.fc(x)
        return x

class LatentHead(nn.Module):
    """
    A simple linear layer that produces mu and logvar for a given
    ↪ latent dimension.
    """
```

```python
    def __init__(self, in_dim, latent_dim):
        super(LatentHead, self).__init__()
        self.mu = nn.Linear(in_dim, latent_dim)
        self.logvar = nn.Linear(in_dim, latent_dim)

    def forward(self, x):
        mu = self.mu(x)
        logvar = self.logvar(x)
        return mu, logvar


# ----------------------------------------------------------------------
# 2) Define the decoder that takes in concatenated z_content and
#    z_style
#    and rebuilds the image.
#
# ----------------------------------------------------------------------
class DecoderCNN(nn.Module):
    """
    A small deconvolutional decoder that reconstructs images from
    a concatenated latent vector.
    """
    def __init__(self, latent_dim_c=16, latent_dim_s=16,
                 out_channels=3, hidden_dim=128):
        super(DecoderCNN, self).__init__()
        total_latent_dim = latent_dim_c + latent_dim_s

        self.fc = nn.Sequential(
            nn.Linear(total_latent_dim, hidden_dim * 4 * 4),
            nn.ReLU(inplace=True)
        )

        self.deconv = nn.Sequential(
            nn.ConvTranspose2d(hidden_dim, 64, kernel_size=4,
                stride=2, padding=1),  # 8x8
            nn.ReLU(inplace=True),
            nn.ConvTranspose2d(64, 32, kernel_size=4, stride=2,
                padding=1),          # 16x16
            nn.ReLU(inplace=True),
            nn.ConvTranspose2d(32, 16, kernel_size=4, stride=2,
                padding=1),          # 32x32
            nn.ReLU(inplace=True),
            nn.Conv2d(16, out_channels, kernel_size=3, padding=1)
                # final recon
        )

    def forward(self, z_c, z_s):
        z = torch.cat([z_c, z_s], dim=1)  # B x (latent_dim_c +
            latent_dim_s)
        x = self.fc(z)  # B x (hidden_dim*4*4)
        x = x.view(x.size(0), -1, 4, 4)  # B x hidden_dim x 4 x 4
        x = self.deconv(x)
        return x
```

```python
#
↳ -----------------------------------------------------------------------
# 3) Assemble the ContentStyleVAE that composes:
#    - one shared CNN
#    - two latent heads (content & style)
#    - one decoder
#
↳ -----------------------------------------------------------------------
class ContentStyleVAE(nn.Module):
    def __init__(self, in_channels=3, shared_feature_dim=128,
                 content_dim=16, style_dim=16):
        super(ContentStyleVAE, self).__init__()
        # Shared feature extractor
        self.shared_encoder = SharedEncoderCNN(in_channels,
        ↳   shared_feature_dim)
        # Separate latent heads
        self.content_head = LatentHead(shared_feature_dim,
        ↳   content_dim)
        self.style_head = LatentHead(shared_feature_dim, style_dim)
        # Decoder
        self.decoder = DecoderCNN(latent_dim_c=content_dim,
                                  latent_dim_s=style_dim,
                                  out_channels=in_channels)

    def encode_content(self, x):
        """
        Encodes x to (mu_c, logvar_c).
        """
        features = self.shared_encoder(x)
        mu_c, logvar_c = self.content_head(features)
        return mu_c, logvar_c

    def encode_style(self, x):
        """
        Encodes x to (mu_s, logvar_s).
        """
        features = self.shared_encoder(x)
        mu_s, logvar_s = self.style_head(features)
        return mu_s, logvar_s

    def reparameterize(self, mu, logvar):
        """
        Reparameterization trick: z = mu + sigma * epsilon
        """
        std = torch.exp(0.5 * logvar)
        eps = torch.randn_like(std)
        return mu + eps * std

    def decode(self, z_c, z_s):
        """
        Decodes the combined latent vectors back to an image.
        """
```

153

```python
        return self.decoder(z_c, z_s)

    def forward(self, x_content, x_style):
        """
        1. Encode content and style
        2. Sample z_c, z_s via reparameterization
        3. Decode to reconstruct
        Returns the reconstructed image and all latents for loss
        ↪ computation.
        """
        mu_c, logvar_c = self.encode_content(x_content)
        mu_s, logvar_s = self.encode_style(x_style)

        z_c = self.reparameterize(mu_c, logvar_c)
        z_s = self.reparameterize(mu_s, logvar_s)

        x_recon = self.decode(z_c, z_s)
        return x_recon, mu_c, logvar_c, mu_s, logvar_s

    def extract_style_code(self, x):
        """
        A helper to get the style latent vector for style matching
        ↪ objective.
        """
        mu_s, logvar_s = self.encode_style(x)
        # For style matching, we take the mean or random sample.
        ↪ We'll take the mean here.
        return mu_s  # or self.reparameterize(mu_s, logvar_s),
        ↪ depending on design


#
↪ -----------------------------------------------------------------------
# 4) Define the key losses: reconstruction, KL, and style matching.
#    We'll do a simple style matching by encouraging the style code
#    of the reconstruction to match the style code of x_style.
#
↪ -----------------------------------------------------------------------
def kl_divergence(mu, logvar):
    """
    KL divergence for Gaussian: 0.5 * sum(1 + logvar - mu^2 -
    ↪ exp(logvar))
    We'll return the mean across the batch for stability.
    """
    return -0.5 * torch.mean(1 + logvar - mu.pow(2) - logvar.exp())

def vae_loss_function(x_recon, x_content, mu_c, logvar_c, mu_s,
↪ logvar_s,
                      style_code_recon, style_code_target,
                      ↪ alpha=1.0, beta=1.0):
    """
    Overall loss includes:
      1) Reconstruction loss: MSE between x_recon and x_content
```

154

```
    2) KL_c: KL divergence for content
    3) KL_s: KL divergence for style
    4) Style matching loss: MSE(style_code_recon,
    ↪    style_code_target)
  alpha, beta allow weighting of content reconstruction vs. style
  ↪    constraints.
  """
  recon_loss = nn.functional.mse_loss(x_recon, x_content)
  kl_c = kl_divergence(mu_c, logvar_c)
  kl_s = kl_divergence(mu_s, logvar_s)
  style_loss = nn.functional.mse_loss(style_code_recon,
  ↪    style_code_target)

  # Weighted sum
  total_loss = recon_loss + kl_c + kl_s + alpha * style_loss
  return total_loss, recon_loss, kl_c, kl_s, style_loss


#
↪    -------------------------------------------------------------------
# 5) Training loop (single epoch).
#    We sample x_content from the batch, x_style from the same batch
#    (possibly different index) to encourage mixing.
#
↪    -------------------------------------------------------------------
def train_one_epoch(model, dataloader, optimizer, device,
↪    alpha=1.0):
    model.train()
    total_loss_epoch = 0
    for batch_idx, (images, _) in enumerate(dataloader):
        images = images.to(device)
        # We'll pick content images from the first half of the batch
        # and style images from the second half to encourage
        ↪    variation.
        # If the batch size is odd, adjust accordingly.
        mid = images.size(0) // 2
        if mid == 0:
            # Not enough data to split, use the same images as both
            ↪    content and style
            x_content = images
            x_style = images
        else:
            x_content = images[:mid]
            x_style = images[mid:]

        # If not enough variety, we can randomize indices instead:
        # idx_style = torch.randperm(images.size(0)).to(device)
        # x_style = images[idx_style]

        # Forward pass
        x_recon, mu_c, logvar_c, mu_s, logvar_s = model(x_content,
        ↪    x_style)

        # We'll extract style code from reconstructed images
```

```python
        style_code_recon = model.extract_style_code(x_recon)
        # We'll also extract style code from x_style as the target
        style_code_target = model.extract_style_code(x_style)

        loss, rec, klc, kls, stl = vae_loss_function(
            x_recon, x_content,
            mu_c, logvar_c,
            mu_s, logvar_s,
            style_code_recon, style_code_target,
            alpha=alpha, beta=1.0
        )

        optimizer.zero_grad()
        loss.backward()
        optimizer.step()

        total_loss_epoch += loss.item()

    return total_loss_epoch / len(dataloader)

#
↪  -----------------------------------------------------------------------
# 6) Main routine: load data, define model, and train.
#
↪  -----------------------------------------------------------------------
def main():
    device = torch.device("cuda" if torch.cuda.is_available() else
    ↪  "cpu")
    print("Running on device:", device)

    # Hyperparameters
    epochs = 5
    batch_size = 64
    lr = 1e-3
    alpha_style_loss = 1.0  # weighting for style matching

    # Create dataset (CIFAR10 for colorful images - style can be
    ↪  color or texture).
    transform = transforms.Compose([
        transforms.Resize((32, 32)),
        transforms.ToTensor(),
    ])
    train_dataset = torchvision.datasets.CIFAR10(root='./data',
    ↪  train=True,
                                                download=True,
                                                ↪  transform=transform)
    train_loader = DataLoader(train_dataset, batch_size=batch_size,
    ↪  shuffle=True)

    # Initialize model, optimizer
    model = ContentStyleVAE(in_channels=3,
                            shared_feature_dim=128,
                            content_dim=16,
```

```python
                   style_dim=16).to(device)
    optimizer = optim.Adam(model.parameters(), lr=lr)

    # Training loop
    for epoch in range(epochs):
        train_loss = train_one_epoch(model, train_loader, optimizer,
        ↪   device, alpha=alpha_style_loss)
        print(f"Epoch [{epoch+1}/{epochs}] - Loss:
        ↪   {train_loss:.4f}")

    # Optional: Save model
    os.makedirs("saved_models", exist_ok=True)
    torch.save(model.state_dict(),
    ↪   "saved_models/content_style_vae.pth")
    print("Training finished and model saved!")

if __name__ == "__main__":
    main()
```

Key Implementation Details:

- **ContentStyleVAE:** Encapsulates two encoders (for content
  and style) and a single decoder. Internally, it uses a shared
  CNN plus separate linear heads for content and style latent
  variables.

- **reparameterize:** Implements $z = + \cdot$, where $= \exp(0.5 \times$
  logvar$)$. This is crucial for backpropagation through stochastic nodes.

- **vae_loss_function:** Combines reconstruction loss, KL divergence for both content and style latents, and a style-matching
  term. The style-matching is computed by encoding the reconstructed image's style and comparing it with the style
  image's code.

- **train_one_epoch:** Splits each batch into content and style
  halves, runs forward passes, and accumulates losses.

- **SharedEncoderCNN / DecoderCNN:** Simple convolutional and
  transposed-convolutional networks for feature extraction and
  image reconstruction. They illustrate how to structure lightweight
  models for experiments in disentanglement.

- **Takeaways:** By splitting content and style latents, it becomes feasible to mix content from one image with style from

157

another, allowing flexible style transfer while preserving semantic structure.

Chapter 20

VQ-VAE for Discrete Latent Representations

Instead of learning a continuous latent space, a Vector Quantized VAE (VQ-VAE) constrains latents to a discrete codebook, simplifying tasks like speech or image generation. This chapter shows how to implement codebook lookups, the commitment loss, and the encoder-decoder pipeline with codebook indices. We detail exactly how to handle the straight-through gradient estimator, set the codebook size, and train with stable updates. By the end, you'll see how discrete latent spaces can capture repeated patterns more effectively.

- We define an `Encoder` to map each input to a continuous latent embedding.

- A `VectorQuantizer` module then projects embeddings onto a discrete set of learnable vectors (the codebook).

- We use the straight-through estimator during backpropagation so code indices are treated as continuous in the backward pass.

- A `Decoder` reconstructs the input image from these discrete embeddings.

- We combine a reconstruction loss with a commitment loss that encourages the encoder output to stay close to the chosen codebook entries.

Python Code Snippet

```python
import torch
import torch.nn as nn
import torch.optim as optim
from torch.utils.data import DataLoader
import torchvision
import torchvision.transforms as transforms
import random
import numpy as np
import os
import matplotlib.pyplot as plt


# ----------------------------------------------------------------
# 1) Set random seed for reproducibility
# ----------------------------------------------------------------
def set_seed(seed=42):
    random.seed(seed)
    np.random.seed(seed)
    torch.manual_seed(seed)
    if torch.cuda.is_available():
        torch.cuda.manual_seed_all(seed)


# ----------------------------------------------------------------
# 2) Define an Encoder and Decoder for VQ-VAE
# ----------------------------------------------------------------
class Encoder(nn.Module):
    """
    Encodes the input image into a latent representation (B,
    ↪ hidden_dim, H', W').
    """
    def __init__(self, in_channels=1, hidden_dim=128,
    ↪ latent_dim=64):
        super(Encoder, self).__init__()
        self.conv1 = nn.Conv2d(in_channels, hidden_dim // 2, 4,
        ↪ stride=2, padding=1)
        self.conv2 = nn.Conv2d(hidden_dim // 2, hidden_dim, 4,
        ↪ stride=2, padding=1)
        self.conv3 = nn.Conv2d(hidden_dim, latent_dim, 1, stride=1,
        ↪ padding=0)
        self.relu = nn.ReLU(inplace=True)

    def forward(self, x):
        x = self.relu(self.conv1(x))   # downsample 2x
        x = self.relu(self.conv2(x))   # downsample 2x
        x = self.conv3(x)              # no downsample, just reduce
        ↪ channels
        return x


class Decoder(nn.Module):
    """
```

```
    Decodes a latent representation back into an image of shape (B,
    ↪  out_channels, H, W).
    """

    def __init__(self, out_channels=1, hidden_dim=128,
    ↪  latent_dim=64):
        super(Decoder, self).__init__()
        self.conv1 = nn.Conv2d(latent_dim, hidden_dim, 1, stride=1,
        ↪  padding=0)
        self.conv2 = nn.ConvTranspose2d(hidden_dim, hidden_dim // 2,
        ↪  4, stride=2, padding=1)
        self.conv3 = nn.ConvTranspose2d(hidden_dim // 2,
        ↪  out_channels, 4, stride=2, padding=1)
        self.relu = nn.ReLU(inplace=True)
        self.tanh = nn.Tanh()

    def forward(self, x):
        x = self.relu(self.conv1(x))
        x = self.relu(self.conv2(x))    # upsample 2x
        x = self.conv3(x)               # upsample 2x
        x = self.tanh(x)
        return x


# ------------------------------------------------------------
# 3) Vector Quantizer (Codebook) and VQ-VAE
# ------------------------------------------------------------
class VectorQuantizer(nn.Module):
    """
    Implements the core VQ layer:
    1) Map continuous latents to nearest codebook entries.
    2) Compute commitment loss.
    3) Straight-through estimator for backprop.
    """

    def __init__(self, num_embeddings=512, embedding_dim=64,
    ↪  commitment_cost=0.25):
        super(VectorQuantizer, self).__init__()
        self.num_embeddings = num_embeddings
        self.embedding_dim = embedding_dim
        self.commitment_cost = commitment_cost

        # Codebook: each embedding is a learnable vector of
        ↪  dimension embedding_dim
        self.embedding = nn.Embedding(num_embeddings, embedding_dim)
        nn.init.uniform_(self.embedding.weight,
        ↪  -1.0/self.num_embeddings, 1.0/self.num_embeddings)

    def forward(self, inputs):
        """
        Inputs have shape: (B, C, H, W)
        We want to flatten over H*W, then find nearest embedding
        ↪  index for each location.
        """
        # Convert inputs from (B, C, H, W) -> (B*H*W, C)
        B, C, H, W = inputs.shape
```

```python
        flat_input = inputs.permute(0, 2, 3, 1).contiguous()
        flat_input = flat_input.view(-1, C)

        # Compute distances to each embedding
        distances = (
            flat_input.pow(2).sum(dim=1, keepdim=True)
            - 2 * flat_input @ self.embedding.weight.t()
            + self.embedding.weight.pow(2).sum(dim=1)
        )  # shape: (B*H*W, num_embeddings)

        # Find nearest embedding index
        encoding_indices = torch.argmin(distances, dim=1)  # shape:
        ↪  (B*H*W)
        encodings = torch.zeros(encoding_indices.shape[0],
        ↪  self.num_embeddings, device=inputs.device)
        encodings.scatter_(1, encoding_indices.unsqueeze(1), 1)

        # Quantize and unflatten
        quantized = self.embedding(encoding_indices).view(B, H, W,
        ↪  C)
        quantized = quantized.permute(0, 3, 1, 2).contiguous()

        # Compute commitment loss
        e_latent_loss = torch.mean((quantized.detach() - inputs)**2)
        q_latent_loss = torch.mean((quantized - inputs.detach())**2)
        loss = q_latent_loss + self.commitment_cost * e_latent_loss

        # Straight-through estimator
        quantized_st = inputs + (quantized - inputs).detach()

        return quantized_st, loss, encoding_indices


class VQVAE(nn.Module):
    """
    The full VQ-VAE model with an encoder, codebook (vector
    ↪  quantizer), and decoder.
    """
    def __init__(self, in_channels=1, hidden_dim=128, latent_dim=64,
                 num_embeddings=512, commitment_cost=0.25):
        super(VQVAE, self).__init__()
        self.encoder = Encoder(in_channels, hidden_dim, latent_dim)
        self.vq_layer = VectorQuantizer(num_embeddings, latent_dim,
        ↪  commitment_cost)
        self.decoder = Decoder(in_channels, hidden_dim, latent_dim)

    def forward(self, x):
        z_e = self.encoder(x)
        z_q, vq_loss, _ = self.vq_layer(z_e)
        x_recon = self.decoder(z_q)
        return x_recon, vq_loss


# -----------------------------------------------------------------
# 4) Training functions
```

162

```
# -------------------------------------------------------------
def train_one_epoch(model, dataloader, optimizer, device):
    model.train()
    total_recon_loss = 0
    total_vq_loss = 0
    for images, _ in dataloader:
        images = images.to(device)
        optimizer.zero_grad()

        x_recon, vq_loss = model(images)
        recon_loss = torch.mean((x_recon - images)**2)
        loss = recon_loss + vq_loss

        loss.backward()
        optimizer.step()

        total_recon_loss += recon_loss.item()
        total_vq_loss += vq_loss.item()

    return total_recon_loss / len(dataloader), total_vq_loss /
    ↪   len(dataloader)


@torch.no_grad()
def evaluate_model(model, dataloader, device):
    model.eval()
    total_recon_loss = 0
    total_vq_loss = 0
    for images, _ in dataloader:
        images = images.to(device)
        x_recon, vq_loss = model(images)
        recon_loss = torch.mean((x_recon - images)**2)
        total_recon_loss += recon_loss.item()
        total_vq_loss += vq_loss.item()
    return total_recon_loss / len(dataloader), total_vq_loss /
    ↪   len(dataloader)


@torch.no_grad()
def visualize_reconstructions(model, dataloader, device, epoch):
    model.eval()
    images, _ = next(iter(dataloader))
    images = images.to(device)
    x_recon, _ = model(images)

    # Move to CPU and scale from [-1,1] to [0,1] if using such
    ↪   normalization.
    # If your dataset is in [0,1], skip the transformation.
    reconstruction = (x_recon * 0.5 + 0.5).clamp(0, 1).cpu()
    original = (images * 0.5 + 0.5).clamp(0, 1).cpu()

    # Concatenate original and reconstruction for visual comparison
    comparison = torch.cat([original[:8], reconstruction[:8]],
    ↪   dim=0)
    grid = torchvision.utils.make_grid(comparison, nrow=8)
```

```python
    os.makedirs("results_vqvae", exist_ok=True)
    plt.figure(figsize=(12, 3))
    plt.axis("off")
    plt.imshow(grid.permute(1, 2, 0).numpy())
    plt.savefig(f"results_vqvae/reconstruction_epoch_{epoch}.png")
    plt.close()

# ------------------------------------------------------------
# 5) Main: load data, initialize model, and train
# ------------------------------------------------------------
def main():
    set_seed(42)
    device = torch.device("cuda" if torch.cuda.is_available() else
    ↪  "cpu")

    # Load MNIST dataset
    transform = transforms.Compose([
        transforms.ToTensor(),
        transforms.Normalize((0.5,), (0.5,))  # map [0,1] to [-1,1]
    ])
    train_dataset = torchvision.datasets.MNIST(root='data',
    ↪  train=True, download=True, transform=transform)
    test_dataset = torchvision.datasets.MNIST(root='data',
    ↪  train=False, download=True, transform=transform)

    train_loader = DataLoader(train_dataset, batch_size=64,
    ↪  shuffle=True)
    test_loader = DataLoader(test_dataset, batch_size=64,
    ↪  shuffle=False)

    # Create VQ-VAE model
    model = VQVAE(in_channels=1, hidden_dim=128, latent_dim=64,
                  num_embeddings=256,
                  ↪  commitment_cost=0.25).to(device)

    optimizer = optim.Adam(model.parameters(), lr=1e-3)

    epochs = 5
    for epoch in range(epochs):
        train_recon_loss, train_vq_loss = train_one_epoch(model,
        ↪  train_loader, optimizer, device)
        val_recon_loss, val_vq_loss = evaluate_model(model,
        ↪  test_loader, device)

        print(f"Epoch [{epoch+1}/{epochs}] ")
        print(f"  Train Recon Loss: {train_recon_loss:.4f}, VQ Loss:
        ↪  {train_vq_loss:.4f}")
        print(f"  Val   Recon Loss: {val_recon_loss:.4f}, VQ Loss:
        ↪  {val_vq_loss:.4f}")

        visualize_reconstructions(model, test_loader, device, epoch)
```

164

```
print("Training complete! Check 'results_vqvae' folder for
↪   sample reconstructions.")

if __name__ == "__main__":
    main()
```

Key Implementation Details:

- **Encoder and Decoder:** We use convolutional layers for downsampling/upscaling. The `Encoder` produces continuous latent codes, while the `Decoder` reconstructs images from the discrete codes.

- **Vector Quantizer:** The `VectorQuantizer` layer maps continuous latents to a discrete codebook. It calculates distances to each embedding, picks the index of the nearest vector, and returns a quantized output.

- **Commitment Loss:** We include a term to encourage the encoder to commit to a specific codebook entry. This is handled in `VectorQuantizer` by adding a cost proportional to $(z - sg[e])^2$, where $sg[...]$ indicates stop-gradient.

- **Straight-Through Estimator:** During backpropagation, the quantized output is replaced with the encoder output's gradient, enabling end-to-end training despite the discrete lookup.

- **Training Objective:** Our total loss is the sum of the reconstruction loss and the codebook commitment loss. Updates jointly adjust the codebook and the encoder/decoder weights.

- **End-to-End Pipeline:** In the `main` function, we load MNIST data, instantiate `VQVAE`, and iterate through epochs. We periodically visualize reconstructions to check training progress.

Chapter 21

Neural Processes with VAE

We integrate VAE principles into Neural Processes to model functions from partial observations. The idea is to learn a latent distribution over functions, using small context sets as input and predicting target sets. Implementation includes designing an encoder that shares context data, a cross-attention or aggregator module, and a decoder that outputs function values. We discuss training loops, sampling strategies, and how to adapt this framework for tasks including regression, few-shot learning, and graphical transformations.

- We first generate a synthetic dataset where each sample is formed by randomly sampling input points and mapping them through a simple function (e.g., a sine wave or polynomial).

- A neural network encoder processes the context points (x_c, y_c) into a global representation which is aggregated to produce parameters for a latent distribution (μ, σ). This aligns with VAE-style reparameterization.

- A decoder decodes the latent sample z, concatenated with target x-coordinates, to predict corresponding y values.

- We train by maximizing the Evidence Lower BOund (ELBO), which includes a reconstruction term (likelihood of the predicted targets) and KL divergence between the inferred latent $q(z|c)$ and a chosen prior $p(z)$.

- The code demonstrates training loops, sampling strategies, and integration with PyTorch for future extensions like few-shot learning, regression tasks, and graphical transformations.

Python Code Snippet

```python
import torch
import torch.nn as nn
import torch.optim as optim
from torch.utils.data import Dataset, DataLoader
import numpy as np
import random
import math
import matplotlib.pyplot as plt


# ----------------------------------------------------------------
# 1) Set random seeds for reproducibility
# ----------------------------------------------------------------
def set_seed(seed=42):
    random.seed(seed)
    np.random.seed(seed)
    torch.manual_seed(seed)
    if torch.cuda.is_available():
        torch.cuda.manual_seed_all(seed)


# ----------------------------------------------------------------
# 2) A synthetic dataset for 1D function regression
# ----------------------------------------------------------------
class SyntheticFunctionDataset(Dataset):
    """
    Creates synthetic 1D function samples.
    Each sample is a function (assume random amplitude & phase for a
    ↪ sine wave).
    We generate a set of input points 'x' and the corresponding 'y'
    ↪ = f(x).
    """
    def __init__(self, num_samples=1000, max_num_points=50):
        super().__init__()
        self.num_samples = num_samples
        self.max_num_points = max_num_points   # Maximum points per
        ↪ function sample

    def __len__(self):
        return self.num_samples

    def __getitem__(self, idx):
        # Randomly choose the number of points
        n_points = np.random.randint(10, self.max_num_points)
```

167

```python
    # Sample x in range [-2,2]
    x = np.random.uniform(-2, 2, n_points)

    # Random amplitude and phase for a sine function
    amplitude = np.random.uniform(0.5, 2.0)
    phase = np.random.uniform(0, 2*math.pi)

    # y = amplitude * sin(x + phase)
    y = amplitude * np.sin(x + phase)

    # Sort by x for clarity (not strictly necessary)
    sort_idx = np.argsort(x)
    x = x[sort_idx]
    y = y[sort_idx]

    return x.astype(np.float32), y.astype(np.float32)

def collate_np(batch):
    """
    Custom collate function to produce context and target sets for
    ↪  Neural Process.
    We randomly split each function's points into context (x_c, y_c)
    ↪  and target (x_t, y_t).
    """
    # Arrays to hold entire batch
    batch_context_x = []
    batch_context_y = []
    batch_target_x = []
    batch_target_y = []

    for (x, y) in batch:
        n_points = len(x)
        # Randomly choose how many in context
        n_context = np.random.randint(3, n_points-1) if n_points > 3
        ↪  else 2

        # Indices for context
        idx_context = np.random.choice(n_points, n_context,
        ↪  replace=False)

        # Indices for target
        idx_target = [i for i in range(n_points) if i not in
        ↪  idx_context]

        x_c = x[idx_context]
        y_c = y[idx_context]
        x_t = x[idx_target]
        y_t = y[idx_target]

        batch_context_x.append(x_c)
        batch_context_y.append(y_c)
        batch_target_x.append(x_t)
        batch_target_y.append(y_t)
```

168

```
        return batch_context_x, batch_context_y, batch_target_x,
        ↪  batch_target_y

# ------------------------------------------------------------
# 3) Helper MLP for encoding / decoding
# ------------------------------------------------------------
class MLP(nn.Module):
    def __init__(self, input_dim, hidden_dim, output_dim,
    ↪  num_layers=3):
        super(MLP, self).__init__()
        layers = []
        in_dim = input_dim
        for _ in range(num_layers - 1):
            layers.append(nn.Linear(in_dim, hidden_dim))
            layers.append(nn.ReLU(inplace=True))
            in_dim = hidden_dim
        layers.append(nn.Linear(in_dim, output_dim))
        self.net = nn.Sequential(*layers)

    def forward(self, x):
        return self.net(x)

# ------------------------------------------------------------
# 4) Encoder, aggregator, decoder
# ------------------------------------------------------------
class NPEncoder(nn.Module):
    """
    Encoder that processes each context point (x_c, y_c) and
    ↪  aggregates to form a global representation.
    Then outputs the parameters of the latent distribution:
    ↪  q(z|context).
    """
    def __init__(self, x_dim=1, y_dim=1, r_dim=128, z_dim=64):
        super(NPEncoder, self).__init__()
        # Encode each point into a representation
        self.point_encoder = MLP(input_dim=x_dim+y_dim,
        ↪  hidden_dim=64, output_dim=r_dim, num_layers=3)
        # MLP for transforming aggregated representation -> (mu,
        ↪  logvar) of z
        self.to_z_params = MLP(input_dim=r_dim, hidden_dim=64,
        ↪  output_dim=2*z_dim, num_layers=2)
        self.z_dim = z_dim

    def forward(self, x_c, y_c):
        """
        x_c, y_c: each is a list of variable-length context sets
        ↪  across the batch.
                    We'll process them in a loop, or we could pad
                    ↪  them, but for clarity we do a loop.
        """
        batch_size = len(x_c)
        device = x_c[0].device
```

```python
        mu_list = []
        logvar_list = []

        for i in range(batch_size):
            # Flatten the context points horizontally
            # shape is (n_context, 1 + 1) in a 1D scenario
            xc_i = x_c[i].unsqueeze(-1)    # shape: (n_context, 1)
            yc_i = y_c[i].unsqueeze(-1)    # shape: (n_context, 1)
            input_i = torch.cat([xc_i, yc_i], dim=-1)  # shape:
            ↪  (n_context, 2)

            # Encode each point, then average
            r_i = self.point_encoder(input_i)  # shape: (n_context,
            ↪  r_dim)
            r_i_agg = torch.mean(r_i, dim=0)    # shape: (r_dim,)

            # Transform aggregated representation to get (mu,
            ↪  logvar)
            z_params = self.to_z_params(r_i_agg)
            mu, logvar = z_params[:self.z_dim],
            ↪  z_params[self.z_dim:]

            mu_list.append(mu.unsqueeze(0))
            logvar_list.append(logvar.unsqueeze(0))

        # Stack them all to shape (B, z_dim)
        mu_batch = torch.cat(mu_list, dim=0).to(device)
        logvar_batch = torch.cat(logvar_list, dim=0).to(device)
        return mu_batch, logvar_batch

class NPDecoder(nn.Module):
    """
    Decoder that, given z and target x, produces a distribution
    ↪  (mu_y, logvar_y) over target y.
    """
    def __init__(self, x_dim=1, z_dim=64, hidden_dim=64):
        super(NPDecoder, self).__init__()
        # We'll decode each target point by concatenating x_t with z
        # Then produce (mu_y, logvar_y)
        self.mlp = MLP(input_dim=x_dim + z_dim,
        ↪  hidden_dim=hidden_dim, output_dim=2, num_layers=3)

    def forward(self, z, x_t):
        """
        z: (B, z_dim)
        x_t: list of length B, each containing (n_target_i,) shape
        ↪  for 1D input
        Returns mu_y, logvar_y for each target.
        """
        all_mu = []
        all_logvar = []
```

170

```python
    for i in range(len(x_t)):
        zi = z[i].unsqueeze(0)  # shape (1, z_dim)
        # Expand z to match the number of target points
        zi_expanded = zi.repeat(len(x_t[i]), 1)   # (n_target_i,
        ↪  z_dim)
        xi = x_t[i].unsqueeze(-1)                  # (n_target_i,
        ↪  1)
        decoder_in = torch.cat([zi_expanded, xi], dim=-1)   #
        ↪  (n_target_i, z_dim + 1)
        out = self.mlp(decoder_in)  # (n_target_i, 2)

        mu = out[:, 0]
        logvar = out[:, 1]
        all_mu.append(mu)
        all_logvar.append(logvar)

    return all_mu, all_logvar


# ------------------------------------------------------------
# 5) Main Neural Process class combining encoder and decoder with
# ↪  VAE logic
# ------------------------------------------------------------
class NeuralProcessVAE(nn.Module):
    def __init__(self, x_dim=1, y_dim=1, r_dim=128, z_dim=64):
        super(NeuralProcessVAE, self).__init__()
        self.encoder = NPEncoder(x_dim=x_dim, y_dim=y_dim,
        ↪  r_dim=r_dim, z_dim=z_dim)
        self.decoder = NPDecoder(x_dim=x_dim, z_dim=z_dim)
        self.z_dim = z_dim

    def reparameterize(self, mu, logvar):
        """
        Reparameterization trick to sample z ~ q(z|x_c, y_c).
        """
        std = torch.exp(0.5 * logvar)
        eps = torch.randn_like(std)
        return mu + eps * std

    def forward(self, x_c, y_c, x_t, y_t=None):
        """
        Forward pass that computes the negative ELBO =
        ↪  -E_{q(z|c)}[log p(y_t|x_t,z)] + KL(q||p).

        x_c, y_c, x_t, y_t are lists of Tensors across the batch
        ↪  dimension.
        """
        device = x_c[0].device

        # Encoder -> get mu_q, logvar_q
        mu_q, logvar_q = self.encoder(x_c, y_c)

        # Reparameterize to get z
```

171

```python
    z = self.reparameterize(mu_q, logvar_q)  # shape: (B,
    ↪  z_dim)

    # prior p(z) ~ N(0,I)
    mu_p = torch.zeros_like(mu_q, device=device)
    logvar_p = torch.zeros_like(logvar_q, device=device)

    # Compute KL term
    kl_div = 0.5 * torch.sum(
        logvar_p - logvar_q + (torch.exp(logvar_q) + (mu_q -
        ↪  mu_p)**2) / torch.exp(logvar_p) - 1,
        dim=1
    )
    kl_div = torch.mean(kl_div)

    # Decode to get mu_y, logvar_y for target
    mu_y_list, logvar_y_list = self.decoder(z, x_t)

    if y_t is None:
        # If there's no target set, just return mu_y_list for
        ↪  prediction
        return mu_y_list, logvar_y_list, kl_div

    # Negative log likelihood of targets (Gaussian)
    # NLL_i = 0.5 * [ log(2*pi) + logvar_y + (y_t - mu_y)^2 /
    ↪  exp(logvar_y) ]
    nll_batch = []
    for i in range(len(x_t)):
        mu_y_i = mu_y_list[i]
        logvar_y_i = logvar_y_list[i]
        y_t_i = y_t[i]
        nll_i = 0.5 * (math.log(2*math.pi) + logvar_y_i +
        ↪  ((y_t_i - mu_y_i)**2 / torch.exp(logvar_y_i)))
        # average over points
        nll_i = torch.mean(nll_i)
        nll_batch.append(nll_i)

    nll = torch.mean(torch.stack(nll_batch))

    # Negative ELBO
    neg_elbo = nll + kl_div
    return neg_elbo, nll, kl_div

# ----------------------------------------------------------------
# 6) Training and utility functions
# ----------------------------------------------------------------
def train_np(model, dataloader, optimizer, device):
    model.train()
    total_loss = 0
    for x_c, y_c, x_t, y_t in dataloader:
        # Convert each list element to torch Tensors on device
        x_c = [torch.tensor(arr, device=device) for arr in x_c]
        y_c = [torch.tensor(arr, device=device) for arr in y_c]
```

172

```
        x_t = [torch.tensor(arr, device=device) for arr in x_t]
        y_t = [torch.tensor(arr, device=device) for arr in y_t]

        optimizer.zero_grad()
        neg_elbo, _, _ = model(x_c, y_c, x_t, y_t)
        neg_elbo.backward()
        optimizer.step()
        total_loss += neg_elbo.item()

    return total_loss / len(dataloader)

def eval_np(model, dataloader, device):
    model.eval()
    total_loss = 0
    with torch.no_grad():
        for x_c, y_c, x_t, y_t in dataloader:
            x_c = [torch.tensor(arr, device=device) for arr in x_c]
            y_c = [torch.tensor(arr, device=device) for arr in y_c]
            x_t = [torch.tensor(arr, device=device) for arr in x_t]
            y_t = [torch.tensor(arr, device=device) for arr in y_t]

            neg_elbo, _, _ = model(x_c, y_c, x_t, y_t)
            total_loss += neg_elbo.item()

    return total_loss / len(dataloader)

def plot_prediction(model, device, n_points=50):
    """
    Plot a single function's context versus predicted function.
    """
    # Build a random function
    x = np.linspace(-2,2,n_points).astype(np.float32)
    amplitude = np.random.uniform(0.5, 2.0)
    phase = np.random.uniform(0, 2*math.pi)
    y_true = amplitude * np.sin(x + phase)

    # Randomly split for context
    n_context = np.random.randint(3, n_points-1)
    idx_context = np.random.choice(n_points, n_context,
    ↪  replace=False)
    idx_target = [i for i in range(n_points) if i not in
    ↪  idx_context]

    x_c_np = torch.tensor(x[idx_context], device=device)
    y_c_np = torch.tensor(y_true[idx_context], device=device)
    x_t_np = torch.tensor(x[idx_target], device=device)

    # Use the model to predict
    model.eval()
    with torch.no_grad():
        mu_q, logvar_q = model.encoder([x_c_np],[y_c_np])
        z_samp = model.reparameterize(mu_q, logvar_q)
        mu_y_list, logvar_y_list = model.decoder(z_samp, [x_t_np])
```

173

```
            mu_y, logvar_y = mu_y_list[0], logvar_y_list[0]
            pred = mu_y.cpu().numpy()

        # Plot
        plt.figure(figsize=(7,5))
        plt.scatter(x[idx_context], y_true[idx_context], color='blue',
        ↪  label='Context')
        plt.scatter(x[idx_target], y_true[idx_target], color='green',
        ↪  label='True Target')
        plt.scatter(x[idx_target], pred, color='red', marker='x',
        ↪  label='Predicted')
        plt.legend()
        plt.title("Neural Process VAE Prediction")
        plt.show()

# ----------------------------------------------------------------
# 7) Main function
# ----------------------------------------------------------------
def main():
    set_seed(42)
    device = torch.device("cuda" if torch.cuda.is_available() else
    ↪  "cpu")

    # Create dataset & dataloader
    dataset = SyntheticFunctionDataset(num_samples=2000,
    ↪  max_num_points=50)
    dataloader = DataLoader(dataset, batch_size=32, shuffle=True,
    ↪  collate_fn=collate_np)

    # Initialize NeuralProcessVAE
    model = NeuralProcessVAE(x_dim=1, y_dim=1, r_dim=128,
    ↪  z_dim=64).to(device)

    optimizer = optim.Adam(model.parameters(), lr=1e-3)

    # Train
    num_epochs = 10
    for epoch in range(num_epochs):
        train_loss = train_np(model, dataloader, optimizer, device)
        val_loss = eval_np(model, dataloader, device)  # Using same
        ↪  set for quick demonstration
        print(f"Epoch [{epoch+1}/{num_epochs}] - Train Loss:
        ↪  {train_loss:.4f}, Val Loss: {val_loss:.4f}")

    # Plot some predictions
    plot_prediction(model, device, n_points=50)

if __name__ == "__main__":
    main()
```

Key Implementation Details

- **Variational Encoder (VAE Principles):** The class `NPEncoder` learns a global latent code by processing context points individually and aggregating them via mean pooling. We then map this aggregated representation to a normal distribution $(\mu\_q, \log \sigma^2\_q)$, employing the reparameterization trick in `reparameterize` to sample from $q(z|c)$.

- **Latent Prior:** We assume a standard normal prior, $p(z) = \mathcal{N}(0, I)$. The KL term in the VAE loss encourages the encoder's posterior to be close to this prior.

- **Decoder for Predictions:** The `NPDecoder` takes a sample z plus target inputs x_t, returning a predictive distribution over y. For simplicity, we output μ and $\log \sigma^2$, using a Gaussian likelihood in our negative log-likelihood.

- **Negative ELBO:** We compute the standard VAE ELBO:

$$-\text{ELBO} = \underbrace{\text{NLL}(y\_t \,\|\, \hat{y}\_t)}\_{\text{reconstruction term}}$$

$$+ \underbrace{\text{KL}(q(z|c) \,\|\, p(z))}\_{\text{KL divergence}}$$

  minimizing NLL for target reconstruction while constraining the latent distribution.

- **Context and Targets:** We randomly split each function's data into a context set (few points) and a target set (the rest). This simulates partial observations and forces the model to generalize function behavior for unseen points.

- **Training Loop:** The `train_np` function samples mini-batches of context-target splits, computes `neg_elbo`, and backpropagates. The `eval_np` function follows the same procedure but does not update parameters.

- **Extensions:** This demo uses a simple aggregator (mean). In practice, cross-attention or advanced aggregator structures can be introduced for improved performance on more complex tasks like few-shot learning or structured data transformations.

Chapter 22

VAE with Normalizing Flows

Normalizing flows can improve the flexibility of the VAE's latent prior. We incorporate a flow-based transformation inside the reparameterization step, allowing the model to learn more complex distributions. The chapter outlines how to build flow layers—like RealNVP or Masked Autoregressive Flows—on top of a standard encoder. Implementation details include integrating the log-determinant of the Jacobian into the ELBO. By adding normalizing flows, your VAE can capture multi-modal data distributions more effectively.

- We first define an encoder (a small MLP) that outputs the approximate posterior's mean and log-variance.

- We then reparameterize this to obtain an initial latent sample.

- Next, we pass the sample through a flow-based transform (e.g., RealNVP) to increase the expressiveness of the approximate posterior.

- We track and add the log-determinant of the Jacobian from each flow transform into the ELBO.

- Finally, a decoder reconstructs data from the transformed latent sample, completing the forward pass.

- Training optimizes the resulting ELBO, which now includes additional terms for the flow (negative sum of log-determinants) alongside the usual reconstruction and KL divergences.

Python Code Snippet

```python
import torch
import torch.nn as nn
import torch.optim as optim
from torch.utils.data import DataLoader
from torchvision import datasets, transforms
import math
import numpy as np


# --------------------------------------------------------------
# 1) Encoder and Decoder for a basic VAE
# --------------------------------------------------------------
class Encoder(nn.Module):
    """
    A simple MLP-based encoder that outputs the mean and
    ↪ log-variance.
    We flatten the input image to a 1D vector.
    """
    def __init__(self, input_dim=28*28, hidden_dim=512,
    ↪ latent_dim=2):
        super(Encoder, self).__init__()
        self.net = nn.Sequential(
            nn.Linear(input_dim, hidden_dim),
            nn.ReLU(),
            nn.Linear(hidden_dim, hidden_dim),
            nn.ReLU()
        )
        self.mu = nn.Linear(hidden_dim, latent_dim)
        self.logvar = nn.Linear(hidden_dim, latent_dim)

    def forward(self, x):
        # x shape: (batch_size, 1, 28, 28) -> flatten ->
        ↪ (batch_size, 784)
        x = x.view(x.size(0), -1)
        h = self.net(x)
        mu = self.mu(h)
        logvar = self.logvar(h)
        return mu, logvar

class Decoder(nn.Module):
    """
    A simple MLP-based decoder that reconstructs from the latent
    ↪ code.
    """
    def __init__(self, latent_dim=2, hidden_dim=512,
    ↪ output_dim=28*28):
        super(Decoder, self).__init__()
        self.net = nn.Sequential(
            nn.Linear(latent_dim, hidden_dim),
            nn.ReLU(),
            nn.Linear(hidden_dim, hidden_dim),
```

177

```python
            nn.ReLU(),
            nn.Linear(hidden_dim, output_dim),
            nn.Sigmoid()
        )

    def forward(self, z):
        # z shape: (batch_size, latent_dim)
        x_recon = self.net(z)
        # reshape into (batch_size, 1, 28, 28)
        return x_recon.view(z.size(0), 1, 28, 28)


# -------------------------------------------------------------
# 2) RealNVP Coupling Layer for the Flow
# -------------------------------------------------------------
class AffineCoupling(nn.Module):
    """
    An affine coupling layer from RealNVP.
    We split the input z into [z1, z2], then shift and scale z2
    based on a neural network conditioned on z1.
    """
    def __init__(self, in_dim, hidden_dim=128, mask=None):
        super(AffineCoupling, self).__init__()
        if mask is None:
            # default mask, first half -> transform second half
            mask = torch.cat([torch.ones(in_dim//2),
                              torch.zeros(in_dim - in_dim//2)],
                             ↪  dim=0)
        self.register_buffer('mask', mask)
        self.scale_net = nn.Sequential(
            nn.Linear(in_dim, hidden_dim),
            nn.ReLU(),
            nn.Linear(hidden_dim, hidden_dim),
            nn.ReLU(),
            nn.Linear(hidden_dim, in_dim)
        )
        self.trans_net = nn.Sequential(
            nn.Linear(in_dim, hidden_dim),
            nn.ReLU(),
            nn.Linear(hidden_dim, hidden_dim),
            nn.ReLU(),
            nn.Linear(hidden_dim, in_dim)
        )

    def forward(self, z):
        """
        z -> z' + log_det
        We apply the affine transform to the elements where mask ==
        ↪  0.
        """
        # mask shape: (in_dim,)
        # z shape: (batch_size, in_dim)
        masked_z = z * self.mask
        s = self.scale_net(masked_z)
```

```python
        t = self.trans_net(masked_z)
        # only transform where mask == 0
        s = s * (1.0 - self.mask)
        t = t * (1.0 - self.mask)

        z_out = z * torch.exp(s) + t
        log_det = torch.sum(s, dim=1)   # sum over dim dimension
        return z_out, log_det

    def inverse(self, z):
        """
        Inverse transform z' -> z.
        """
        masked_z = z * self.mask
        s = self.scale_net(masked_z)
        t = self.trans_net(masked_z)
        s = s * (1.0 - self.mask)
        t = t * (1.0 - self.mask)

        z_in = (z - t) * torch.exp(-s)
        log_det = -torch.sum(s, dim=1)
        return z_in, log_det


# ------------------------------------------------------------
# 3) RealNVP Flow Module (composing multiple layers)
# ------------------------------------------------------------
class RealNVP(nn.Module):
    """
    A container for multiple affine coupling layers.
    Each layer has an associated mask.
    """
    def __init__(self, latent_dim=2, num_coupling_layers=2):
        super(RealNVP, self).__init__()
        # Create alternating binary masks to alternate which part is
        ↪   transformed
        masks = []
        for i in range(num_coupling_layers):
            # alternate between first half and second half
            # e.g., [1,1,0,0,...] -> [0,0,1,1,...]
            mask_pattern = [1]*(latent_dim//2) + [0]*(latent_dim -
            ↪   latent_dim//2)
            if i % 2 == 1:
                mask_pattern = [1 - m for m in mask_pattern]
            mask_ts = torch.tensor(mask_pattern, dtype=torch.float)
            masks.append(mask_ts)

        self.coupling_layers = nn.ModuleList(
            [AffineCoupling(in_dim=latent_dim, mask=masks[i])
             for i in range(num_coupling_layers)]
        )

    def forward(self, z):
        """
```

179

```
    Pass z forward through all coupling layers.
    Returns the transformed z_out and sum of log determinants.
    """
    log_det_sum = 0.0
    for coupling in self.coupling_layers:
        z, log_det = coupling(z)
        log_det_sum += log_det
    return z, log_det_sum

def inverse(self, z):
    """
    Invert z by going in reverse order of the coupling layers.
    """
    log_det_sum = 0.0
    for coupling in reversed(self.coupling_layers):
        z, log_det = coupling.inverse(z)
        log_det_sum += log_det
    return z, log_det_sum


# ------------------------------------------------------------------
# 4) Full VAE with Flow
# ------------------------------------------------------------------
class VAEwithFlow(nn.Module):
    """
    A VAE that uses Normalizing Flows to transform the latent
    ↪    distribution.
    We have an encoder -> (mu, logvar)
    then we sample z0 (reparameterization trick),
    then pass z0 through RealNVP -> zK, log_det,
    and decode zK.
    """
    def __init__(self, input_dim=28*28, hidden_dim=512,
    ↪    latent_dim=2, num_flows=2):
        super(VAEwithFlow, self).__init__()
        self.latent_dim = latent_dim
        self.encoder = Encoder(input_dim, hidden_dim, latent_dim)
        self.decoder = Decoder(latent_dim, hidden_dim, input_dim)
        self.flow = RealNVP(latent_dim,
        ↪    num_coupling_layers=num_flows)

    def encode(self, x):
        mu, logvar = self.encoder(x)
        return mu, logvar

    def reparameterize(self, mu, logvar):
        std = torch.exp(0.5 * logvar)
        eps = torch.randn_like(std)
        return mu + eps * std

    def forward(self, x):
        """
        Returns reconstruction, mu, logvar, zK, sum_log_det.
        """
```

```
        mu, logvar = self.encode(x)
        z0 = self.reparameterize(mu, logvar)
        # Flow transform
        zK, sum_log_det = self.flow(z0)
        recon = self.decoder(zK)
        return recon, mu, logvar, z0, zK, sum_log_det


# -------------------------------------------------------------
# 5) ELBO and training helpers
# -------------------------------------------------------------
def flow_vae_loss_function(x, recon_x, mu, logvar, z0, zK,
↪   sum_log_det):
    """

    Computes the negative ELBO for a VAE with normalizing flows.
    Terms:
    1) Reconstruction loss: binary cross-entropy or MSE
    2) KL-like term that includes flow's log-det
    """
    batch_size = x.size(0)
    # Reconstruction loss (e.g., BCELoss)
    # Flatten images to compare
    recon_flat = recon_x.view(batch_size, -1)
    x_flat = x.view(batch_size, -1)

    bce = nn.functional.binary_cross_entropy(
        recon_flat, x_flat, reduction='sum'
    )

    # Standard Gaussian prior on zK:
    # log p(zK) = -0.5 * (zK^2 + log(2*pi)) integrated over zK
    ↪   dimensions
    # but we won't explicitly compute it if we handle the usual VAE
    ↪   KL + flow terms
    # Standard VAE KL for q(z0|x) ~ diag Normal:
    # KL(q(z0|x) || p(z0)) = 0.5 * sum( exp(logvar) + mu^2 - 1 -
    ↪   logvar )
    # Then we incorporate the flow log-det correction:

    kl_vae = 0.5 * torch.sum(mu**2 + torch.exp(logvar) - 1.0 -
    ↪   logvar)

    # Flow introduces an extra term: - E[ sum_log_det ]
    # Minimizing negative sum_log_det is like penalizing expansions
    # and rewarding compressions in the flow's transform.
    # The sign is negative because we want to *subtract* log_det
    ↪   from KL.
    # We'll treat it like: kl_flow = - sum of log_det. Then total
    ↪   KL is kl_vae - sum_log_det.
    kl_flow = - torch.sum(sum_log_det)

    # Negative ELBO:
    loss = (bce + kl_vae + kl_flow)
    return loss / batch_size
```

```python
def train_one_epoch(model, dataloader, optimizer, device):
    model.train()
    epoch_loss = 0.0
    for x, _ in dataloader:
        x = x.to(device)
        recon, mu, logvar, z0, zK, sum_log_det = model(x)
        loss = flow_vae_loss_function(x, recon, mu, logvar, z0, zK,
         ↪  sum_log_det)

        optimizer.zero_grad()
        loss.backward()
        optimizer.step()

        epoch_loss += loss.item()
    return epoch_loss / len(dataloader)

def test_one_epoch(model, dataloader, device):
    model.eval()
    epoch_loss = 0.0
    with torch.no_grad():
        for x, _ in dataloader:
            x = x.to(device)
            recon, mu, logvar, z0, zK, sum_log_det = model(x)
            loss = flow_vae_loss_function(x, recon, mu, logvar, z0,
             ↪  zK, sum_log_det)
            epoch_loss += loss.item()
    return epoch_loss / len(dataloader)


# ----------------------------------------------------------------
# 6) Main function to load data, train, and test the model
# ----------------------------------------------------------------
def main():
    # Hyperparameters
    batch_size = 64
    latent_dim = 2
    num_flows = 2
    learning_rate = 1e-3
    epochs = 5

    # Device
    device = torch.device("cuda" if torch.cuda.is_available() else
     ↪  "cpu")

    # Data
    transform = transforms.Compose([
        transforms.ToTensor()
    ])
    train_dataset = datasets.MNIST(root="./data", train=True,
     ↪  transform=transform, download=True)
    test_dataset = datasets.MNIST(root="./data", train=False,
     ↪  transform=transform, download=True)
```

182

```
    train_loader = DataLoader(train_dataset, batch_size=batch_size,
    ↪   shuffle=True)
    test_loader = DataLoader(test_dataset, batch_size=batch_size,
    ↪   shuffle=False)

    # Model
    model = VAEwithFlow(input_dim=28*28, hidden_dim=512,
    ↪   latent_dim=latent_dim, num_flows=num_flows)
    model.to(device)

    # Optimizer
    optimizer = optim.Adam(model.parameters(), lr=learning_rate)

    # Training loop
    for epoch in range(1, epochs+1):
        train_loss = train_one_epoch(model, train_loader, optimizer,
        ↪   device)
        test_loss = test_one_epoch(model, test_loader, device)
        print(f"Epoch [{epoch}/{epochs}] - Train Loss:
        ↪   {train_loss:.4f} | Test Loss: {test_loss:.4f}")

    print("Training complete!")

if __name__ == "__main__":
    main()
```

Key Implementation Details:

- **Encoder/Decoder:** The Encoder outputs a mean and log-variance for a diagonal Gaussian in latent space, while the Decoder reconstructs data from the latent code.

- **Normalizing Flow:** We introduce a RealNVP-based flow (RealNVP) that transforms the initial latent sample z0 to a final sample zK, tracking the sum of log-determinants via affine coupling layers.

- **Reparameterization Trick:** reparameterize samples z0 from the encoder's Gaussian distribution, ensuring gradients flow through mu and logvar.

- **Flow VAE Loss:** In flow_vae_loss_function, we combine BCE reconstruction with the KL-like term that now includes the negative sum of log-determinants from the flow. This encourages the learned distribution to match the standard normal prior while leveraging the expressiveness of normalizing flows.

- **Full Pipeline:** The `main` procedure loads MNIST, instantiates the `VAEwithFlow`, and trains for multiple epochs. Checking `test_one_epoch` helps ensure generalization, and the final model can generate or reconstruct samples with the powerful latent distribution learned via normalizing flows.

Chapter 23

VAE for Inverse Problem Solving

We use a VAE to solve inverse problems such as image inpainting or tomography where we only observe partial data and need to infer what is missing. The encoder learns a latent distribution of complete samples, and during testing, we infer latents that best explain the partial observations. The chapter details how to create objective functions that mix data fidelity with the VAE's prior, and how to perform optimization in latent space. Python examples show how to adapt the dataset and integrate iterative solvers for improved reconstructions.

- We first train a Variational Autoencoder (VAE) on complete images to learn a compact latent representation.

- For inverse tasks such as inpainting, we create a partial observation by masking out sections of an image.

- During test time, we optimize over the latent variables to match the visible portions of the corrupted image while also respecting the learned VAE prior.

- This procedure can be extended to other inverse problems by adjusting the fidelity term to incorporate domain-specific constraints (e.g., tomography projections).

Python Code Snippet

```python
import torch
import torch.nn as nn
import torch.optim as optim
import torchvision
import torchvision.transforms as transforms
from torch.utils.data import DataLoader, Dataset

import matplotlib.pyplot as plt
import numpy as np
import random
import os

# ----------------------------------------------------------------
# 1) Set seeds and device for reproducibility
# ----------------------------------------------------------------
def set_seed(seed=42):
    random.seed(seed)
    np.random.seed(seed)
    torch.manual_seed(seed)
    if torch.cuda.is_available():
        torch.cuda.manual_seed_all(seed)

# ----------------------------------------------------------------
# 2) Define a simple VAE architecture
# ----------------------------------------------------------------
class VAE(nn.Module):
    """
    A Variational Autoencoder for 28x28 grayscale images (e.g.,
    ↪  MNIST).
    Encodes an image to a latent distribution, then decodes a sample
    back to the image space.
    """
    def __init__(self, latent_dim=20):
        super(VAE, self).__init__()
        self.latent_dim = latent_dim

        # Encoder layers
        self.encoder = nn.Sequential(
            nn.Conv2d(1, 32, 3, stride=2, padding=1),
            nn.ReLU(),
            nn.Conv2d(32, 64, 3, stride=2, padding=1),
            nn.ReLU(),
            nn.Flatten()
        )
        # After two strides of 2, we go from 28x28 to 7x7 with 64
        ↪  channels => 64*7*7 = 3136
        self.fc_mu = nn.Linear(3136, latent_dim)
        self.fc_logvar = nn.Linear(3136, latent_dim)

        # Decoder layers
```

186

```python
        self.fc_decode = nn.Linear(latent_dim, 3136)
        self.decoder = nn.Sequential(
            nn.ConvTranspose2d(64, 32, 3, stride=2, padding=1,
            ↪  output_padding=1),
            nn.ReLU(),
            nn.ConvTranspose2d(32, 1, 3, stride=2, padding=1,
            ↪  output_padding=1),
            nn.Sigmoid()  # Map output to [0,1]
        )

    def encode(self, x):
        """
        Encode input x into a latent distribution (mu, logvar).
        """
        x_encoded = self.encoder(x)
        mu = self.fc_mu(x_encoded)
        logvar = self.fc_logvar(x_encoded)
        return mu, logvar

    def reparameterize(self, mu, logvar):
        """
        Reparameterization trick to sample from N(mu, var).
        """
        std = torch.exp(0.5 * logvar)
        eps = torch.randn_like(std)
        return mu + eps * std

    def decode(self, z):
        """
        Decode latent vector z back to an image.
        """
        z_decoded = self.fc_decode(z)
        z_decoded = z_decoded.view(-1, 64, 7, 7)
        return self.decoder(z_decoded)

    def forward(self, x):
        """
        Complete forward pass: returns reconstructed x and (mu,
        ↪  logvar).
        """
        mu, logvar = self.encode(x)
        z = self.reparameterize(mu, logvar)
        x_recon = self.decode(z)
        return x_recon, mu, logvar


# -------------------------------------------------------------
# 3) VAE loss: reconstruction + KL divergence
# -------------------------------------------------------------
def vae_loss_function(x_recon, x, mu, logvar):
    """
    Compute the VAE loss as the sum of reconstruction loss (binary
    ↪  cross-entropy)
    and KL divergence.
```

```python
    """
    bce = nn.functional.binary_cross_entropy(
        x_recon, x, reduction='sum'
    )
    # KL divergence: measure how far q(z|x) is from the prior p(z).
    kld = -0.5 * torch.sum(1 + logvar - mu.pow(2) - logvar.exp())
    return bce + kld


# -------------------------------------------------------------
# 4) Train the VAE
# -------------------------------------------------------------
def train_vae(model, dataloader, optimizer, device):
    """
    One epoch of training the VAE.
    """
    model.train()
    running_loss = 0.0
    for imgs, _ in dataloader:
        imgs = imgs.to(device)
        optimizer.zero_grad()
        x_recon, mu, logvar = model(imgs)
        loss = vae_loss_function(x_recon, imgs, mu, logvar)
        loss.backward()
        optimizer.step()
        running_loss += loss.item()
    return running_loss / len(dataloader.dataset)

def test_vae(model, dataloader, device):
    """
    Evaluate the VAE on a test set.
    """
    model.eval()
    test_loss = 0.0
    with torch.no_grad():
        for imgs, _ in dataloader:
            imgs = imgs.to(device)
            x_recon, mu, logvar = model(imgs)
            loss = vae_loss_function(x_recon, imgs, mu, logvar)
            test_loss += loss.item()
    return test_loss / len(dataloader.dataset)


# -------------------------------------------------------------
# 5) Create partial observations (inpainting scenario)
# -------------------------------------------------------------
def create_random_mask(batch_size, img_size=(28, 28),
↪   prop_missing=0.3):
    """
    Generate a random mask of size img_size with a certain
    ↪   proportion of missing pixels.
    Returns a tensor of shape [batch_size, 1, H, W].
    """
    total_pixels = img_size[0] * img_size[1]
    num_missing = int(total_pixels * prop_missing)
```

188

```
    masks = []
    for _ in range(batch_size):
        mask = torch.ones(total_pixels, dtype=torch.float32)
        # Randomly choose indices for missing
        missing_indices = torch.randperm(total_pixels)[:num_missing]
        mask[missing_indices] = 0.0
        mask = mask.view(*img_size)
        masks.append(mask.unsqueeze(0))
    return torch.stack(masks, dim=0)

# -------------------------------------------------------------
# 6) Inference / inpainting: Latent optimization
# -------------------------------------------------------------
def inpaint_image(model, partial_img, mask, device, steps=200,
↪    lr=0.01, lambda_prior=1.0):
    """
    Given a partial image (pixels are 0 for unknown areas), we
    ↪    optimize a latent vector z
    to best reconstruct the known pixels while respecting the VAE
    ↪    prior.
    Args:
      model: trained VAE model
      partial_img: shape [1, 1, H, W], partial observation
      mask: shape [1, 1, H, W], 1 for known, 0 for missing
      steps: number of gradient steps
      lr: learning rate for latent optimization
      lambda_prior: weighting for the prior term (roughly encourages
      ↪    z to stay near N(0,I))
    """
    model.eval()
    with torch.no_grad():
        # We'll just pick one forward pass to get dimension for z
        mu, logvar = model.encode(partial_img)
        z_init = model.reparameterize(mu, logvar)

    # Make z_init a parameter so we can optimize it directly
    z_opt = nn.Parameter(z_init.clone().detach(),
    ↪    requires_grad=True)
    optimizer = optim.Adam([z_opt], lr=lr)

    for _ in range(steps):
        optimizer.zero_grad()

        # Decode current z
        x_hat = model.decode(z_opt)

        # Compute fidelity loss only on known pixels
        fidelity_loss = ((x_hat * mask - partial_img *
        ↪    mask)**2).sum()

        # Encourage z to stay near zero -- basic prior penalty
        prior_loss = (z_opt**2).sum()
```

```python
        loss = fidelity_loss + lambda_prior * prior_loss
        loss.backward()
        optimizer.step()

    # Return the completed image
    with torch.no_grad():
        inpainted = model.decode(z_opt)
    return inpainted


# ---------------------------------------------------------------
# 7) Visualization utility
# ---------------------------------------------------------------
def visualize_inpainting(original, masked, inpainted, mask,
↪  filename="inpainting_result.png"):
    """
    Save a side-by-side comparison of the original, partial, and
    ↪  inpainted result.
    """
    fig, axs = plt.subplots(1, 3, figsize=(9, 3))

    axs[0].imshow(original[0, 0].cpu().numpy(), cmap='gray')
    axs[0].set_title("Original")
    axs[0].axis('off')

    # Show masked image
    axs[1].imshow(masked[0, 0].cpu().numpy(), cmap='gray')
    axs[1].set_title("Partial Obs")
    axs[1].axis('off')

    # Show inpainted image
    axs[2].imshow(inpainted[0, 0].cpu().numpy(), cmap='gray')
    axs[2].set_title("Inpainted")
    axs[2].axis('off')

    plt.tight_layout()
    os.makedirs("results_inverse", exist_ok=True)
    plt.savefig(os.path.join("results_inverse", filename))
    plt.close()


# ---------------------------------------------------------------
# 8) Main script
# ---------------------------------------------------------------
def main():
    set_seed(42)
    device = torch.device("cuda" if torch.cuda.is_available() else
    ↪  "cpu")

    # Load MNIST for demonstration
    transform = transforms.Compose([
        transforms.ToTensor()
    ])
```

```python
    train_dataset = torchvision.datasets.MNIST(root="./data",
    ↪    train=True, download=True, transform=transform)
    test_dataset = torchvision.datasets.MNIST(root="./data",
    ↪    train=False, download=True, transform=transform)
    train_loader = DataLoader(train_dataset, batch_size=64,
    ↪    shuffle=True)
    test_loader = DataLoader(test_dataset, batch_size=64,
    ↪    shuffle=False)

    # Initialize the VAE
    model = VAE(latent_dim=20).to(device)
    optimizer = optim.Adam(model.parameters(), lr=1e-3)

    # Train VAE for a few epochs
    epochs = 5
    for epoch in range(epochs):
        train_loss = train_vae(model, train_loader, optimizer,
        ↪    device)
        val_loss = test_vae(model, test_loader, device)
        print(f"Epoch [{epoch+1}/{epochs}] - Train Loss:
        ↪    {train_loss:.2f}, Val Loss: {val_loss:.2f}")

    # Demonstration of inpainting on a few samples from test set
    model.eval()
    for i in range(3):
        # Grab a single test image
        img, _ = test_dataset[i]
        img = img.unsqueeze(0).to(device)  # shape [1,1,28,28]

        # Create random mask
        mask = create_random_mask(batch_size=1, img_size=(28,28),
        ↪    prop_missing=0.5).to(device)
        partial_img = img * mask

        # Inpaint
        reconstructed = inpaint_image(
            model=model,
            partial_img=partial_img,
            mask=mask,
            device=device,
            steps=300,
            lr=0.01,
            lambda_prior=0.001
        )

        # Visualize
        visualize_inpainting(img, partial_img, reconstructed, mask,
        ↪    filename=f"inpainting_{i}.png")

    print("Inpainting demo complete. Results saved to
    ↪    'results_inverse' folder.")

if __name__ == "__main__":
```

Key Implementation Details:

- **VAE Architecture:** We define a convolutional encoder that reduces the image dimension twice via strides. Latent parameters (`mu` and `logvar`) come from fully connected layers. The decoder mirrors this process with transposed convolutions.

- **Loss Function:** The objective combines binary cross-entropy for reconstruction and a KL divergence term that regularizes the latent space toward a standard normal prior.

- **Inverse Problem Setup (Inpainting):** We create a mask with `create_random_mask` to simulate missing pixels. The partial observation is the elementwise product of the mask and the original image.

- **Latent Optimization:** In `inpaint_image`, we treat the latent code `z_opt` as a learnable parameter and optimize a loss that balances:
  - data fidelity on known pixels,
  - a prior penalty (keeping `z_opt` close to zero as a simple approximation of the KL term).

- **Practical Considerations:**
  - `lambda_prior` can be tuned to control how strictly we adhere to the prior vs. matching the partial observation.
  - We use a small set of gradient steps (`steps=300`) in the example, but real-world problems might require more iterations or advanced solvers.

- **Visualization:** The `visualize_inpainting` function shows side-by-side comparisons of the original, partial, and inpainted images.

Chapter 24

Sparse VAE for High-Dimensional Data

This chapter tackles the challenge of extremely high-dimensional datasets, such as large-scale text or gene expression profiles. We add sparsity-inducing penalties or constraints on the latent space and potentially the weights. Implementation involves a custom regularization term or specialized layers that encourage sparse codes. We explore trade-offs between reconstruction fidelity and interpretability, showing how to modify standard VAE training loops to handle dimensionalities in the tens or hundreds of thousands.

- We construct a standard Variational Autoencoder capable of handling large input dimensions.

- We add an L1 penalty on the latent means to encourage sparse representations, thus balancing reconstruction and interpretability.

- We rely on a multi-layer perceptron (MLP) that can scale to thousands of input features.

- We show how to implement the reparameterization trick, the KL term, and the sparse penalty term in a single training loop.

- This approach can be extended for real datasets like text (bag-of-words vectors) or high-dimensional biological data, e.g., gene expression.

Python Code Snippet

```python
import torch
import torch.nn as nn
import torch.optim as optim
from torch.utils.data import Dataset, DataLoader
import numpy as np

#
↳   ------------------------------------------------------------------
# 1) Synthetic high-dimensional dataset
#
↳   ------------------------------------------------------------------
class SyntheticHighDimDataset(Dataset):
    """
    A simple synthetic dataset that yields random high-dimensional
    ↳   vectors.
    This can mimic large-scale text or gene expression data.
    """
    def __init__(self, num_samples=10000, dim=1000, seed=42):
        super().__init__()
        np.random.seed(seed)
        self.data = np.random.randn(num_samples,
        ↳   dim).astype(np.float32)

    def __len__(self):
        return self.data.shape[0]

    def __getitem__(self, idx):
        x = self.data[idx]
        return x, 0    # dummy label


#
↳   ------------------------------------------------------------------
# 2) Define the SparseVAE model
#
↳   ------------------------------------------------------------------
class SparseVAE(nn.Module):
    """
    A Variational Autoencoder with an MLP encoder and decoder.
    Additionally, we apply an L1 penalty on the latent means to
    ↳   encourage sparsity.
    """
    def __init__(self, input_dim=1000, latent_dim=32,
    ↳   hidden_dim=256):
        super(SparseVAE, self).__init__()

        # Encoder
        self.encoder = nn.Sequential(
            nn.Linear(input_dim, hidden_dim),
            nn.ReLU(),
```

194

```python
            nn.Linear(hidden_dim, hidden_dim),
            nn.ReLU()
        )

        # Latent space parameters: mu and logvar
        self.fc_mu = nn.Linear(hidden_dim, latent_dim)
        self.fc_logvar = nn.Linear(hidden_dim, latent_dim)

        # Decoder
        self.decoder = nn.Sequential(
            nn.Linear(latent_dim, hidden_dim),
            nn.ReLU(),
            nn.Linear(hidden_dim, hidden_dim),
            nn.ReLU(),
            nn.Linear(hidden_dim, input_dim)
        )

    def reparameterize(self, mu, logvar):
        """
        Reparameterization trick:
        z = mu + sigma * eps, where eps ~ N(0, I).
        """
        std = torch.exp(0.5 * logvar)
        eps = torch.randn_like(std)
        return mu + eps * std

    def forward(self, x):
        """
        Forward pass: encode input x to latent distribution,
        sample z, and decode to reconstruction.
        Returns reconstruction, mu, logvar.
        """
        enc_out = self.encoder(x)
        mu = self.fc_mu(enc_out)
        logvar = self.fc_logvar(enc_out)

        z = self.reparameterize(mu, logvar)
        reconstruction = self.decoder(z)
        return reconstruction, mu, logvar


#
↪ -----------------------------------------------------------------------
# 3) Training and evaluation routines
#
↪ -----------------------------------------------------------------------
def train_one_epoch(model, data_loader, optimizer, device,
↪ alpha=1e-4):
    """
    Train for one epoch.
    alpha controls the strength of the L1 sparsity penalty on the
    ↪ latent means.
    """
```

```python
    model.train()
    total_loss = 0.0

    for batch_x, _ in data_loader:
        batch_x = batch_x.to(device)
        optimizer.zero_grad()

        # Forward pass
        reconstruction, mu, logvar = model(batch_x)

        # Reconstruction loss (MSE)
        recon_loss = nn.functional.mse_loss(reconstruction, batch_x,
        ↪   reduction='sum') / batch_x.size(0)

        # KL divergence
        # KL = 0.5 * sum( exp(logvar) + mu^2 - 1 - logvar ) /
        ↪   batch_size
        kl_loss = 0.5 * torch.mean(torch.sum(torch.exp(logvar) +
        ↪   mu**2 - 1.0 - logvar, dim=1))

        # L1 sparsity penalty on mu
        l1_sparsity = alpha * mu.abs().mean()

        # Total VAE loss
        loss = recon_loss + kl_loss + l1_sparsity

        loss.backward()
        optimizer.step()

        total_loss += loss.item()

    return total_loss / len(data_loader)


def evaluate_model(model, data_loader, device, alpha=1e-4):
    """
    Evaluate on a validation/test set, returning average total loss
    ↪   over the dataset.
    """
    model.eval()
    total_loss = 0.0
    with torch.no_grad():
        for batch_x, _ in data_loader:
            batch_x = batch_x.to(device)

            reconstruction, mu, logvar = model(batch_x)

            recon_loss = nn.functional.mse_loss(reconstruction,
            ↪   batch_x, reduction='sum') / batch_x.size(0)
            kl_loss = 0.5 * torch.mean(torch.sum(torch.exp(logvar) +
            ↪   mu**2 - 1.0 - logvar, dim=1))
            l1_sparsity = alpha * mu.abs().mean()
```

```
            loss = recon_loss + kl_loss + l1_sparsity
            total_loss += loss.item()

    return total_loss / len(data_loader)


def sample_from_vae(model, n_samples=5, latent_dim=32,
 ↪  device='cpu'):
    """
    Sample new points by drawing z ~ N(0,I) and decoding them.
    Returns a torch tensor of shape [n_samples, input_dim].
    """
    model.eval()
    with torch.no_grad():
        z = torch.randn(n_samples, latent_dim, device=device)
        samples = model.decoder(z)
    return samples


#
 ↪  -----------------------------------------------------------------------
# 4) Main script to demonstrate usage
#
 ↪  -----------------------------------------------------------------------
def main():
    # Configuration
    device = torch.device("cuda" if torch.cuda.is_available() else
     ↪  "cpu")
    input_dim = 1000
    latent_dim = 32
    hidden_dim = 256
    alpha = 1e-4    # L1 penalty coefficient
    lr = 1e-3
    batch_size = 128
    epochs = 5

    # Create synthetic dataset
    train_dataset = SyntheticHighDimDataset(num_samples=8000,
     ↪  dim=input_dim)
    val_dataset = SyntheticHighDimDataset(num_samples=2000,
     ↪  dim=input_dim, seed=123)

    train_loader = DataLoader(train_dataset, batch_size=batch_size,
     ↪  shuffle=True, drop_last=True)
    val_loader = DataLoader(val_dataset, batch_size=batch_size,
     ↪  shuffle=False, drop_last=False)

    # Initialize model and optimizer
    model = SparseVAE(input_dim=input_dim, latent_dim=latent_dim,
     ↪  hidden_dim=hidden_dim).to(device)
    optimizer = optim.Adam(model.parameters(), lr=lr)

    # Training loop
```

197

```
for epoch in range(epochs):
    train_loss = train_one_epoch(model, train_loader, optimizer,
    ↪    device, alpha=alpha)
    val_loss = evaluate_model(model, val_loader, device,
    ↪    alpha=alpha)
    print(f"Epoch [{epoch+1}/{epochs}] - Train Loss:
    ↪    {train_loss:.4f}, Val Loss: {val_loss:.4f}")

# Sample from the trained VAE
samples = sample_from_vae(model, n_samples=3,
↪    latent_dim=latent_dim, device=device)
print("Sampled new data points shape:", samples.shape)
print("A few sample values:\n", samples[0][:10].cpu().numpy())

if __name__ == "__main__":
    main()
```

Key Implementation Details:

- **Encoder and Decoder:** The MLP-based encoder and decoder in `SparseVAE` each have multiple linear layers with ReLU activation, flexible enough to handle high-dimensional inputs.

- **Latent Distribution:** We parameterize the Gaussian latent distribution with `fc_mu` and `fc_logvar`, storing the mean and log-variance.

- **Reparameterization Trick:** The `reparameterize` function performs z = mu + sigma * eps, where eps is drawn from a standard normal distribution.

- **Sparse Penalty:** An L1 penalty on the latent mean (`mu`) is added in `train_one_epoch` and `evaluate_model` to encourage distributing energy across fewer latent units.

- **Training Objective:** In `train_one_epoch`, we combine reconstruction loss (MSE), KL divergence, and the L1 sparsity term to form the total VAE loss.

- **Data Loader and Synthetic Dataset:**
  `SyntheticHighDimDataset` provides random high-dimensional vectors to mimic large feature spaces. `DataLoader` is used for batching.

- **Inference/Sampling:** The function `sample_from_vae` draws random latent vectors and decodes them into the input space, illustrating generative capability.

Chapter 25

VAE for Federated Learning

Extending VAEs to distributed or federated environments requires careful handling of partial data from different clients. We implement a federated training loop using libraries like PySyft or TensorFlow Federated, sharing model weights while keeping local data private. The chapter focuses on coordinating updates, handling heterogeneous data distributions, and ensuring communication efficiency. By balancing local reconstruction losses with a global KL prior, we achieve a VAE that can learn across multiple devices without centralizing data.

- We define a simple Variational Autoencoder (VAE) with fully-connected layers for demonstration.

- Each client holds a local subset of the dataset and trains a local copy of the model.

- We then average the resulting weights across clients to obtain a global model (a naive "FedAvg" approach).

- This global model is distributed back to clients for further local training, improving performance without requiring data to leave each client device.

Python Code Snippet

```python
import torch
import torch.nn as nn
import torch.optim as optim
from torch.utils.data import DataLoader, Subset
import torchvision
import torchvision.transforms as transforms
import numpy as np
import copy


# ------------------------------------------------------------------
# 1) Define VAE Architecture
# ------------------------------------------------------------------
class VAE(nn.Module):
    """
    A simple Variational Autoencoder with fully-connected encoder
    ↪   and decoder.
    Latent dimension is smaller than input dimension to learn
    ↪   compressed representations.
    """
    def __init__(self, input_dim=784, hidden_dim=400,
    ↪   latent_dim=20):
        super(VAE, self).__init__()

        # Encoder
        self.fc1 = nn.Linear(input_dim, hidden_dim)
        self.fc2_mean = nn.Linear(hidden_dim, latent_dim)
        self.fc2_logvar = nn.Linear(hidden_dim, latent_dim)

        # Decoder
        self.fc3 = nn.Linear(latent_dim, hidden_dim)
        self.fc4 = nn.Linear(hidden_dim, input_dim)

        self.relu = nn.ReLU()
        self.sigmoid = nn.Sigmoid()

    def encode(self, x):
        h = self.relu(self.fc1(x))
        mean = self.fc2_mean(h)
        logvar = self.fc2_logvar(h)
        return mean, logvar

    def reparameterize(self, mean, logvar):
        """
        The reparameterization trick: sample z ~ N(mean,
        ↪   exp(logvar))
        with random epsilon ~ N(0,1).
        """
        std = torch.exp(0.5 * logvar)
        eps = torch.randn_like(std)
        return mean + eps * std
```

```
    def decode(self, z):
        h = self.relu(self.fc3(z))
        return self.sigmoid(self.fc4(h))

    def forward(self, x):
        mean, logvar = self.encode(x)
        z = self.reparameterize(mean, logvar)
        reconstruction = self.decode(z)
        return reconstruction, mean, logvar


# ---------------------------------------------------------------
# 2) Loss Function: Reconstruction + KL Divergence
# ---------------------------------------------------------------
def vae_loss(reconstruction, x, mean, logvar):
    """
    The VAE loss is composed of:
    1) BCE or MSE reconstruction loss
    2) KL divergence term

    KL divergence = 0.5 * sum(1 + logvar - mean^2 - exp(logvar))
    """
    # We flatten inputs and reconstructions for simpler MSE usage
    mse = nn.MSELoss(reduction='sum')
    recon_loss = mse(reconstruction, x)

    # KL divergence
    kl_div = -0.5 * torch.sum(1 + logvar - mean.pow(2) -
    ↪   logvar.exp())

    return (recon_loss + kl_div) / x.size(0)


# ---------------------------------------------------------------
# 3) Local Client Training
# ---------------------------------------------------------------
def train_local(model, train_loader, epochs, lr=1e-3, device='cpu'):
    """
    Trains the model on a local dataset for a specified number of
    ↪   epochs.
    Returns the updated model parameters.
    """
    model = copy.deepcopy(model)
    model.to(device)
    optimizer = optim.Adam(model.parameters(), lr=lr)
    model.train()

    for _ in range(epochs):
        for batch_data, _ in train_loader:
            # Flatten images: e.g., 1 x 28 x 28 -> 784
            batch_data = batch_data.view(batch_data.size(0), -1)
            batch_data = batch_data.to(device)

            optimizer.zero_grad()
```

202

```
                    reconstruction, mean, logvar = model(batch_data)
                    loss = vae_loss(reconstruction, batch_data, mean,
                    ↪    logvar)
                    loss.backward()
                    optimizer.step()

        return model.state_dict()


    # -------------------------------------------------------------
    # 4) Federated Averaging
    # -------------------------------------------------------------
    def federated_averaging(global_model, client_params_list):
        """
        A simple FedAvg approach: we average parameters across all
        ↪    clients.
        """
        new_global_params = copy.deepcopy(global_model.state_dict())
        for key in new_global_params.keys():
            new_global_params[key] = torch.mean(
                torch.stack([params[key] for params in
                ↪    client_params_list]), dim=0
            )
        return new_global_params


    # -------------------------------------------------------------
    # 5) Evaluation
    # -------------------------------------------------------------
    def evaluate_global_model(global_model, data_loader, device='cpu'):
        """
        Evaluate the global model by computing the reconstruction loss
        on a held-out set.
        """
        global_model.eval()
        global_model.to(device)
        total_loss = 0
        with torch.no_grad():
            for batch_data, _ in data_loader:
                batch_data = batch_data.view(batch_data.size(0),
                ↪    -1).to(device)
                reconstruction, mean, logvar = global_model(batch_data)
                loss = vae_loss(reconstruction, batch_data, mean,
                ↪    logvar)
                total_loss += loss.item()
        return total_loss / len(data_loader)


    # -------------------------------------------------------------
    # 6) Main Federated Learning Loop
    # -------------------------------------------------------------
    def main():
        device = torch.device('cuda' if torch.cuda.is_available() else
        ↪    'cpu')

        # Hyperparameters
```

203

```
input_dim = 784   # for MNIST
hidden_dim = 400
latent_dim = 20
local_epochs = 1
federated_rounds = 5
num_clients = 2   # Simple example with 2 clients

# Load dataset
transform = transforms.Compose([
    transforms.ToTensor(),
    # scale from [0,1] to [0,1], flattening later in training
])
full_dataset = torchvision.datasets.MNIST(root='data',
↪   train=True, download=True, transform=transform)
test_dataset = torchvision.datasets.MNIST(root='data',
↪   train=False, download=True, transform=transform)

# Split dataset among clients
indices = np.arange(len(full_dataset))
np.random.shuffle(indices)
split_size = len(full_dataset) // num_clients
client_loaders = []

for i in range(num_clients):
    start_idx = i * split_size
    end_idx = len(full_dataset) if i == (num_clients - 1) else
    ↪   (i+1) * split_size
    subset_indices = indices[start_idx:end_idx]
    subset_data = Subset(full_dataset, subset_indices)
    loader = DataLoader(subset_data, batch_size=64,
    ↪   shuffle=True)
    client_loaders.append(loader)

# Test loader for global evaluation
test_loader = DataLoader(test_dataset, batch_size=64,
↪   shuffle=False)

# Initialize global model
global_model = VAE(input_dim=input_dim, hidden_dim=hidden_dim,
↪   latent_dim=latent_dim)

# Federated training
for round_idx in range(federated_rounds):
    client_params_list = []

    # Each client trains locally on its subset
    for c in range(num_clients):
        local_params = train_local(global_model,
        ↪   client_loaders[c], epochs=local_epochs, lr=1e-3,
        ↪   device=device)
        client_params_list.append(local_params)

    # Aggregate updates into the global model
```

```
new_global_params = federated_averaging(global_model,
↪   client_params_list)
global_model.load_state_dict(new_global_params)

# Evaluate global model
val_loss = evaluate_global_model(global_model, test_loader,
↪   device=device)
print(f"Round {round_idx+1}/{federated_rounds} - Global Val
↪   Loss: {val_loss:.4f}")

    print("Federated training completed.")
    # Optionally, save or use the final global model for inference.

if __name__ == "__main__":
    main()
```

Key Implementation Details:

- The `VAE` class implements a simple encoder-decoder structure with a reparameterization trick. Fully-connected layers are used for clarity, though convolutional variants may be used for image data.

- The `train_local` function runs a local training loop on a client's subset of the data, computing a standard VAE loss (sum of reconstruction and KL divergence terms) and returning updated model parameters.

- `federated_averaging` aggregates the locally updated model parameters by simply averaging corresponding weights (FedAvg). More advanced methods could incorporate weighting by dataset size or momentum.

- `evaluate_global_model` computes the average VAE loss on the test set, helping monitor global performance improvements over federated rounds.

- In `main`, we split MNIST into a simple 2-client scenario, initialize a global VAE, and iteratively perform local updates and global averaging. This demonstrates how a VAE can be trained in a federated manner without sharing raw data between clients.

Chapter 26

Few-Shot Learning with VAE

Using VAE latent spaces for few-shot tasks involves quickly adapting to new classes with minimal labeled examples. We show how to initialize the encoder and decoder with a generic dataset, then perform rapid fine-tuning or latent adaptation for novel classes. Implementation details include specialized loss setups for classification plus reconstruction, meta-learning loops, and guidelines for data arrangement. By the end, you'll have a prototype that can generalize from few examples by leveraging the VAE's learned features.

- We first train a Variational Autoencoder on a set of "base classes" for representation learning.

- We incorporate a simple classification head on top of the VAE latent space to guide semi-supervised or supervised tasks.

- We then fine-tune the VAE with minimal labeled data for "novel classes," demonstrating how quickly the learned latent representation adapts to unseen categories.

Python Code Snippet

```
import torch
import torch.nn as nn
import torch.optim as optim
```

```python
import torch.nn.functional as F
from torch.utils.data import DataLoader, Subset
import torchvision
import torchvision.transforms as transforms
import numpy as np
import random


#
↳   --------------------------------------------------------------------
# 1) Utility Functions
#
↳   --------------------------------------------------------------------
def set_seed(seed=42):
    """
    Set random seed for reproducibility.
    """
    random.seed(seed)
    np.random.seed(seed)
    torch.manual_seed(seed)
    if torch.cuda.is_available():
        torch.cuda.manual_seed_all(seed)


def filter_mnist(mnist_dataset, keep_classes):
    """
    Return a filtered subset of MNIST containing only the digits in
    ↳   keep_classes.
    """
    indices = []
    for i in range(len(mnist_dataset)):
        _, label = mnist_dataset[i]
        if label in keep_classes:
            indices.append(i)
    return Subset(mnist_dataset, indices)


#
↳   --------------------------------------------------------------------
# 2) VAE with Classification Head
#
↳   --------------------------------------------------------------------
class VAEClassifier(nn.Module):
    """
    A Variational Autoencoder that outputs a latent representation
    ↳   z,
    and an additional classification head for digit classification.
    We assume the input is 28x28; we use a simple MLP for
    ↳   demonstration.
    """
    def __init__(self, latent_dim=16, n_classes=10):
        super(VAEClassifier, self).__init__()
        self.latent_dim = latent_dim
        self.n_classes = n_classes

        # ----------------------------
```

207

```python
        # Encoder
        # -------------------------
        # Flatten 28x28 into 784
        self.enc_fc1 = nn.Linear(784, 256)
        self.enc_fc2 = nn.Linear(256, 128)
        self.mu_layer = nn.Linear(128, latent_dim)
        self.logvar_layer = nn.Linear(128, latent_dim)

        # -------------------------
        # Decoder
        # -------------------------
        self.dec_fc1 = nn.Linear(latent_dim, 128)
        self.dec_fc2 = nn.Linear(128, 256)
        self.dec_out = nn.Linear(256, 784)

        # -------------------------
        # Classifier head
        # -------------------------
        self.classifier = nn.Linear(latent_dim, n_classes)

    def encode(self, x):
        """
        Encode the input image x into a latent distribution (mu,
        ↪  logvar).
        """
        h = F.relu(self.enc_fc1(x))
        h = F.relu(self.enc_fc2(h))
        mu = self.mu_layer(h)
        logvar = self.logvar_layer(h)
        return mu, logvar

    def reparameterize(self, mu, logvar):
        """
        Reparameterization trick to sample z ~ N(mu, sigma^2).
        """
        std = torch.exp(0.5 * logvar)
        eps = torch.randn_like(std)
        return mu + eps * std

    def decode(self, z):
        """
        Decode the latent variable z back to image space.
        """
        h = F.relu(self.dec_fc1(z))
        h = F.relu(self.dec_fc2(h))
        x_recon = torch.sigmoid(self.dec_out(h))
        return x_recon

    def forward_classifier(self, z):
        """
        Forward pass of the classification head given a latent
        ↪  vector z.
        """
```

```
        logits = self.classifier(z)
        return logits

    def forward(self, x):
        """
        Forward pass through the entire model for reconstruction +
        ↪  classification.
        Used mainly for convenience. For separate usage, call
        ↪  `encode` or `forward_classifier` as needed.
        """
        # Encode
        mu, logvar = self.encode(x)
        z = self.reparameterize(mu, logvar)
        # Decode
        x_recon = self.decode(z)
        # Classify
        logits = self.forward_classifier(z)
        return x_recon, mu, logvar, logits

#
↪  ------------------------------------------------------------------------
# 3) Training Helpers
#
↪  ------------------------------------------------------------------------
def vae_classification_loss(x, x_recon, mu, logvar, logits, labels,
↪  alpha=1.0):
    """
    Compute VAE loss (reconstruction + KL) plus classification loss
    ↪  if labels exist.
    alpha: weighting factor for classification loss.
    """
    # Reconstruction loss (MSE or BCE). Here we use BCE since
    ↪  x_recon in [0, 1].
    recon_loss = F.binary_cross_entropy(x_recon, x, reduction='sum')
    ↪  / x.size(0)

    # KL Divergence
    kld = -0.5 * torch.mean(1 + logvar - mu.pow(2) - logvar.exp())

    # Classification loss (cross-entropy), apply only if labels is
    ↪  not None
    if labels is not None:
        class_loss = F.cross_entropy(logits, labels)
    else:
        class_loss = 0.0

    # Total loss merges them; alpha scales the classification
    ↪  component
    total_loss = recon_loss + kld + alpha * class_loss
    return total_loss, recon_loss, kld, class_loss

def train_vae_classifier(model, loader, optimizer, device,
↪  alpha=1.0):
```

209

```python
    """
    Train the VAE + classifier for one epoch on the given loader.
    """
    model.train()
    epoch_loss = 0
    for images, labels in loader:
        images = images.to(device)
        labels = labels.to(device)

        # Flatten images from [B,1,28,28] -> [B,784]
        images_flat = images.view(images.size(0), -1)
        x_recon, mu, logvar, logits = model(images_flat)

        loss, _, _, _ = vae_classification_loss(images_flat,
        ↪ x_recon, mu, logvar, logits, labels, alpha)
        optimizer.zero_grad()
        loss.backward()
        optimizer.step()

        epoch_loss += loss.item()
    return epoch_loss / len(loader)

def eval_vae_classifier(model, loader, device):
    """
    Evaluate reconstruction and classification performance on the
    ↪ given loader.
    Returns average classification accuracy and reconstruction loss.
    """
    model.eval()
    correct = 0
    total = 0
    recon_sum = 0.0
    with torch.no_grad():
        for images, labels in loader:
            images = images.to(device)
            labels = labels.to(device)
            images_flat = images.view(images.size(0), -1)

            x_recon, mu, logvar, logits = model(images_flat)
            # Classification accuracy
            preds = logits.argmax(dim=1)
            correct += (preds == labels).sum().item()
            total += labels.size(0)

            # Recon loss (BCE)
            recon_loss = F.binary_cross_entropy(x_recon,
            ↪ images_flat, reduction='sum') / images.size(0)
            recon_sum += recon_loss.item()

    acc = 100.0 * correct / total if total > 0 else 0
    recon_avg = recon_sum / len(loader) if len(loader) > 0 else 0
    return acc, recon_avg
```

```python
def fine_tune_on_few_shot(model, loader, optimizer, device,
    epochs=2, alpha=1.0):
    """
    Fine-tune the VAE + classifier on a few-shot loader for novel
        classes.
    Typically fewer epochs are used to avoid overfitting.
    """
    for ep in range(epochs):
        loss_val = train_vae_classifier(model, loader, optimizer,
            device, alpha=alpha)
        # Optionally evaluate or just keep training
    return


#
    ----------------------------------------------------------------
# 4) Main Routine
#
    ----------------------------------------------------------------
def main():
    set_seed()

    device = torch.device("cuda" if torch.cuda.is_available() else
        "cpu")
    print(f"Using device: {device}")

    # Load MNIST
    transform = transforms.Compose([transforms.ToTensor()])
    train_data = torchvision.datasets.MNIST(root="data", train=True,
        download=True, transform=transform)
    test_data = torchvision.datasets.MNIST(root="data", train=False,
        download=True, transform=transform)

    # Separate base classes (0..7) and novel classes (8..9)
    base_classes = [0,1,2,3,4,5,6,7]
    novel_classes = [8,9]

    # Filter the datasets
    base_train_data = filter_mnist(train_data, base_classes)
    novel_train_data = filter_mnist(train_data, novel_classes)
    base_test_data = filter_mnist(test_data, base_classes)
    novel_test_data = filter_mnist(test_data, novel_classes)

    # DataLoaders
    base_train_loader = DataLoader(base_train_data, batch_size=64,
        shuffle=True)
    base_test_loader = DataLoader(base_test_data, batch_size=64,
        shuffle=False)

    # We will artificially limit the novel classes to few-shot
        examples
    # e.g., pick 50 examples from novel classes
    few_shot_indices = list(range(min(len(novel_train_data), 50)))
    novel_few_shot_data = Subset(novel_train_data, few_shot_indices)
```

211

```python
novel_few_shot_loader = DataLoader(novel_few_shot_data,
↪   batch_size=32, shuffle=True)

novel_test_loader = DataLoader(novel_test_data, batch_size=64,
↪   shuffle=False)

# Initialize the VAE + Classifier
model = VAEClassifier(latent_dim=16, n_classes=10).to(device)
optimizer = optim.Adam(model.parameters(), lr=1e-3)

# Step A: Train on base classes
print("Training on base classes...")
epochs_base = 5
for epoch in range(epochs_base):
    train_loss = train_vae_classifier(model, base_train_loader,
↪       optimizer, device, alpha=1.0)
    acc, recon_loss = eval_vae_classifier(model,
↪       base_test_loader, device)
    print(f"Epoch [{epoch+1}/{epochs_base}] | Loss:
↪       {train_loss:.3f} | "
        f"Base Test Acc: {acc:.2f}% | Recon Loss:
↪           {recon_loss:.3f}")

# Step B: Fine-tune on novel classes (few-shot data)
print("\nFine-tuning on novel classes (digits 8,9)...")
fine_tune_on_few_shot(model, novel_few_shot_loader, optimizer,
↪   device, epochs=3, alpha=1.0)

# Evaluate on full novel test set
novel_acc, novel_recon = eval_vae_classifier(model,
↪   novel_test_loader, device)
print(f"Novel Classes Test Acc: {novel_acc:.2f}% | Recon Loss:
↪   {novel_recon:.3f}\n")

print("Few-shot adaptation complete!")

if __name__ == "__main__":
    main()
```

Key Implementation Details:

- **VAE Architecture:** In the above code, the encoder maps images to a latent distribution $(\mu, \log \sigma^2)$. The reparameterization trick ensures gradients pass correctly by sampling $z = \mu + \sigma \cdot \epsilon$.

- **Reconstruction + KL Loss:** We use a binary cross-entropy between the reconstructed image and the original, plus a KL term to regularize the latent space.

- **Classification Head:** A linear layer (logits) is applied on the latent vector z, enabling digit prediction. When labels exist, a cross-entropy loss is added to guide the latent embedding toward class-discriminative representations.

- **Data Partitioning:** We split MNIST into base classes (0–7) and novel classes (8–9), training the VAE primarily on base classes. Later, a few-shot subset of novel classes is used to fine-tune the same VAE quickly.

- **Few-Shot Adaptation:** The function `fine_tune_on_few_shot` further optimizes both reconstruction and classification terms on a small subset of examples from novel classes. This rapid fine-tuning demonstrates the VAE's capacity to adapt to new classes with minimal labeled data.

- **Evaluation:** We compute classification accuracy and reconstruction error on both base and novel classes to confirm the model's adaptability and representation quality.

Chapter 27

Graphical Models with VAE

We extend Variational Autoencoders (VAEs) to more traditional graphical models by mixing latent variable dependencies. The encoder essentially learns approximate posterior factors, while the decoder becomes a conditional likelihood. Implementation strategies include:

- Representing dependencies in a factor graph, such as a factorized prior $p(z_1)p(z_2| z_1)$.

- Leveraging library modules or custom code for structured variational inference.

- Adding constraints to the decoder or the prior for improved interpretability.

- Using hierarchical or factorized latents instead of a single monolithic latent space.

By forming a structured latent space, we can improve interpretability and handle more complex data than a purely feed-forward VAE.

Python Code Snippet

```
import torch
import torch.nn as nn
import torch.optim as optim
```

```python
import torch.nn.functional as F
from torch.utils.data import DataLoader
import torchvision
import torchvision.transforms as transforms
import matplotlib.pyplot as plt
import os
import random


# ------------------------------------------------------------
# 1) Set random seed for reproducibility
# ------------------------------------------------------------
def set_seed(seed=42):
    random.seed(seed)
    torch.manual_seed(seed)
    if torch.cuda.is_available():
        torch.cuda.manual_seed_all(seed)


# ------------------------------------------------------------
# 2) Reparameterization trick
# ------------------------------------------------------------
def reparameterize(mu, logvar):
    """
    Given a Normal distribution N(mu, sigma^2), we sample
    using z = mu + std * eps, where std = exp(0.5 * logvar)
    """
    std = torch.exp(0.5 * logvar)
    eps = torch.randn_like(std)
    return mu + eps * std


# ------------------------------------------------------------
# 3) Define small MLP blocks
# ------------------------------------------------------------
class MLP(nn.Module):
    """
    A simple feed-forward network that can be used
    for encoder or decoder layers.
    """
    def __init__(self, input_dim, hidden_dim, output_dim,
    ↪   num_hidden_layers=1):
        super(MLP, self).__init__()
        layers = []
        current_dim = input_dim
        for _ in range(num_hidden_layers):
            layers.append(nn.Linear(current_dim, hidden_dim))
            layers.append(nn.ReLU(True))
            current_dim = hidden_dim
        layers.append(nn.Linear(current_dim, output_dim))
        self.net = nn.Sequential(*layers)

    def forward(self, x):
        return self.net(x)


    # ------------------------------------------------------------
```

```python
# 4) Structured VAE model
# --------------------------------------------------------------
class StructuredVAE(nn.Module):
    """
    A VAE that factors the prior as p(z1) p(z2|z1).
    The encoder approximates q(z1|x) q(z2|x,z1).
    The decoder is p(x|z1,z2).
    """

    def __init__(self,
                 input_dim=784,
                 hidden_dim=256,
                 latent_dim1=8,
                 latent_dim2=8):
        super(StructuredVAE, self).__init__()

        self.latent_dim1 = latent_dim1
        self.latent_dim2 = latent_dim2

        # Encoder for z1 -> q(z1|x)
        # outputs [mu_z1, logvar_z1]
        self.encoder_z1 = MLP(input_dim, hidden_dim, 2*latent_dim1,
        ↪  num_hidden_layers=2)

        # Encoder for z2 -> q(z2|z1, x)
        # inputs are z1 plus x, so total dimension is latent_dim1 +
        ↪  input_dim
        self.encoder_z2 = MLP(latent_dim1 + input_dim, hidden_dim,
        ↪  2*latent_dim2, num_hidden_layers=2)

        # Prior net for z2 -> p(z2|z1)
        # inputs are z1, outputs [prior_mu_z2, prior_logvar_z2]
        self.prior_z2 = MLP(latent_dim1, hidden_dim, 2*latent_dim2,
        ↪  num_hidden_layers=2)

        # Decoder: p(x|z1,z2)
        # returns either logits or means for x
        # input dimension is latent_dim1 + latent_dim2
        self.decoder = MLP(latent_dim1 + latent_dim2, hidden_dim,
        ↪  input_dim, num_hidden_layers=2)

    def forward(self, x):
        """
        Forward pass used during training.
        Returns reconstruction and distribution parameters.
        """
        # Flatten the input x: (B, 1, 28, 28) -> (B, 784)
        x = x.view(x.size(0), -1)

        # 1) Encode to get q(z1|x)
        out_z1 = self.encoder_z1(x)
        mu_z1, logvar_z1 = torch.chunk(out_z1, chunks=2, dim=1)
        z1 = reparameterize(mu_z1, logvar_z1)
```

216

```python
        # 2) Encode to get q(z2|x,z1)
        concat_z1x = torch.cat([z1, x], dim=1)
        out_z2 = self.encoder_z2(concat_z1x)
        mu_z2, logvar_z2 = torch.chunk(out_z2, chunks=2, dim=1)
        z2 = reparameterize(mu_z2, logvar_z2)

        # 3) Prior for z2: p(z2|z1)
        prior_out = self.prior_z2(z1)
        prior_mu_z2, prior_logvar_z2 = torch.chunk(prior_out,
        ↪  chunks=2, dim=1)

        # 4) Decode to get p(x|z1,z2)
        concat_z = torch.cat([z1, z2], dim=1)
        x_recon_logits = self.decoder(concat_z)

        return (x_recon_logits,
                mu_z1, logvar_z1,
                mu_z2, logvar_z2,
                prior_mu_z2, prior_logvar_z2)

# ---------------------------------------------------------------
# 5) Define the losses
# ---------------------------------------------------------------
def kl_divergence_normal(mu_q, logvar_q, mu_p, logvar_p):
    """
    KL( q(z) || p(z) ) for diagonal Gaussians
    = 0.5 * sum( logvar_p - logvar_q +
                 (exp(logvar_q) + (mu_q - mu_p)^2) / exp(logvar_p) -
                 ↪  1 )
    """
    return 0.5 * torch.sum(
        logvar_p - logvar_q
        + (torch.exp(logvar_q) + (mu_q - mu_p)**2) /
        ↪  torch.exp(logvar_p)
        - 1,
        dim=1
    )


def structured_vae_loss(x,
                        x_recon_logits,
                        mu_z1, logvar_z1,
                        mu_z2, logvar_z2,
                        prior_mu_z2, prior_logvar_z2):
    """
    Computes the ELBO = - E_q[log p(x|z1,z2)] + KL(q(z1,z2|x) ||
    ↪  p(z1,z2))
    Factorized as:
      KL(q(z1|x) || p(z1)) + E_{q(z1|x)} [ KL( q(z2|x,z1) ||
      ↪  p(z2|z1) ) ]
    plus the reconstruction loss.
    """
    # Reconstruction (Bernoulli or cross-entropy from logits)
    # x is in [0,1], we used logit decoders
```

```python
    x = x.view(x.size(0), -1)
    recon_loss = F.binary_cross_entropy_with_logits(
        x_recon_logits, x, reduction='none'
    ).sum(dim=1)

    # KL for z1 ~ q(z1|x) vs p(z1)=N(0,I)
    mu_0 = torch.zeros_like(mu_z1)
    logvar_0 = torch.zeros_like(logvar_z1)
    kl_z1 = kl_divergence_normal(mu_z1, logvar_z1, mu_0, logvar_0)

    # KL for z2 ~ q(z2|x,z1) vs p(z2|z1)
    # We approximate E_{z1 ~ q(z1|x)} [ KL(...) ] by sampling one z1
    kl_z2 = kl_divergence_normal(mu_z2, logvar_z2, prior_mu_z2,
    ↪   prior_logvar_z2)

    # Sum all parts of the loss for the final objective
    total_kl = kl_z1 + kl_z2
    elbo = recon_loss + total_kl
    return elbo.mean()

# ----------------------------------------------------------------
# 6) Training and evaluation loops
# ----------------------------------------------------------------
def train_one_epoch(model, dataloader, optimizer, device):
    model.train()
    epoch_loss = 0
    for x, _ in dataloader:
        x = x.to(device)

        (x_recon_logits,
         mu_z1, logvar_z1,
         mu_z2, logvar_z2,
         prior_mu_z2, prior_logvar_z2) = model(x)

        loss = structured_vae_loss(x,
                                   x_recon_logits,
                                   mu_z1, logvar_z1,
                                   mu_z2, logvar_z2,
                                   prior_mu_z2, prior_logvar_z2)

        optimizer.zero_grad()
        loss.backward()
        optimizer.step()

        epoch_loss += loss.item()
    return epoch_loss / len(dataloader)

def evaluate_model(model, dataloader, device):
    model.eval()
    epoch_loss = 0
    with torch.no_grad():
        for x, _ in dataloader:
            x = x.to(device)
```

218

```
            (x_recon_logits,
             mu_z1, logvar_z1,
             mu_z2, logvar_z2,
             prior_mu_z2, prior_logvar_z2) = model(x)

            loss = structured_vae_loss(x,
                                       x_recon_logits,
                                       mu_z1, logvar_z1,
                                       mu_z2, logvar_z2,
                                       prior_mu_z2, prior_logvar_z2)
            epoch_loss += loss.item()
    return epoch_loss / len(dataloader)

def sample_from_model(model, device, num_samples=16):
    """
    Sample from the factorized prior p(z1), p(z2|z1),
    and generate new images from p(x|z1,z2).
    """
    model.eval()
    with torch.no_grad():
        # p(z1) = N(0, I)
        z1 = torch.randn(num_samples, model.latent_dim1,
        ↪   device=device)

        # p(z2|z1) -> get mu_z2, logvar_z2 from prior_net
        prior_out = model.prior_z2(z1)
        prior_mu_z2, prior_logvar_z2 = torch.chunk(prior_out,
        ↪   chunks=2, dim=1)
        z2 = reparameterize(prior_mu_z2, prior_logvar_z2)

        # Decode
        concat_z = torch.cat([z1, z2], dim=1)
        x_recon_logits = model.decoder(concat_z)
        x_recon = torch.sigmoid(x_recon_logits)  # in [0,1]
        return x_recon

def save_samples(samples, epoch):
    """
    Save a grid of generated samples to
    ↪   "results/sample_epoch_{epoch}.png".
    """
    os.makedirs("results", exist_ok=True)
    samples = samples.view(-1, 1, 28, 28).cpu()
    grid_img = torchvision.utils.make_grid(samples, nrow=4)
    plt.figure(figsize=(4,4))
    plt.imshow(grid_img.permute(1, 2, 0).numpy(), cmap='gray')
    plt.axis('off')
    plt.savefig(f"results/sample_epoch_{epoch}.png")
    plt.close()

# ------------------------------------------------------------------
# 7) Main function
# ------------------------------------------------------------------
```

```python
def main():
    set_seed(42)
    device = torch.device("cuda" if torch.cuda.is_available() else
    ↪  "cpu")

    # Load MNIST
    transform = transforms.Compose([
        transforms.ToTensor()
    ])
    train_dataset = torchvision.datasets.MNIST(root='data',
                                               train=True,
                                               download=True,
                                               transform=transform)
    test_dataset = torchvision.datasets.MNIST(root='data',
                                              train=False,
                                              download=True,
                                              transform=transform)
    train_loader = DataLoader(train_dataset, batch_size=64,
    ↪  shuffle=True)
    test_loader = DataLoader(test_dataset, batch_size=64,
    ↪  shuffle=False)

    # Initialize model
    model = StructuredVAE(input_dim=784, hidden_dim=256,
    ↪  latent_dim1=8, latent_dim2=8)
    model.to(device)

    # Optimizer
    optimizer = optim.Adam(model.parameters(), lr=1e-3)

    # Training
    epochs = 5
    for epoch in range(epochs):
        train_loss = train_one_epoch(model, train_loader, optimizer,
        ↪  device)
        val_loss = evaluate_model(model, test_loader, device)
        print(f"Epoch [{epoch+1}/{epochs}] - Train Loss:
        ↪  {train_loss:.4f}, Val Loss: {val_loss:.4f}")

        # Sample new images from the prior
        samples = sample_from_model(model, device, num_samples=16)
        save_samples(samples, epoch)

    print("Training finished! Check the 'results' folder for
    ↪  generated samples.")

if __name__ == "__main__":
    main()
```

Key Implementation Details:

- **Factorized Prior:** We define p(z_1) as a standard Normal, and p($z\_2 \mid z\_1$) by a small neural network (`prior_z2`) mapping z_1 to a mean and log-variance.

- **Approximate Posterior:** The encoder splits into two parts: `encoder_z1` to estimate q($z\_1 \mid x$), and `encoder_z2` that uses both x and sampled z_1 to produce q($z\_2 \mid x, z\_1$).

- **Decoder:** `decoder` models p($x \mid z\_1, z\_2$) by mapping the concatenated latents back to a flattened image representation. A standard sigmoid or Bernoulli observation model can then be applied.

- **ELBO Computation:** The loss combines reconstruction error with the sum of KL divergences: KL(q($z\_1 \mid x$) $\|$ p(z_1)) + E$\_q$($z\_1 \mid x$)[KL(q($z\_2 \mid x, z\_1$) $\|$ p($z\_2 \mid z\_1$))].

- **Sampling:** To generate new samples, we first draw $z\_1 \sim \mathcal{N}(0, I)$, then $z\_2 \sim p(z\_2 \mid z\_1)$, and finally decode to get $\hat{x}$.

- **Interpretability:** This factorized approach can yield more interpretable latent variables and accommodates scenarios where hierarchical or conditional structures are important for data modeling.

Chapter 28

Probabilistic Reasoning with VAE

In this chapter, we treat the Variational Autoencoder (VAE) as a framework for Bayesian inference and reasoning under uncertainty. We demonstrate how to:

- Incorporate additional latent variables to encode prior beliefs or domain constraints.

- Interpret the latent space as a distribution over possible outcomes and use it for posterior inference.

- Leverage a probabilistic programming library to automatically differentiate the Evidence Lower Bound (ELBO).

- Diagnose model convergence and perform posterior predictive checks.

We rely on PyTorch and Pyro to implement a VAE on a toy version of the MNIST dataset. The key modifications include adding an additional positively constrained latent variable for demonstration of domain constraints. You'll observe how this latent variable can be viewed as encoding prior knowledge about the generation process.

Python Code Snippet

```
import os
import torch
```

```python
import torch.nn as nn
import torch.nn.functional as F
from torch.utils.data import DataLoader
from torchvision.datasets import MNIST
import torchvision.transforms as transforms

# Pyro for probabilistic modeling
import pyro
import pyro.distributions as dist
from pyro.infer import SVI, Trace_ELBO
from pyro.optim import ClippedAdam


# ------------------------------------------------------------
# 1) Utilities: Setting seeds and preparing data
# ------------------------------------------------------------
def set_seed(seed=42):
    """
    Set random seeds for reproducibility.
    """
    torch.manual_seed(seed)
    pyro.set_rng_seed(seed)
    if torch.cuda.is_available():
        torch.cuda.manual_seed(seed)


def get_data_loaders(batch_size=64):
    """
    Download and prepare MNIST data loaders.
    """
    transform = transforms.Compose([
        transforms.ToTensor(),
        transforms.Normalize((0.1307,), (0.3081,))
    ])
    train_dataset = MNIST(root="data", train=True, download=True,
    ↪    transform=transform)
    test_dataset  = MNIST(root="data", train=False, download=True,
    ↪    transform=transform)

    train_loader = DataLoader(train_dataset, batch_size=batch_size,
    ↪    shuffle=True)
    test_loader  = DataLoader(test_dataset,  batch_size=batch_size,
    ↪    shuffle=False)
    return train_loader, test_loader


# ------------------------------------------------------------
# 2) Define an MLP encoder and decoder
# ------------------------------------------------------------
class EncoderNet(nn.Module):
    """
    Approximate posterior (encoder) network:
    Transforms an input image into distributions over latent
    ↪    variables.
    """
    def __init__(self, hidden_size=400, z_dim=20):
```

```python
        super(EncoderNet, self).__init__()
        self.fc1 = nn.Linear(28*28, hidden_size)
        self.fc2 = nn.Linear(hidden_size, hidden_size)

        # Mean and scale for main latent z
        self.z_loc = nn.Linear(hidden_size, z_dim)
        self.z_scale = nn.Linear(hidden_size, z_dim)

        # Mean and scale for additional positively constrained
        ↪ latent z_pos
        self.z_pos_loc = nn.Linear(hidden_size, 1)
        self.z_pos_scale = nn.Linear(hidden_size, 1)

        self.relu = nn.ReLU()

    def forward(self, x):
        x = x.view(-1, 28*28)  # Flatten
        h = self.relu(self.fc1(x))
        h = self.relu(self.fc2(h))

        loc = self.z_loc(h)
        scale = F.softplus(self.z_scale(h)) + 1e-7  # ensure
        ↪ positivity

        loc_pos = self.z_pos_loc(h)
        scale_pos = F.softplus(self.z_pos_scale(h)) + 1e-7

        return loc, scale, loc_pos, scale_pos

class DecoderNet(nn.Module):
    """
    Likelihood (decoder) network:
    Takes latent variables and reconstructs images via Bernoulli or
    ↪ similar distribution.
    """
    def __init__(self, hidden_size=400, z_dim=20):
        super(DecoderNet, self).__init__()
        self.fc1 = nn.Linear(z_dim + 1, hidden_size)
        self.fc2 = nn.Linear(hidden_size, hidden_size)
        self.fc3 = nn.Linear(hidden_size, 28*28)
        self.relu = nn.ReLU()

    def forward(self, z, z_pos):
        """
        z: main latent (B, z_dim)
        z_pos: additional positively constrained latent (B, 1)
        """
        # Concatenate both latents
        combined = torch.cat([z, z_pos], dim=-1)
        h = self.relu(self.fc1(combined))
        h = self.relu(self.fc2(h))
        logits = self.fc3(h)
        return logits
```

224

```python
# ------------------------------------------------------------
# 3) The VAE model and guide in Pyro
# ------------------------------------------------------------
class VAE(nn.Module):
    """
    A VAE that uses an approximate posterior network (encoder)
    and a likelihood network (decoder). Incorporates an additional
    latent variable with constraints as a demonstration of
    domain knowledge or prior beliefs.
    """
    def __init__(self, z_dim=20, hidden_size=400):
        super(VAE, self).__init__()
        self.z_dim = z_dim
        self.encoder = EncoderNet(hidden_size, z_dim)
        self.decoder = DecoderNet(hidden_size, z_dim)

    def model(self, x):
        """
        p(x, z, z_pos) = p(z, z_pos) p(x|z, z_pos).

        z ~ Normal(0,1),
        z_pos ~ LogNormal(0,1)   (positive constraint),
        x ~ Bernoulli(decoder(z, z_pos)).
        """
        pyro.module("decoder", self.decoder)
        batch_size = x.size(0)

        # Prior for main latent z
        with pyro.plate("data_plate", batch_size):
            z = pyro.sample("z",
                        dist.Normal(torch.zeros([batch_size,
                        ↪ self.z_dim]).to(x.device),
                                    torch.ones([batch_size,
                                    ↪ self.z_dim]).to(x.device))
                        .to_event(1))

            # Prior for z_pos (for domain constraint, positivity)
            z_pos = pyro.sample("z_pos",
            dist.LogNormal(torch.zeros([batch_size,1]).to(x.device),
                        torch.ones([batch_size,1]).to(x.device))
            .to_event(1))

            # Decoder forward pass
            logits = self.decoder(z, z_pos).view(-1, 28*28)

            # Likelihood using Bernoulli (for normalized MNIST)
            pyro.sample("obs",
            ↪ dist.Bernoulli(logits=logits).to_event(1),
            ↪ obs=x.view(-1, 28*28))

    def guide(self, x):
        """
```

```
        q(z, z_pos | x) = Normal(z_loc, z_scale^2) *
        ↪  LogNormal(z_pos_loc, z_pos_scale^2).
        Both are learned distributions from the encoder.
        """

        pyro.module("encoder", self.encoder)
        batch_size = x.size(0)

        with pyro.plate("data_plate", batch_size):
            z_loc, z_scale, z_pos_loc, z_pos_scale = self.encoder(x)

            z = pyro.sample("z",
                            dist.Normal(z_loc, z_scale)
                            .to_event(1))

            # Additional latent with positivity constraint
            pyro.sample("z_pos",
                        dist.LogNormal(z_pos_loc, z_pos_scale)
                        .to_event(1))

# -----------------------------------------------------------
# 4) Training loop with Pyro SVI
# -----------------------------------------------------------
def train_epoch(data_loader, vae, svi, device):
    """
    Single epoch over the training dataset.
    """
    epoch_loss = 0.0
    vae.train()
    for x, _ in data_loader:
        x = x.to(device)
        loss = svi.step(x)
        epoch_loss += loss
    return epoch_loss / len(data_loader.dataset)

def evaluate(data_loader, vae, svi, device):
    """
    Evaluate on held-out data by computing the ELBO.
    """
    total_loss = 0.0
    vae.eval()
    with torch.no_grad():
        for x, _ in data_loader:
            x = x.to(device)
            loss = svi.evaluate_loss(x)
            total_loss += loss
    return total_loss / len(data_loader.dataset)

def posterior_predictive_check(vae, data_loader, device):
    """
    Simple demonstration of how to do a posterior predictive check.
    We do a forward sample of z, z_pos, then decode, and compare
    reconstruction visually or via aggregated errors.
    """
```

```
    vae.eval()
    x_batch, _ = next(iter(data_loader))
    x_batch = x_batch.to(device)

    # Sample from posterior (approx) given x
    with torch.no_grad(), pyro.plate("data_plate", x_batch.size(0)):
        # Encode
        z_loc, z_scale, z_pos_loc, z_pos_scale =
        ↪   vae.encoder(x_batch)
        z_post = dist.Normal(z_loc, z_scale).sample()
        z_pos_post = dist.LogNormal(z_pos_loc, z_pos_scale).sample()

        # Decode
        logits = vae.decoder(z_post, z_pos_post)
        probs = torch.sigmoid(logits)

    # Evaluate a simple reconstruction difference
    recon = probs.view(-1, 1, 28, 28)
    recon_error = (recon - x_batch).abs().mean().item()
    print(f"Posterior predictive check - average reconstruction L1
    ↪   error: {recon_error:.4f}")

# ------------------------------------------------------------
# 5) Main function: put it all together
# ------------------------------------------------------------
def main():
    set_seed(42)
    device = torch.device("cuda" if torch.cuda.is_available() else
    ↪   "cpu")

    # Data
    train_loader, test_loader = get_data_loaders(batch_size=64)

    # Create VAE
    z_dim = 20
    vae = VAE(z_dim=z_dim).to(device)

    # Setup optimizer
    pyro.clear_param_store()
    optimizer = ClippedAdam({"lr": 1e-3, "clip_norm": 10.0})

    # SVI with ELBO
    svi = SVI(model=vae.model,
              guide=vae.guide,
              optim=optimizer,
              loss=Trace_ELBO())

    # Train for a few epochs
    num_epochs = 5
    for epoch in range(num_epochs):
        train_loss = train_epoch(train_loader, vae, svi, device)
        val_loss = evaluate(test_loader, vae, svi, device)
```

```
print(f"Epoch [{epoch+1}/{num_epochs}] - Train ELBO:
↪  {train_loss:.4f}, Val ELBO: {val_loss:.4f}")

# Posterior predictive check after each epoch (simple
↪   demonstration)
posterior_predictive_check(vae, test_loader, device)

print("Training complete! You can use the model for sampling or
↪   further inference.")

if __name__ == "__main__":
    main()
```

Key Implementation Details:

- **Model Definition:** The `model` imposes priors on both `z` (a standard normal) and `z_pos` (a log-normal distribution) to illustrate how domain constraints or prior beliefs can be encoded.

- **Guide (Encoder):** Within `guide`, the encoder network outputs the parameters of approximate posteriors for both latent variables, allowing efficient amortized inference.

- **ELBO Optimization:** We employ Pyro's `SVI` to minimize the ELBO, ensuring that both the decoder likelihood and KL terms are learned end-to-end.

- **Domain Constraints:** By using `LogNormal` for `z_pos`, we model a latent variable constrained to be positive—mimicking a scenario where domain knowledge restricts possible values.

- **Posterior Predictive Checks:** The function `posterior_predictive_check` demonstrates how to draw samples from the approximate posterior and visualize or compute reconstruction errors, a key practice in Bayesian reasoning.

- **Implementation Practicalities:**
    - We rely on `pyro.module` to register parameters within Pyro's scope.
    - `ClippedAdam` helps stabilize training by bounding large gradients.

- The model can be extended to other distributions, architectures, or domain-specific constraints without altering the core inference procedure.

Chapter 29

VAE for Bayesian Optimization

We apply a VAE to represent a design space for global optimization tasks (e.g., molecule design or hyperparameter tuning). By sampling from the latent space and decoding candidates, we can explore new solutions. We demonstrate constructing a combined approach with a surrogate model (like Gaussian Processes) that guides sampling toward promising regions in latent space. Practical code snippets highlight how to train the VAE, incorporate acquisition functions, and iterate the cycle of propose-evaluate-update to find optimum solutions efficiently. In summary, our approach follows these main steps:

- Train a Variational Autoencoder (VAE) on existing samples to encode them into a latent space and decode them back to the original design space.

- Fit a surrogate model (e.g., a Gaussian Process) on the latent codes and their objective (or reward) scores.

- Use an acquisition function to select promising latent points given the surrogate model's predictions.

- Decode candidate latent points back to the original design space, evaluate them, and incorporate the new data into subsequent iterations.

Python Code Snippet

```python
import torch
import torch.nn as nn
import torch.optim as optim
from torch.utils.data import DataLoader, TensorDataset
import numpy as np

# For the surrogate model
from sklearn.gaussian_process import GaussianProcessRegressor
from sklearn.gaussian_process.kernels import Matern

# Set a random seed for reproducibility
def set_seed(seed=123):
    np.random.seed(seed)
    torch.manual_seed(seed)


# ---------------------------------------------------------------
# 1) Define a simple toy objective function to optimize
# ---------------------------------------------------------------
def toy_objective_function(x):
    """
    A simple 2D function with a global minimum or maximum.
    x is assumed to be shape [N, 2], each row is a design.
    This function returns shape [N,].
    You can replace this with a more complex domain-specific
    ↪ function.
    """
    # Example: a shifted, scaled "Rastrigin-like" function
    # Just for demonstration. Lower is "better" in this toy example.
    A = 10
    return A * 2 + (x[:, 0]**2 - A * torch.cos(2 * np.pi * x[:, 0]))
    ↪ \
            + (x[:, 1]**2 - A * torch.cos(2 * np.pi * x[:, 1]))


# ---------------------------------------------------------------
# 2) Create VAE architecture
# ---------------------------------------------------------------
class VAE(nn.Module):
    """
    A simple VAE with a 2D input space and a latent dimension
    ↪ (z_dim).
    The encoder and decoder are small MLPs.
    """

    def __init__(self, input_dim=2, z_dim=2, hidden_dim=64):
        super().__init__()
        # Encoder
        self.encoder = nn.Sequential(
            nn.Linear(input_dim, hidden_dim),
            nn.ReLU(),
            nn.Linear(hidden_dim, hidden_dim),
            nn.ReLU()
```

```python
    )
    # Latent space parameters
    self.fc_mu = nn.Linear(hidden_dim, z_dim)
    self.fc_var = nn.Linear(hidden_dim, z_dim)

    # Decoder
    self.decoder = nn.Sequential(
        nn.Linear(z_dim, hidden_dim),
        nn.ReLU(),
        nn.Linear(hidden_dim, hidden_dim),
        nn.ReLU(),
        nn.Linear(hidden_dim, input_dim)
    )

def encode(self, x):
    """ Encodes x into the latent distribution parameters (mu,
    ↪   log_var). """
    h = self.encoder(x)
    mu = self.fc_mu(h)
    log_var = self.fc_var(h)
    return mu, log_var

def reparameterize(self, mu, log_var):
    """ Reparameterization trick to sample z from N(mu,
    ↪   sigma^2). """
    std = torch.exp(0.5 * log_var)
    eps = torch.randn_like(std)
    return mu + eps * std

def decode(self, z):
    """ Decodes latent variable z back to original space. """
    return self.decoder(z)

def forward(self, x):
    """ Full VAE forward: encode -> reparameterize -> decode.
    ↪      """
    mu, log_var = self.encode(x)
    z = self.reparameterize(mu, log_var)
    x_recon = self.decode(z)
    return x_recon, mu, log_var

def vae_loss_function(x, x_recon, mu, log_var):
    """
    The standard VAE loss = reconstruction loss + KL divergence.
    Here we use MSE as the reconstruction term.
    """
    recon_loss = nn.functional.mse_loss(x_recon, x, reduction='sum')
    # KL divergence: D_KL(q(z|x) || p(z)) = 0.5 * sum(1 + log_var -
    ↪   mu^2 - exp(log_var))
    kl_loss = 0.5 * torch.sum(log_var.exp() + mu**2 - 1.0 - log_var)
    return (recon_loss + kl_loss) / x.size(0)

# ----------------------------------------------------------------
```

```python
# 3) Train the VAE on available data
# ----------------------------------------------------------------
def train_vae(model, data, epochs=100, batch_size=32, lr=1e-3):
    """
    Train the VAE on a given dataset (data: torch.Tensor shape
    ↪   [N,2]).
    This function returns the trained model.
    """
    dataset = TensorDataset(data)
    dataloader = DataLoader(dataset, batch_size=batch_size,
    ↪   shuffle=True)

    optimizer = optim.Adam(model.parameters(), lr=lr)
    model.train()
    for epoch in range(epochs):
        total_loss = 0.0
        for (batch_x,) in dataloader:
            batch_x = batch_x
            optimizer.zero_grad()
            x_recon, mu, log_var = model(batch_x)
            loss = vae_loss_function(batch_x, x_recon, mu, log_var)
            loss.backward()
            optimizer.step()
            total_loss += loss.item()
        if (epoch+1) % 20 == 0:
            print(f"Epoch {epoch+1}/{epochs}, Loss:
            ↪   {total_loss/len(dataloader):.4f}")
    return model


# ----------------------------------------------------------------
# 4) Train or update the GP on the encoded data
# ----------------------------------------------------------------
def train_gp(latent_z, scores):
    """
    Trains a Gaussian Process regressor using the latent points
    ↪   'latent_z' as input
    and the 'scores' as the target. Returns the trained model.
    """
    # Convert to numpy for sklearn
    X = latent_z.detach().cpu().numpy()
    y = scores.detach().cpu().numpy()

    kernel = Matern(nu=2.5)
    gp = GaussianProcessRegressor(kernel=kernel, alpha=1e-3,
    ↪   normalize_y=True)
    gp.fit(X, y)
    return gp


# ----------------------------------------------------------------
# 5) Acquisition function: Expected Improvement (simplified)
# ----------------------------------------------------------------
def acquisition_ei(latent_candidates, gp, best_score):
    """
```

```python
    Compute a simplified Expected Improvement.
    latent_candidates: torch.Tensor shape [M, z_dim]
    best_score: float or scalar Tensor specifying the best known
    ↪ score so far (lower is better).
    """
    # Convert to numpy
    Xc = latent_candidates.detach().cpu().numpy()

    # The GP predictor returns mean and std
    mean, std = gp.predict(Xc, return_std=True)
    std = np.clip(std, 1e-9, None)  # avoid division by zero
    improvement = best_score - mean  # since lower is better in toy
    ↪ example
    Z = improvement / std
    from scipy.stats import norm
    ei = improvement * norm.cdf(Z) + std * norm.pdf(Z)
    ei[std < 1e-9] = 0.0
    return ei


# ----------------------------------------------------------------
# 6) Propose-evaluate-update loop
# ----------------------------------------------------------------
def propose_new_point(model, gp, z_dim=2, n_candidates=1000,
↪ best_score=None):
    """
    Sample random points in the latent space, evaluate the EI,
    and pick the best candidate in terms of highest EI.
    """
    latents = torch.randn(n_candidates, z_dim)
    ei_vals = acquisition_ei(latents, gp, best_score)
    idx_best = np.argmax(ei_vals)
    return latents[idx_best]


def decode_and_evaluate(model, latent_point):
    """
    Decode the latent point to original space, evaluate the
    ↪ objective.
    """
    with torch.no_grad():
        design = model.decode(latent_point.unsqueeze(0))
        fx = toy_objective_function(design).item()
    return design.squeeze(0), fx


# ----------------------------------------------------------------
# 7) Main demonstration
# ----------------------------------------------------------------
def main():
    set_seed(123)

    # ----------------------------------------------------------------
    # Generate initial data from random samples in [-2, 2]
    # ----------------------------------------------------------------
    N_init = 20
```

```
X_init = -2 + 4 * torch.rand(N_init, 2)   # shape [20,2]
y_init = toy_objective_function(X_init)

# We treat lower y as "better" for this demonstration
best_score = y_init.min().item()
print("Initial best score:", best_score)

# --------------------------------------------------------------
# Create and train VAE on initial data
# --------------------------------------------------------------
vae_model = VAE(input_dim=2, z_dim=2, hidden_dim=64)
vae_model = train_vae(vae_model, X_init, epochs=100,
 ↪ batch_size=10, lr=1e-3)

# Encode X_init to latent space
with torch.no_grad():
    mu, log_var = vae_model.encode(X_init)
    z_init = mu  # use mean as latent representation

# --------------------------------------------------------------
# Train GP on the latent codes
# --------------------------------------------------------------
gp_model = train_gp(z_init, y_init)

# --------------------------------------------------------------
# Optimization loop
# --------------------------------------------------------------
n_iter = 10  # number of BO iterations
all_X = [X_init]
all_y = [y_init]

for i in range(n_iter):
    # Propose new latent point
    new_latent = propose_new_point(vae_model, gp_model, z_dim=2,
     ↪ best_score=best_score)

    # Decode to original space, evaluate objective
    x_new, y_new = decode_and_evaluate(vae_model, new_latent)

    # Update dataset
    X_curr = torch.cat([all_X[-1], x_new.unsqueeze(0)], dim=0)
    y_curr = torch.cat([all_y[-1], torch.tensor([y_new])],
     ↪ dim=0)

    best_score = min(best_score, y_new)
    print(f"Iteration {i+1}/{n_iter}, Proposed
     ↪ X={x_new.numpy()}, f(X)={y_new:.4f}, Best
     ↪ Score={best_score:.4f}")

    # Retrain VAE with updated dataset
    vae_model = train_vae(vae_model, X_curr, epochs=50,
     ↪ batch_size=10, lr=1e-3)
```

```
# Encode new dataset into latent space
with torch.no_grad():
    mu, _ = vae_model.encode(X_curr)
    Z_new = mu

# Retrain GP
gp_model = train_gp(Z_new, y_curr)

# Store for next iteration
all_X.append(X_curr)
all_y.append(y_curr)

if __name__ == "__main__":
    main()
```

Key Implementation Details:

- **Variational Autoencoder Layout:** The VAE class includes
  an encoder that outputs distribution parameters (mu, log_var)
  and a decoder that reconstructs from a sampled latent vector.

- **Reparameterization Trick:** reparameterize adds nor-
  mally distributed noise to mu scaled by std to allow gradient
  flow through the sampling process.

- **Loss Computation:** vae_loss_function balances an MSE
  reconstruction error with the KL divergence to maintain a
  smooth latent space.

- **GP Surrogate Model:** train_gp uses latent representations and their scores to fit a GaussianProcessRegressor; we
  employ the Matern kernel for flexibility.

- **Acquisition Function (EI):** acquisition_ei calculates ex-
  pected improvement based on GP predictions. Higher values
  suggest more promising latent directions.

- **Propose-Evaluate-Update Loop:** propose_new_point samples latent points and selects the one with maximal EI. The
  chosen latent is decoded back to original space, evaluated,
  and appended to the training set. The VAE and GP are then
  retrained, continuing the global optimization cycle.

Chapter 30

Mixture-of-Experts VAE

Mixture-of-Experts VAEs use multiple encoder and decoder pairs (experts) to better model diverse datasets. We combine expert outputs by weighting their contribution to the latent distribution or reconstruction. This chapter shows how to organize your code into separate sub-encoders, unify their latent distributions, and train the decoders to produce ensemble outputs. We discuss advanced weighting schemes and specialized loss terms for gating. By harnessing multiple experts, your model can better handle complex, multimodal data domains.

In summary:

- We define multiple encoder-decoder pairs, each one acting as an expert for the data.

- A gating network outputs a set of mixture weights for each input, indicating which expert should dominate for that sample.

- Latent codes from these experts are combined (in this example, via a weighted sum) to form a single VAE-style representation.

- The decoders also combine their results based on the gating weights to produce a final reconstruction.

Python Code Snippet

```python
import torch
import torch.nn as nn
import torch.optim as optim
from torch.utils.data import DataLoader
import torchvision
import torchvision.transforms as transforms


# --------------------------------------------------------------
# 1) Hyperparameters and Setup
# --------------------------------------------------------------
BATCH_SIZE = 64
EPOCHS = 5
LATENT_DIM = 20
N_EXPERTS = 2   # Number of mixture experts
HIDDEN_DIM = 400
LEARNING_RATE = 1e-3

device = torch.device("cuda" if torch.cuda.is_available() else
↪    "cpu")


# --------------------------------------------------------------
# 2) Data Loading (MNIST)
#     We'll use a simple MLP approach on flattened images.
# --------------------------------------------------------------
transform = transforms.Compose([
    transforms.ToTensor(),
    # Convert values from [0,1] range to [-1,1] for stability
    transforms.Normalize((0.5,), (0.5,))
])

train_dataset = torchvision.datasets.MNIST(
    root="./data",
    train=True,
    download=True,
    transform=transform
)
test_dataset = torchvision.datasets.MNIST(
    root="./data",
    train=False,
    download=True,
    transform=transform
)

train_loader = DataLoader(train_dataset, batch_size=BATCH_SIZE,
↪    shuffle=True)
test_loader = DataLoader(test_dataset, batch_size=BATCH_SIZE,
↪    shuffle=False)

INPUT_DIM = 28 * 28   # Flattened MNIST images
```

```python
# ----------------------------------------------------------------
# 3) Define the gating network
#     This small MLP outputs logits of size N_EXPERTS, then
#     we use softmax to get mixture weights for each sample.
# ----------------------------------------------------------------
class GatingNetwork(nn.Module):
    def __init__(self, input_dim=INPUT_DIM, hidden_dim=128,
    ↪ n_experts=N_EXPERTS):
        super(GatingNetwork, self).__init__()
        self.net = nn.Sequential(
            nn.Linear(input_dim, hidden_dim),
            nn.ReLU(),
            nn.Linear(hidden_dim, n_experts)
        )
        self.softmax = nn.Softmax(dim=1)

    def forward(self, x):
        # x shape: (batch_size, input_dim)
        logits = self.net(x)
        weights = self.softmax(logits)  # shape: (batch_size,
        ↪ n_experts)
        return weights


# ----------------------------------------------------------------
# 4) Define a single Expert Encoder
#     Each expert outputs a (mu, logvar) for the latent space.
# ----------------------------------------------------------------
class ExpertEncoder(nn.Module):
    def __init__(self, input_dim=INPUT_DIM, hidden_dim=HIDDEN_DIM,
    ↪ latent_dim=LATENT_DIM):
        super(ExpertEncoder, self).__init__()
        self.fc_mu = nn.Sequential(
            nn.Linear(input_dim, hidden_dim),
            nn.ReLU(),
            nn.Linear(hidden_dim, latent_dim)
        )
        self.fc_logvar = nn.Sequential(
            nn.Linear(input_dim, hidden_dim),
            nn.ReLU(),
            nn.Linear(hidden_dim, latent_dim)
        )

    def forward(self, x):
        # x shape: (batch_size, input_dim)
        mu = self.fc_mu(x)
        logvar = self.fc_logvar(x)
        return mu, logvar


# ----------------------------------------------------------------
# 5) Define a single Expert Decoder
#     Each expert decodes from latent_dim back to input_dim.
# ----------------------------------------------------------------
class ExpertDecoder(nn.Module):
```

```python
    def __init__(self, latent_dim=LATENT_DIM, hidden_dim=HIDDEN_DIM,
    ↪  output_dim=INPUT_DIM):
        super(ExpertDecoder, self).__init__()
        self.net = nn.Sequential(
            nn.Linear(latent_dim, hidden_dim),
            nn.ReLU(),
            nn.Linear(hidden_dim, output_dim),
            nn.Tanh()  # outputs roughly in [-1, 1]
        )

    def forward(self, z):
        # z shape: (batch_size, latent_dim)
        return self.net(z)

# -------------------------------------------------------------
# 6) Mixture-of-Experts VAE
#    - We hold N_EXPERTS encoders and N_EXPERTS decoders.
#    - The gating network provides mixture weights.
#    - We'll create a weighted latent code & reconstruction.
# -------------------------------------------------------------
class MoEVAE(nn.Module):
    def __init__(self, n_experts=N_EXPERTS, input_dim=INPUT_DIM,
    ↪  latent_dim=LATENT_DIM, hidden_dim=HIDDEN_DIM):
        super(MoEVAE, self).__init__()
        self.n_experts = n_experts

        # Create a list of encoders and decoders
        self.encoders = nn.ModuleList([
            ExpertEncoder(input_dim, hidden_dim, latent_dim) for _
            ↪  in range(n_experts)
        ])
        self.decoders = nn.ModuleList([
            ExpertDecoder(latent_dim, hidden_dim, input_dim) for _
            ↪  in range(n_experts)
        ])

        # Gating network
        self.gating_net = GatingNetwork(input_dim, 128, n_experts)

    def reparameterize(self, mu, logvar):
        # Standard reparameterization trick
        std = torch.exp(0.5 * logvar)
        eps = torch.randn_like(std)
        return mu + eps * std

    def forward(self, x):
        """
        x: shape (batch_size, input_dim)
        Returns:
          recon: the mixture reconstruction
          mus: list of mu for each expert
          logvars: list of logvar for each expert
          w: mixture weights for each sample
```

```python
    """
    # Get gating weights: w has shape (batch_size, n_experts)
    w = self.gating_net(x)

    # Collect each expert's mean & logvar
    mus = []
    logvars = []
    zs = []
    recons = []

    for i in range(self.n_experts):
        mu_i, logvar_i = self.encoders[i](x)
        z_i = self.reparameterize(mu_i, logvar_i)
        recon_i = self.decoders[i](z_i)
        mus.append(mu_i)
        logvars.append(logvar_i)
        zs.append(z_i)
        recons.append(recon_i)

    # Weighted combination of reconstructions
    # recons[i] shape: (batch_size, input_dim)
    # w shape: (batch_size, n_experts)
    # We'll do a per-sample weighting:
    # final_recon[k] = sum_i (w[k, i] * recons[i][k])

    # Stack recons into (batch_size, n_experts, input_dim)
    recons_stacked = torch.stack(recons, dim=1)
    # recons_stacked shape: (batch_size, n_experts, input_dim)
    # w needs to broadcast to match
    w_3d = w.unsqueeze(-1)   # shape: (batch_size, n_experts, 1)
    recon = (recons_stacked * w_3d).sum(dim=1)   # shape:
    ↪  (batch_size, input_dim)

    return recon, mus, logvars, w

# ----------------------------------------------------------------
# 7) Loss Function for MoEVAE
#    We'll treat the final reconstruction as a mixture and
#    the KL as a weighted average of the experts' KL terms.
#    Simple MSE reconstruction, plus standard VAE KL.
# ----------------------------------------------------------------
def moe_vae_loss(x, recon, mus, logvars, w):
    """
    x: (batch_size, input_dim)
    recon: (batch_size, input_dim)
    mus, logvars: lists of length n_experts
    w: mixture weights (batch_size, n_experts)
    """
    batch_size = x.size(0)

    # Reconstruction loss (MSE)
    recon_loss = nn.functional.mse_loss(recon, x, reduction="sum") /
    ↪  batch_size
```

241

```python
# Weighted sum of KL for each expert:
# KL_i(x) = -0.5 * sum(1 + logvar_i - mu_i^2 - exp(logvar_i))
# We'll multiply each KL_i by the gating weight w_i for each
↪    sample
# and take an average across the batch.
kl_total = 0.0
for i in range(len(mus)):
    mu_i = mus[i]
    logvar_i = logvars[i]

    kl_i = -0.5 * torch.sum(1 + logvar_i - mu_i.pow(2) -
↪        logvar_i.exp(), dim=1)
    # kl_i shape: (batch_size,)

    # Weighted by w[:, i]
    kl_i_weighted = w[:, i] * kl_i
    kl_total += kl_i_weighted.mean()

loss = recon_loss + kl_total
return loss, recon_loss, kl_total


# ------------------------------------------------------------
# 8) Training and Testing Routines
# ------------------------------------------------------------
def train_one_epoch(model, optimizer, dataloader):
    model.train()
    total_loss = 0.0
    total_recon_loss = 0.0
    total_kl_loss = 0.0
    for batch, (images, _) in enumerate(dataloader):
        # Flatten images
        images = images.view(-1, INPUT_DIM).to(device)

        optimizer.zero_grad()

        recon, mus, logvars, w = model(images)
        loss, recon_loss, kl_loss = moe_vae_loss(images, recon, mus,
↪            logvars, w)

        loss.backward()
        optimizer.step()

        total_loss += loss.item()
        total_recon_loss += recon_loss.item()
        total_kl_loss += kl_loss.item()

    avg_loss = total_loss / len(dataloader)
    avg_recon = total_recon_loss / len(dataloader)
    avg_kl = total_kl_loss / len(dataloader)
    return avg_loss, avg_recon, avg_kl

def test_model(model, dataloader):
```

242

```python
        model.eval()
        total_loss = 0.0
        total_recon_loss = 0.0
        total_kl_loss = 0.0
        with torch.no_grad():
            for images, _ in dataloader:
                images = images.view(-1, INPUT_DIM).to(device)
                recon, mus, logvars, w = model(images)
                loss, recon_loss, kl_loss = moe_vae_loss(images, recon,
                ↪   mus, logvars, w)
                total_loss += loss.item()
                total_recon_loss += recon_loss.item()
                total_kl_loss += kl_loss.item()
        avg_loss = total_loss / len(dataloader)
        avg_recon = total_recon_loss / len(dataloader)
        avg_kl = total_kl_loss / len(dataloader)
        return avg_loss, avg_recon, avg_kl

# Optional: function to sample new images from the
↪   mixture-of-experts VAE
def sample_images(model, n_samples=16):
    """
    We sample by first picking an expert using gating = uniform
    ↪   random,
    or we can simply pick the first expert for demonstration.
    Then we decode from a standard Normal in latent space.
    """
    model.eval()

    # For demonstration, let's sample from each expert with uniform
    ↪   probability
    samples = []
    with torch.no_grad():
        for _ in range(n_samples):
            # Choose an expert index randomly
            expert_idx = torch.randint(0, N_EXPERTS, (1,)).item()

            z = torch.randn(1, LATENT_DIM, device=device)
            x_gen = model.decoders[expert_idx](z)
            samples.append(x_gen.cpu())

    # Return shape: [n_samples, input_dim]
    return torch.cat(samples, dim=0)


# --------------------------------------------------------------
# 9) Main Function to Train and Evaluate
# --------------------------------------------------------------
def main():
    # Initialize the MoEVAE
    model = MoEVAE(
        n_experts=N_EXPERTS,
        input_dim=INPUT_DIM,
        latent_dim=LATENT_DIM,
```

```
        hidden_dim=HIDDEN_DIM
    ).to(device)

    optimizer = optim.Adam(model.parameters(), lr=LEARNING_RATE)

    for epoch in range(EPOCHS):
        train_loss, train_recon, train_kl = train_one_epoch(model,
        ↪   optimizer, train_loader)
        test_loss, test_recon, test_kl = test_model(model,
        ↪   test_loader)

        print(f"Epoch [{epoch+1}/{EPOCHS}] "
            f"Train Loss: {train_loss:.4f} (Recon:
            ↪   {train_recon:.4f}, KL: {train_kl:.4f}) "
            f"| Test Loss: {test_loss:.4f} (Recon:
            ↪   {test_recon:.4f}, KL: {test_kl:.4f})")

    # Quick sampling demonstration
    gen_samples = sample_images(model, n_samples=8)
    print("Sampled images (tensor shape):", gen_samples.shape)
    print("Training complete!")

if __name__ == "__main__":
    main()
```

Key Implementation Details:

- **Multiple Encoders and Decoders:** Each expert has a `forward` method producing a mean and log-variance. A corresponding decoder reconstructs from the latent. This allows learning different modes of the data distribution.

- **Gating Network:** The `GatingNetwork` calculates softmax weights for each expert, capturing which expert is best suited for a given sample.

- **Weighted Mixture:** In `MoEVAE.forward`, each sample is processed by all experts. Their reconstructions are combined with gating weights, and the KL divergences are also weighted.

- **VAE Objective:** We compute a mean-squared-error based reconstruction term plus a weighted KL term for each expert. The `kl_total` is integrated via gate-specific weighting, following the standard VAE reparameterization trick.

244

- **Training Loop:** The `train_one_epoch` function runs a forward pass, calculates the mixture loss, performs a backward pass, and updates parameters. The `test_model` function evaluates the model's performance on a held-out set.

- **Sampling:** In `sample_images`, we randomly choose an expert, sample a latent, and decode. This can be adapted to other strategies (e.g., gating-based mixture sampling) for more nuanced generation.

Chapter 31

Materials Discovery with VAE

We focus on applying Variational Autoencoders (VAEs) to scientific domains such as materials and chemistry, where the goal is to discover novel compounds. We gather atomic configurations or formula descriptors, embed them in an encoder, and train the VAE to reconstruct known materials. The latent space can then be searched or sampled to propose new candidate compounds. The chapter explains data preprocessing for scientific formats, specialized loss functions for constraint satisfaction, and evaluating candidate materials. By analyzing the latent representations, researchers can identify patterns conducive to guided exploration of the materials space.

- We define a VAE with an encoder that maps high-dimensional material descriptors to a latent distribution (mean and logvar) and a decoder that reconstructs the original descriptors.

- We incorporate domain transformations (e.g., normalization, feature engineering) to handle various materials data (e.g., atomic features, formula strings).

- We introduce a specialized constraint term that helps enforce domain-specific validity (e.g., stoichiometric constraints, physically plausible ranges).

- A training loop optimizes the combined reconstruction loss and the KL divergence, with optional constraint terms.

- Once trained, we can sample from the learned latent space to propose novel compounds or transform existing ones by latent-space interpolation.

Python Code Snippet

```python
import torch
import torch.nn as nn
import torch.optim as optim
from torch.utils.data import Dataset, DataLoader
import numpy as np
import os

# -----------------------------------------------------------------
# 1) Custom dataset class for materials
# -----------------------------------------------------------------
class MaterialsDataset(Dataset):
    """
    A simple dataset that simulates loading descriptors for
    ↪ materials.
    Each descriptor is a float vector, which we want to reconstruct
    ↪ using a VAE.
    In practice, you might load from a .csv file or specialized data
    ↪ format.
    """
    def __init__(self, num_samples=1000, descriptor_dim=64,
    ↪ transform=None):
        super().__init__()
        self.transform = transform
        # Simulate dummy data: random float vectors
        # Real case might read from a file with known material
        ↪ properties or descriptors
        self.data = np.random.rand(num_samples,
        ↪ descriptor_dim).astype(np.float32)
        # For demonstration, we normalize these features to [0,1]
        # More advanced transformations (e.g., domain knowledge) can
        ↪ be applied
        self.data /= np.max(self.data, axis=0, keepdims=True) + 1e-8

    def __len__(self):
        return len(self.data)

    def __getitem__(self, idx):
        x = self.data[idx]
        if self.transform:
            x = self.transform(x)
        return x

# -----------------------------------------------------------------
# 2) Define a Variational Autoencoder
```

```python
# ------------------------------------------------------------------
class VAE(nn.Module):
    """
    A simple feed-forward VAE for materials descriptor data.
    Encoder:  (descriptor_dim) -> hidden -> (latent_dim)
    Decoder:  (latent_dim) -> hidden -> (descriptor_dim)
    """
    def __init__(self, descriptor_dim=64, latent_dim=16,
    ↪   hidden_dim=128):
        super(VAE, self).__init__()
        # Encoder layers
        self.fc1 = nn.Linear(descriptor_dim, hidden_dim)
        self.fc2_mean = nn.Linear(hidden_dim, latent_dim)
        self.fc2_logvar = nn.Linear(hidden_dim, latent_dim)

        # Decoder layers
        self.fc3 = nn.Linear(latent_dim, hidden_dim)
        self.fc4 = nn.Linear(hidden_dim, descriptor_dim)

        # Activation
        self.relu = nn.ReLU()

    def encode(self, x):
        """
        Encoder network: produce mean and log-variance for the
        ↪   distribution q(z/x).
        """
        h = self.relu(self.fc1(x))
        mean = self.fc2_mean(h)
        logvar = self.fc2_logvar(h)
        return mean, logvar

    def reparameterize(self, mean, logvar):
        """
        Reparameterization trick: z = mean + eps * exp(0.5*logvar).
        """
        std = torch.exp(0.5 * logvar)
        eps = torch.randn_like(std)
        return mean + eps * std

    def decode(self, z):
        """
        Decoder network: reconstruct x from latent z.
        """
        h = self.relu(self.fc3(z))
        return self.fc4(h)

    def forward(self, x):
        """
        Forward pass: encode -> reparam -> decode.
        Returns reconstructed x, plus mean and logvar for KL
        ↪   divergence.
        """
```

248

```
        mean, logvar = self.encode(x)
        z = self.reparameterize(mean, logvar)
        x_recon = self.decode(z)
        return x_recon, mean, logvar

# ----------------------------------------------------------------
# 3) Loss function with optional constraint
# ----------------------------------------------------------------
def vae_loss_function(x, x_recon, mean, logvar,
↪    constraint_loss=None, lambda_c=1.0):
    """
    Standard VAE loss: reconstruction term + KL divergence.
    We add an optional constraint_loss if domain constraints are
    ↪ needed.
    """
    # Reconstruction loss (MSE on descriptors)
    recon_loss = nn.functional.mse_loss(x_recon, x, reduction='sum')

    # KL Divergence: D_KL(q(z|x) || p(z)) = -0.5 * sum(1 + logvar -
    ↪  mean^2 - exp(logvar))
    kl_div = -0.5 * torch.sum(1 + logvar - mean.pow(2) -
    ↪  logvar.exp())

    # Optional domain-specific constraint
    c_loss = 0.0
    if constraint_loss is not None:
        c_loss = constraint_loss

    total_loss = recon_loss + kl_div + lambda_c * c_loss
    return total_loss, recon_loss, kl_div, c_loss

def material_constraint(x):
    """
    Placeholder for a domain-specific constraint function.
    Example: penalize descriptor values that exceed a certain
    ↪   threshold
    or stoichiometric constraints for certain tasks.
    In practice, you'd incorporate meaningful domain logic here.
    """
    # For demonstration, let's just compute a small penalty if any
    ↪   element is > 0.9
    # This is contrived and would be replaced by real physical or
    ↪   chemical constraints.
    penalty = (x > 0.9).float().sum(dim=1).mean()   # average number
    ↪   of features > 0.9
    return penalty


# ----------------------------------------------------------------
# 4) Training and evaluation loops
# ----------------------------------------------------------------
def train_vae(model, dataloader, optimizer, device,
↪    lambda_constraint=0.1):
    """
```

```
    One epoch training routine for the VAE.
    """
    model.train()
    total_loss = 0.0
    for batch in dataloader:
        batch = batch.to(device)

        # Forward pass
        x_recon, mean, logvar = model(batch)

        # Example constraint: we apply a penalty on the original
        ↪  input or reconstruction
        c_loss = material_constraint(batch) +
        ↪  material_constraint(x_recon)

        loss, recon_l, kl_l, c_l = vae_loss_function(
            batch, x_recon, mean, logvar,
            constraint_loss=c_loss,
            lambda_c=lambda_constraint
        )

        optimizer.zero_grad()
        loss.backward()
        optimizer.step()

        total_loss += loss.item()
    return total_loss / len(dataloader)

def evaluate_vae(model, dataloader, device):
    """
    Compute average validation loss for the VAE.
    """
    model.eval()
    total_loss = 0.0
    with torch.no_grad():
        for batch in dataloader:
            batch = batch.to(device)
            x_recon, mean, logvar = model(batch)
            loss, _, _, _ = vae_loss_function(batch, x_recon, mean,
            ↪  logvar)
            total_loss += loss.item()
    return total_loss / len(dataloader)


# ----------------------------------------------------------------
# 5) Sampling routines
# ----------------------------------------------------------------
def sample_from_vae(model, n_samples, latent_dim, device):
    """
    Generate new samples by sampling from the prior p(z) ~ N(0,I).
    """
    model.eval()
    with torch.no_grad():
        z = torch.randn(n_samples, latent_dim).to(device)
```

```
            samples = model.decode(z)
            return samples

# ----------------------------------------------------------------
# 6) Main script: data preparation, model creation, training
# ----------------------------------------------------------------
def main():
    # Hyperparameters
    descriptor_dim = 64
    latent_dim = 16
    hidden_dim = 128
    batch_size = 32
    epochs = 5
    lambda_constraint = 0.1  # scale factor for domain/thematic
    ↪    constraints

    device = torch.device("cuda" if torch.cuda.is_available() else
    ↪    "cpu")

    # Create synthetic dataset
    train_dataset = MaterialsDataset(num_samples=800,
    ↪    descriptor_dim=descriptor_dim)
    test_dataset = MaterialsDataset(num_samples=200,
    ↪    descriptor_dim=descriptor_dim)
    train_loader = DataLoader(train_dataset, batch_size=batch_size,
    ↪    shuffle=True)
    test_loader = DataLoader(test_dataset, batch_size=batch_size,
    ↪    shuffle=False)

    # Model and optimizer
    model = VAE(descriptor_dim=descriptor_dim,
    ↪    latent_dim=latent_dim, hidden_dim=hidden_dim).to(device)
    optimizer = optim.Adam(model.parameters(), lr=1e-3)

    # Create output directory
    os.makedirs("materials_vae_results", exist_ok=True)

    # Training loop
    for epoch in range(epochs):
        train_loss = train_vae(model, train_loader, optimizer,
        ↪    device, lambda_constraint=lambda_constraint)
        val_loss = evaluate_vae(model, test_loader, device)

        print(f"Epoch [{epoch+1}/{epochs}] - Train Loss:
        ↪    {train_loss:.2f}, Val Loss: {val_loss:.2f}")

        # Sample new data from latent space
        samples = sample_from_vae(model, n_samples=5,
        ↪    latent_dim=latent_dim, device=device)
        samples_np = samples.detach().cpu().numpy()

        # For demonstration, let's just save them as .npy files
```

```
      ↪   np.save(f"materials_vae_results/epoch_{epoch+1}_samples.npy",
      ↪   samples_np)

   print("Training complete! Sampled data is saved in
      ↪   'materials_vae_results' folder.")

if __name__ == "__main__":
    main()
```

Key Implementation Details:

- **Data Loading and Preprocessing:** The class `MaterialsDataset` simulates loading material descriptors. In real scenarios, it might parse domain-specific file formats, normalize feature ranges, and apply physical constraints.

- **VAE Architecture:** The model `VAE` uses an MLP encoder-decoder pair. The encoder outputs a mean and log-variance (`encode`), from which we sample a latent vector via `reparameterize`. The decoder (`decode`) reconstructs the input descriptor.

- **Loss Function:** `vae_loss_function` combines the reconstruction loss (MSE) and KL divergence. An optional `constraint_loss` can be used to incorporate domain-specific conditions (e.g., stoichiometry, stability thresholds).

- **Training Loop:** For each mini-batch, we compute the forward pass, then backpropagate the total loss which includes reconstruction, KL, and constraints. Functions `train_vae` and `evaluate_vae` manage these details.

- **Sampling Novel Compounds:** We draw random latent vectors from the Gaussian prior in `sample_from_vae`, decode them, and save as potential "new" material descriptors for further analysis or property predictions.

252

Chapter 32

Meta-Learning with VAE

Meta-learning approaches can leverage VAE latent spaces to quickly adapt to new tasks. We integrate the VAE in a meta-learning loop, using an outer loop to update parameters that generalize across tasks, and an inner loop to adapt the latent representation to each new task. Implementation details include how to structure training data into tasks, define the meta-objective, and manage shared vs. task-specific parameters. By the end, you will have a blueprint for quickly learning generative models under shifting task distributions.

- We create multiple simple synthetic tasks, each providing data samples with distinct underlying distributions.

- A Variational Autoencoder (VAE) is chosen as the main model that learns a latent representation of these data samples.

- We adopt a lightweight meta-learning strategy (in the style of first-order MAML/Reptile) that:

  - Performs an inner-loop update on task-specific data (support set).
  - Performs an outer-loop update across many tasks, adjusting shared parameters to enhance generalization.

- Crucially, the VAE's encoder-decoder architecture is emphasized, showing how the reparameterization trick and ELBO-based loss function are integrated in a meta-learning context.

- By iterating between inner (per-task adaptation) and outer (meta-update) loops, the VAE quickly adapts to new task distributions.

Python Code Snippet

```python
import torch
import torch.nn as nn
import torch.optim as optim
import random
import math
import copy

# -------------------------------------------------------------
# 1) Set seed for reproducibility
# -------------------------------------------------------------
def set_seed(seed=42):
    random.seed(seed)
    torch.manual_seed(seed)
    if torch.cuda.is_available():
        torch.cuda.manual_seed_all(seed)

# -------------------------------------------------------------
# 2) Define a simple VAE in an MLP style for 2D data
# -------------------------------------------------------------
class SimpleVAE(nn.Module):
    """
    A straightforward Variational Autoencoder for 2D inputs.
    Encoder -> latent mean/logvar -> latent sampling -> Decoder.
    """

    def __init__(self, input_dim=2, hidden_dim=32, latent_dim=2):
        super(SimpleVAE, self).__init__()

        # Encoder
        self.enc_fc1 = nn.Linear(input_dim, hidden_dim)
        self.enc_fc2 = nn.Linear(hidden_dim, hidden_dim)
        self.enc_mu = nn.Linear(hidden_dim, latent_dim)
        self.enc_logvar = nn.Linear(hidden_dim, latent_dim)

        # Decoder
        self.dec_fc1 = nn.Linear(latent_dim, hidden_dim)
        self.dec_fc2 = nn.Linear(hidden_dim, hidden_dim)
        self.dec_out = nn.Linear(hidden_dim, input_dim)

        self.relu = nn.ReLU()

    def encode(self, x):
        h = self.relu(self.enc_fc1(x))
        h = self.relu(self.enc_fc2(h))
        mu = self.enc_mu(h)
```

254

```python
        logvar = self.enc_logvar(h)
        return mu, logvar

    def reparameterize(self, mu, logvar):
        std = torch.exp(0.5 * logvar)
        eps = torch.randn_like(std)
        return mu + eps * std

    def decode(self, z):
        h = self.relu(self.dec_fc1(z))
        h = self.relu(self.dec_fc2(h))
        return self.dec_out(h)

    def forward(self, x):
        mu, logvar = self.encode(x)
        z = self.reparameterize(mu, logvar)
        recon = self.decode(z)
        return recon, mu, logvar

def vae_loss_function(recon, x, mu, logvar):
    """
    Computes the VAE loss: reconstruction loss + KL divergence.
    Using MSE for reconstruction to keep it simple.
    """
    mse = nn.MSELoss(reduction='sum')
    recon_loss = mse(recon, x)

    # KL divergence term
    kl = -0.5 * torch.sum(1 + logvar - mu.pow(2) - logvar.exp())

    return (recon_loss + kl) / x.size(0)


# ----------------------------------------------------------------
# 3) Generate tasks and data
# ----------------------------------------------------------------
def generate_tasks(num_tasks=5, num_samples=100, input_dim=2):
    """
    Creates multiple tasks, each representing a different 2D
    ↪ distribution.
    For simplicity, each task has a random mean offset for a
    ↪ Gaussian.
    """
    tasks = []
    for _ in range(num_tasks):
        mean_offset = 2.0 * (torch.rand(input_dim) - 0.5)   # random
        ↪ mean in [-1,1] range
        data = torch.randn(num_samples, input_dim) + mean_offset
        tasks.append(data)
    return tasks

def split_support_query(data, support_size=20):
    """
```

```
    Splits a given task's data into a support set (inner loop)
    and query set (outer loop).
    """
    indices = torch.randperm(data.size(0))
    support_idx = indices[:support_size]
    query_idx = indices[support_size:]
    return data[support_idx], data[query_idx]


# ------------------------------------------------------------
# 4) Meta-Learning (First-Order) Routines
# ------------------------------------------------------------
def clone_model(model):
    """
    Creates a copy of the given model with the same parameters.
    """
    cloned = copy.deepcopy(model)
    return cloned

def inner_update(model, support_data, inner_lr=0.01):
    """
    Performs a few gradient steps on the support set for a single
    ↪   task.
    Returns an updated model (in first-order style).
    """
    optimizer = optim.SGD(model.parameters(), lr=inner_lr)
    # We'll do a small fixed number of steps for simplicity
    steps = 5

    for _ in range(steps):
        recon, mu, logvar = model(support_data)
        loss = vae_loss_function(recon, support_data, mu, logvar)

        optimizer.zero_grad()
        loss.backward()
        optimizer.step()

    return model

def meta_update(global_model, adapted_model, meta_lr=0.001):
    """
    Updates the global_model parameters toward the adapted model
    ↪   parameters
    using a simple first-order approach (Reptile-style).
    """
    for global_param, adapted_param in
    ↪   zip(global_model.parameters(), adapted_model.parameters()):
        global_param.data = global_param.data + meta_lr *
        ↪   (adapted_param.data - global_param.data)


# ------------------------------------------------------------
# 5) Main Training (Outer Loop)
# ------------------------------------------------------------
```

```python
def main():
    set_seed(42)

    device = torch.device("cuda" if torch.cuda.is_available() else
    ↪   "cpu")
    # Hyperparameters
    num_tasks = 5
    samples_per_task = 100
    support_size = 20
    outer_steps = 10  # number of meta-iterations
    meta_lr = 0.001
    inner_lr = 0.01

    # Create a global model
    global_vae = SimpleVAE(input_dim=2, hidden_dim=32,
    ↪   latent_dim=2).to(device)

    # Generate tasks
    tasks = generate_tasks(num_tasks=num_tasks,
    ↪   num_samples=samples_per_task, input_dim=2)

    # Outer loop: meta-training
    for epoch in range(outer_steps):
        for task_data in tasks:
            # Move data to device
            task_data = task_data.to(device)

            # Split into support and query sets
            support_data, query_data =
            ↪   split_support_query(task_data, support_size)

            # Clone the global model and adapt it to this task
            ↪   (inner-update)
            adapted_vae = clone_model(global_vae).to(device)
            adapted_vae = inner_update(adapted_vae, support_data,
            ↪   inner_lr=inner_lr)

            # Evaluate on query set
            # (Not strictly needed in a Reptile approach for the
            ↪   parameter update,
            # but we can do so to track performance or extend for
            ↪   second-order MAML)
            with torch.no_grad():
                recon_q, mu_q, logvar_q = adapted_vae(query_data)
                query_loss = vae_loss_function(recon_q, query_data,
                ↪   mu_q, logvar_q)

            # Meta-update: move global parameters toward the adapted
            ↪   parameters
            meta_update(global_vae, adapted_vae, meta_lr=meta_lr)

        # End of one meta-epoch
```

```
        print(f"Epoch {epoch+1}/{outer_steps}, last task query loss
        ↪  = {query_loss.item():.4f}")

    print("Meta-training complete.")

if __name__ == "__main__":
    main()
```

Key Implementation Details:

- **VAE Architecture:** We define a simple fully-connected VAE for 2D inputs. The class "SimpleVAE" has an encoder (two hidden layers) producing and $\log(^2)$, applies the reparameterization trick, and then decodes back to 2D space.

- **VAE Loss Function:** The `vae_loss_function` combines mean-squared error for reconstruction and the KL divergence on latent variables (classic ELBO formulation).

- **Task Generation:** Each task is a small 2D dataset sampled from a Gaussian with a random mean offset. This simulates "different but related" tasks for meta-learning.

- **Meta-Learning Routine:**

  - In the inner loop (`inner_update`), the VAE is quickly specialized to a single task using support data.

  - The outer loop (`main`) aggregates adaptations across multiple tasks to update global (shared) parameters in a first-order (Reptile-style) approach via `meta_update`.

- **Shared vs. Task-Specific Parameters:** The global parameters represent the knowledge common across all tasks, while the inner loop adaptation to each task modifies a copy of those parameters. Finally, the global parameters are nudged toward the adapted model.

Chapter 33

Symbolic Regression with VAE

Finally, we explore using a VAE to represent mathematical expressions or symbolic formulas. We encode parse trees or string tokens into latent space and decode them to symbolic forms. Implementation involves specialized tokenization procedures, an attention-based encoder, and a decoder that predicts operator and operand tokens step by step. We also discuss strategies to prune invalid formulas, combine the VAE with search algorithms, and discover concise expressions. With this approach, you can automate symbolic regression tasks in Python.

- We generate or collect symbolic expressions (e.g., random arithmetic formulas).

- We tokenize these expressions into discrete tokens for easier processing by the model.

- Our encoder (in this example, a Transformer) takes a token sequence, producing a mean and log-variance for the latent distribution.

- Using the reparameterization trick, we sample from the latent space, then feed it into our decoder to reconstruct the original symbolic sequence.

- Invalid formulas can be pruned at generation or after reconstruction, and the model can be integrated with search algorithms to discover simpler or more accurate formulas.

Python Code Snippet

```python
import math
import random
import re
import torch
import torch.nn as nn
import torch.optim as optim
from torch.utils.data import Dataset, DataLoader
import numpy as np


# ---------------------------------------------------------------
# 1) Generate Random Expressions for Demonstration
# ---------------------------------------------------------------
OPERATORS = ['+', '-', '*', '/']
MAX_NUM = 9
MIN_LEN = 3
MAX_LEN = 7

def generate_random_expression():
    """
    Generate a random arithmetic expression consisting of
    ↪ single-digit operands
    (1..9) and operators (+, -, *, /). Ensures random length within
    ↪ a range.
    """
    length = random.randint(MIN_LEN, MAX_LEN)
    expr_tokens = []
    for i in range(length):
        if i % 2 == 0:
            # operand
            expr_tokens.append(str(random.randint(1, MAX_NUM)))
        else:
            # operator
            expr_tokens.append(random.choice(OPERATORS))
    # Example: "3+8-1"
    return "".join(expr_tokens)


# ---------------------------------------------------------------
# 2) Tokenizer and Special Tokens
# ---------------------------------------------------------------
PAD_TOKEN = "<pad>"
BOS_TOKEN = "<bos>"
EOS_TOKEN = "<eos>"

class Tokenizer:
    """
    Basic tokenizer that maps tokens to integer ids and back.
    Includes special tokens for padding, beginning-of-sequence, and
    ↪ end-of-sequence.
    """
    def __init__(self):
```

```python
        self.token2id = {}
        self.id2token = []
        self.add_token(PAD_TOKEN)   # 0
        self.add_token(BOS_TOKEN)   # 1
        self.add_token(EOS_TOKEN)   # 2

    def add_token(self, token):
        if token not in self.token2id:
            self.token2id[token] = len(self.id2token)
            self.id2token.append(token)

    def build_vocab(self, expressions):
        # Derive distinct tokens from all expressions
        for expr in expressions:
            for ch in expr:
                self.add_token(ch)

    def encode(self, expr):
        # map each character to an id
        return [self.token2id[BOS_TOKEN]] + [self.token2id[ch] for
        ↪   ch in expr] + [self.token2id[EOS_TOKEN]]

    def decode(self, tokens):
        # map ids to characters, ignoring PAD
        result = []
        for tid in tokens:
            if self.id2token[tid] == PAD_TOKEN:
                continue
            if self.id2token[tid] in (BOS_TOKEN, EOS_TOKEN):
                continue
            result.append(self.id2token[tid])
        return "".join(result)

    def __len__(self):
        return len(self.id2token)


# ---------------------------------------------------------------
# 3) Dataset and Collation
# ---------------------------------------------------------------
class ExpressionDataset(Dataset):
    """
    A PyTorch dataset that yields symbolic expressions and their
    ↪   token IDs.
    """

    def __init__(self, tokenizer, size=1000):
        super().__init__()
        self.tokenizer = tokenizer
        self.size = size

        # Generate random expressions for demonstration
        self.expressions = [generate_random_expression() for _ in
        ↪   range(size)]
```

261

```python
    def __len__(self):
        return self.size

    def __getitem__(self, idx):
        expr = self.expressions[idx]
        token_ids = self.tokenizer.encode(expr)
        return torch.tensor(token_ids, dtype=torch.long)

def collate_fn(batch):
    """
    Collate a batch of sequences by padding to the longest sequence
    ↪  length.
    """
    lens = [len(seq) for seq in batch]
    max_len = max(lens)
    padded = []
    for seq in batch:
        padded_seq = torch.cat([seq, torch.full((max_len -
        ↪  len(seq),), 0, dtype=torch.long)])
        padded.append(padded_seq)
    return torch.stack(padded, dim=0)


# ----------------------------------------------------------------
# 4) VAE Model with Attention (Transformer)
# ----------------------------------------------------------------
class ExpressionVAE(nn.Module):
    """
    An end-to-end model that encodes symbolic expressions into a
    ↪  latent space
    using a Transformer encoder, then reconstructs them with a
    ↪  Transformer decoder.
    """
    def __init__(self, vocab_size, d_model=128, nhead=4,
    ↪  num_layers=2, dim_feedforward=256, latent_dim=32):
        super().__init__()
        self.d_model = d_model
        self.latent_dim = latent_dim

        # Embeddings
        self.embed = nn.Embedding(vocab_size, d_model)

        # Positional encoding (simple learnable approach)
        self.pos_encoding = nn.Parameter(torch.zeros(1, 100,
        ↪  d_model))  # max length 100 for demonstration

        # Transformer Encoder
        encoder_layer = nn.TransformerEncoderLayer(
            d_model=d_model, nhead=nhead,
            ↪  dim_feedforward=dim_feedforward
        )
        self.encoder = nn.TransformerEncoder(encoder_layer,
        ↪  num_layers=num_layers)
```

```python
        # For computing mean and logvar
        self.to_mean = nn.Linear(d_model, latent_dim)
        self.to_logvar = nn.Linear(d_model, latent_dim)

        # Transform latent back to hidden dims
        self.from_latent = nn.Linear(latent_dim, d_model)

        # Transformer Decoder
        decoder_layer = nn.TransformerDecoderLayer(
            d_model=d_model, nhead=nhead,
            ↪    dim_feedforward=dim_feedforward
        )
        self.decoder = nn.TransformerDecoder(decoder_layer,
        ↪    num_layers=num_layers)

        # Decoder final output
        self.out = nn.Linear(d_model, vocab_size)

    def forward(self, src, tgt):
        """
        Full forward pass:
          1) Encode src into hidden
          2) Extract global latent
          3) Reparam trick (z = mean + exp(logvar/2)*eps)
          4) Decode z + tgt (teacher forcing)
        """
        # src, tgt: shape [batch_size, seq_len]
        # We need [seq_len, batch_size, d_model] for Transformer
        src_emb = self.embed(src) + self.pos_encoding[:,
        ↪    :src.size(1), :]
        src_emb = src_emb.transpose(0, 1)   # (seq_len, batch,
        ↪    d_model)

        # Transformer Encoder
        enc_out = self.encoder(src_emb)   # shape [seq_len, batch,
        ↪    d_model]

        # We'll take the last token's output as a "global"
        ↪    representation
        last_hidden = enc_out[-1]   # shape [batch, d_model]

        # Map to mean and logvar
        mean = self.to_mean(last_hidden)
        logvar = self.to_logvar(last_hidden)

        # Reparameterize
        std = torch.exp(0.5 * logvar)
        eps = torch.randn_like(std)
        z = mean + eps * std

        # Expand z to seq_len dimension for decoder
        z_context = self.from_latent(z).unsqueeze(0)   # shape [1,
        ↪    batch, d_model]
```

263

```python
    # Prepare decoder input
    tgt_emb = self.embed(tgt) + self.pos_encoding[:,
    ↪  :tgt.size(1), :]
    tgt_emb = tgt_emb.transpose(0, 1)  # shape [tgt_seq_len,
    ↪  batch, d_model]

    # The decoder attends to z_context repeated or appended
    # For demonstration, we treat z_context as "memory" the
    ↪  decoder can attend to
    out_dec = self.decoder(tgt_emb,
    ↪  z_context.repeat(tgt_emb.size(0), 1, 1))
    logits = self.out(out_dec)  # shape [tgt_seq_len, batch,
    ↪  vocab_size]

    return logits.transpose(0, 1), mean, logvar  # shape [batch,
    ↪  tgt_seq_len, vocab_size]

def encode_latent(self, src):
    """
    Obtain latent sample from source expression only (for
    ↪  inference).
    """
    src_emb = self.embed(src) + self.pos_encoding[:,
    ↪  :src.size(1), :]
    src_emb = src_emb.transpose(0, 1)
    enc_out = self.encoder(src_emb)
    last_hidden = enc_out[-1]
    mean = self.to_mean(last_hidden)
    logvar = self.to_logvar(last_hidden)
    std = torch.exp(0.5 * logvar)
    eps = torch.randn_like(std)
    z = mean + eps * std
    return z, mean, logvar

def decode_from_latent(self, z, max_len=20, start_id=1,
↪  end_id=2):
    """
    Given a latent vector z, generate an expression token by
    ↪  token.
    """
    z_context = self.from_latent(z).unsqueeze(0)  # [1, batch,
    ↪  d_model]
    generated_tokens = []

    # Start with BOS
    current_token = torch.tensor([[start_id]], device=z.device)

    for _ in range(max_len):
        tgt_emb = self.embed(current_token) +
        ↪  self.pos_encoding[:, :current_token.size(1), :]
        tgt_emb = tgt_emb.transpose(0, 1)
```

264

```
        out_dec = self.decoder(tgt_emb,
        ↪   z_context.repeat(tgt_emb.size(0), 1, 1))
        logits = self.out(out_dec[-1])  # last token's logits =>
        ↪   shape [batch, vocab_size]
        next_token = torch.argmax(logits, dim=-1, keepdim=True)
        ↪   # greedy decoding
        generated_tokens.append(next_token.item())
        # Stop if we hit EOS
        if next_token.item() == end_id:
            break
        current_token = torch.cat([current_token, next_token],
        ↪   dim=1)

    return generated_tokens  # list of token IDs

# ---------------------------------------------------------------
# 5) Training Routines
# ---------------------------------------------------------------
def vae_loss_fn(pred_logits, target, mean, logvar, pad_idx=0,
↪   beta=1.0):
    """
    Standard VAE loss: cross-entropy reconstruction +
    ↪   KL(divergence).
    beta parameter can scale the KL term for 'beta-VAE' style
    ↪   training.
    """
    # Flatten preds: [batch * seq_len, vocab_size]
    pred_flat = pred_logits.reshape(-1, pred_logits.size(-1))
    target_flat = target.view(-1)

    # Mask out PAD tokens in loss
    ce_loss = nn.CrossEntropyLoss(ignore_index=pad_idx)(pred_flat,
    ↪   target_flat)

    # KL divergence
    kl_loss = -0.5 * torch.mean(1 + logvar - mean.pow(2) -
    ↪   logvar.exp())

    return ce_loss + beta * kl_loss, ce_loss, kl_loss

def train_vae(model, dataloader, optimizer, device, beta=1.0):
    """
    One epoch of VAE training: iterate over the DataLoader, compute
    ↪   forward pass,
    and update parameters.
    """
    model.train()
    total_loss = 0.0
    for batch in dataloader:
        batch = batch.to(device)
        # We use the same sequence as src and tgt (auto-encoding)
        logits, mean, logvar = model(batch, batch)
```

```python
        loss, ce, kl = vae_loss_fn(logits, batch, mean, logvar,
        ↪  pad_idx=0, beta=beta)

        optimizer.zero_grad()
        loss.backward()
        optimizer.step()

        total_loss += loss.item()
    return total_loss / len(dataloader)

def evaluate_vae(model, dataloader, device, beta=1.0):
    model.eval()
    total_loss = 0.0
    with torch.no_grad():
        for batch in dataloader:
            batch = batch.to(device)
            logits, mean, logvar = model(batch, batch)
            loss, _, _ = vae_loss_fn(logits, batch, mean, logvar,
            ↪  pad_idx=0, beta=beta)
            total_loss += loss.item()
    return total_loss / len(dataloader)

def sample_expressions(model, tokenizer, device, num_samples=5):
    """
    Samples a few expressions by randomly encoding a batch from the
    ↪  dataset or just
    sampling from random Z to see the reconstructed or new
    ↪  expressions.
    """
    model.eval()
    with torch.no_grad():
        # Sample random latent vectors
        latents = torch.randn(num_samples,
        ↪  model.latent_dim).to(device)
        for i in range(num_samples):
            z = latents[i].unsqueeze(0)   # shape [1, latent_dim]
            gen_ids = model.decode_from_latent(z)
            decoded_str = tokenizer.decode(gen_ids)
            print(f"Sample {i+1}: {decoded_str}")

# ----------------------------------------------------------------
# 6) Main Driver Function
# ----------------------------------------------------------------
def main():
    device = torch.device("cuda" if torch.cuda.is_available() else
    ↪  "cpu")
    print("Using device:", device)

    # Prepare a small random dataset
    random_expressions = [generate_random_expression() for _ in
    ↪  range(2000)]

    # Build tokenizer
```

```
tokenizer = Tokenizer()
tokenizer.build_vocab(random_expressions)

# Create dataset and dataloader
train_size = 1800
test_size = 200
train_data = random_expressions[:train_size]
test_data = random_expressions[train_size:]

train_dataset = ExpressionDataset(tokenizer, size=train_size)
train_dataset.expressions = train_data

test_dataset = ExpressionDataset(tokenizer, size=test_size)
test_dataset.expressions = test_data

train_loader = DataLoader(train_dataset, batch_size=32,
↪    shuffle=True, collate_fn=collate_fn)
test_loader = DataLoader(test_dataset, batch_size=32,
↪    shuffle=False, collate_fn=collate_fn)

# Initialize the VAE
vocab_size = len(tokenizer)
model = ExpressionVAE(vocab_size=vocab_size, d_model=128,
↪    nhead=4, num_layers=2, dim_feedforward=256, latent_dim=32)
model.to(device)

optimizer = optim.Adam(model.parameters(), lr=1e-3)

# Train
epochs = 5
for epoch in range(epochs):
    train_loss = train_vae(model, train_loader, optimizer,
↪        device, beta=1.0)
    val_loss = evaluate_vae(model, test_loader, device,
↪        beta=1.0)
    print(f"Epoch [{epoch+1}/{epochs}] - Train Loss:
↪        {train_loss:.4f}, Val Loss: {val_loss:.4f}")

# Sample from the model
sample_expressions(model, tokenizer, device, num_samples=5)

if __name__ == "__main__":
    main()
```

Key Implementation Details:

- **Tokenization and Dataset:** The Tokenizer maps each unique character (operand or operator) to an integer ID. The ExpressionDataset auto-encodes expressions to learn a continuous latent representation.

- **Transformer-based VAE:** The `ExpressionVAE` employs a `TransformerEncoder` to encode the input tokens, producing a global latent distribution. The mean and log-variance define the latent space, sampled via the reparameterization trick.

- **Decoding Strategy:** The `TransformerDecoder` receives the latent code as "memory," reconstructing the expression. We demonstrate greedy decoding for simplicity, though beam search or sampling could be used.

- **Loss Function:** We sum the cross-entropy reconstruction error and the KL divergence with a `beta` coefficient for potential disentanglement tuning.

- **Sampling New Expressions:** The function `sample_expressions` randomly generates latent vectors and passes them to `decode_from_latent`, returning novel symbolic formulas which can be pruned or combined with search algorithms for symbolic regression.

www.ingramcontent.com/pod-product-compliance
Lightning Source LLC
LaVergne TN
LVHW012320060326
832904LV00028B/343